D1527928

Land Use
Planning

Volume 187   Sage Library of Social Research

RECENT VOLUMES IN . . .
SAGE LIBRARY OF SOCIAL RESEARCH

Land Use Planning

The Ballot Box Revolution

Roger W. Caves

Sage Library of Social Research 187

SAGE PUBLICATIONS
The International Professional Publishers
Newbury Park   London   New Delhi

For information address:

SAGE Publications, Inc.
2455 Teller Road
Newbury Park, California 91320

SAGE Publications Ltd.
6 Bonhill Street
London EC2A 4PU
United Kingdom

SAGE Publications India Pvt. Ltd.
M-32 Market
Greater Kailash I
New Delhi 110 048 India

Printed in the United States of America

Library of Congress Cataloging-in-Publication Data

Caves, Roger W.
    Land use planning : the ballot box revolution / Roger W. Caves.
        p.   cm. — (Sage library of social research ; v. 187)
    Includes bibliographical references and index.
    ISBN 0-8039-3824-1. — ISBN 0-8039-3825-X (pbk.)
    1. Land use—Government policy—United States—Citizen
participation.   I. Title.   II. Series.
HD205.C38   1992
333.73'13'0973—dc20   91-17548

FIRST PRINTING, 1992

Sage Production Editor: Michelle R. Starika

Contents

Preface

In many areas of the United States, citizens are no longer sitting idly by and watching state and local legislative bodies make all of the public policy decisions. The trend toward using direct democracy or direct legislation has some individuals applauding its use and others questioning its need, intent, and legality. For various reasons citizens have taken to developing state and city legislation and ordinances instead of letting their elected officials do so. We have seen an increasing number of citizens and interest groups develop land use policies and ordinances at the local level; follow the appropriate procedures, as required by law, for getting the measure on the ballot; and then let the voters decide whether the measure will be approved or rejected. If approved, the measure must be adhered to and enforced by the various local bodies.

The two most commonly used direct democracy devices employed by citizens and interest groups are the *initiative* and *referendum*. Prior to any substantive discussion of the devices, it is imperative that the terms be defined. Although *referendum* has been occasionally used as a generic term, the terms do have different meanings.

An *initiative* is a citizen proposed legislative measure that is put before the electorate for approval or rejection. It represents a way of obtaining direct voter opinion on a specific issue. At the state level, we have seen citizens decide such issues as the murder penalty, official state language, state lottery, bond issues, property taxes, and oil and gas conservation. At the local level, with an emphasis placed on land use matters, we have seen the passage of legislation that calls for a change in a zoning ordinance—limiting the number of building permits in an area, decreasing density on hillsides, or requiring voter approval on certain zoning changes in specific areas of the city. Some areas may also distinguish between two types of initiatives—direct and indirect. A direct initiative follows the required procedures for getting the measure placed on the ballot and goes straight from the petitioners to the voters and bypasses the appropriate legislative body. In contrast, an indirect initiative must first be submitted to the legislative body, which can either adopt the measure or reject it, but is not allowed to alter the initiative in any form. If the legislative body fails to act on the initiative and the petitioners possess enough signatures to get the measure placed on the ballot, it will go before the electorate for its approval or rejection. A local legislative body could also sponsor a measure and place it on the ballot with the citizen sponsored measure. One intent of such an act might be to provide the voters with an alternative to the citizen measure. Its use has become somewhat commonplace in California in recent years.

There is also a third type of initiative that may be used—the advisory initiative. This type of initiative is simply advisory in nature and serves to alert public officials about citizen feelings on a particular issue. For instance, in an area experiencing rapid population growth, citizens may become increasingly concerned that individual cities are planning only for the area inside their boundaries and ignoring the impacts of their actions on the surrounding region—so they turn to the ballot box as a last resort. This concern might result in the formulation of an advisory initiative that advocates planning for growth at the regional level.

In comparison, the *referendum* follows an action by the legislative body and allows citizens to approve or reject an ordinance already adopted by the legislative body. Voters must approve the change before it becomes law. The referendum can be permissive—voters must file a petition to review the action—or in some areas it could be mandatory—required for certain actions such as zoning amendments.

The difference between the *initiative* and *referendum* is not always easy to detect, especially because some individuals use the terms interchangeably. And it becomes more confusing when we find out that an initiative could be used as a substitute for a referendum. As Mandelker (1988, p. 274) has indicated, "If a municipality adopts an amendment to the zoning ordinance that upzones land to a more intensive use, the voters may petition for an initiative in the form of a repeal of the zoning amendment." Nevertheless, the general conclusion appears to be, as Oberholtzer (1971, p. 369) suggested, that "the referendum has been described as a condition precedent to the taking effect of the law; the initiative is a condition precedent to the referendum."

This book is intended to improve our understanding and appreciation of the use of direct democracy, in general, and the growing use of the initiative and referendum in local land use planning matters in the United States. It examines broad-scale planning issues, not rezonings of single parcels of land. Although citizens turn to the initiative or referendum for reasons unique to their areas, we may be able to identify similarities or commonalities in how they are used. However, before this can be accomplished, we need to examine the concept of direct democracy. Putting direct democracy in a historical context is the focus of Chapter 1. Among the topics addressed in this chapter are the evolution of direct democracy in the United States and the arguments for and against its use.

The use of the initiative and referendum in land use planning matters, better known as "electoral land use planning" or "ballot box planning," is the subject of Chapter 2. This chapter examines how ballot box planning has been used in the United States, traditional means of deciding land use planning issues, the role of citizen participation in the planning process, general actions subject to possible initiative or referendum, the procedures that must be followed to have a measure placed on the ballot, and the reasons why citizens might turn to a direct democracy device to decide a land use planning issue. A special emphasis is placed on California—the locale for an enormous number of initiatives and referendums on planning matters at the local level.

Any action, whether traditional planning tool or initiative or referendum, that places restrictions on how a piece of property can be used is bound to come under legal scrutiny by property owners and their attorneys. Chapter 3 explores various legal issues raised whenever an initiative or referendum is employed in a land use planning context. Among the topics examined in this chapter are the legislative/administrative distinction, due process and equal protection concerns, exclusionary impacts, improper use of the police power, and whether the ballot measure is consistent with the general plan.

The next four chapters provide case studies of how ballot box planning has been used in areas around the United States. These chapters illustrate how four distinct areas have used ballot box planning to decide important questions involving growth and growth control. Chapter 4 examines two measures from Barnstable County, Massachusetts, an area better known as Cape Cod, that called both for the creation of a regional planning body and for a moratorium on most construction until a regulating agency could begin enforcement. Chapter 5 analyzes a ballot measure in Portland, Maine, which sought to limit all waterfront-area development to buildings associated with marine use. Chapter 6 examines a managed growth initiative that was developed in San Diego, California. This measure required a vote of the people before land designated for future development could be changed to any other land-use designation. The measure represents only one of San Diego's ventures into ballot box planning. Chapter 7 discusses an initiative in Seattle, Washington, which sought to control downtown development by reducing permitted building height; reducing bulk by reducing development bonuses for public and development benefits; limiting the development of new office space, with exceptions for small buildings; and requiring the preparation of a study regarding future management of downtown growth. The central questions addressed in each case study are:

What event(s) prompted citizens to turn to the ballot box to decide the particular land use action?
Who was involved in the campaign for and against the ballot measure?
How were the campaigns financed?
What types of campaign tactics were used by the proponents and opponents of the ballot measure?
Were outside influences present during the campaign?
How active was the media in covering the campaign?
What lessons can be learned from the campaign?
What happened after the measure was approved or rejected by the voters?

Chapter 8, the final chapter, provides a summary of the findings of the research. It discusses the implications of continued ballot box planning as well as recommendations for future research on the topic.

A number of concerns inspired me to develop this book. Living in a rapidly growing area like San Diego, California, and seeing citizens becoming more and more frustrated over increasing housing costs, air pollution, highway congestion, and a general lessening in the area's quality of life, I was interested in finding out why citizens were turning to the ballot box as a means of deciding land use issues, instead of letting their elected officials make the decisions. In California and elsewhere, citizens possess the power to use the initiative or referendum to decide a number of legislative matters, including land use policy.

After observing an increase in the number of initiatives and referendums appearing on ballots, I came up with several questions. First of all, have the citizens lost faith in the decisions of their elected officials? Are they turning to the ballot box as a last resort, or are they simply wanting to participate more in deciding matters that will impact their lives?

Second, seeing that ballot box planning is apparently in vogue in California, I wondered whether citizens in other states were turning to the ballot box. If so, were there common reasons why citizens have turned to ballot box planning? If not, why were citizens prevented from using the initiative and referendum to decide land use matters?

Third, having investigated the literature on direct democracy and direct legislation, I was struck by the fact that most of the research on the topic has been conducted at the state level. Little research has been conducted on direct democracy on the local level, particularly regarding its use to resolve land use matters. Therefore, a book on direct democracy and ballot box planning at the local level would fill a significant research gap in the literature.

The preparation of this book could not have been completed without the help, encouragement, and assistance of a number of individuals. First, I would like to thank the many individuals in Barnstable County, Massachusetts; Portland, Maine; San Diego, California; and Seattle, Washington, for allowing me the opportunity to interview them and get their thoughts and concerns about various aspects of ballot box planning in their areas. Second, I thank San Diego State University for a Research, Scholarship, Creative Activity Award that enabled me to complete a portion of this manuscript. Third, I am grateful to Professor Scott Bollens, University of Massachusetts, for his assistance and insights on the ballot measures in Barnstable County. Fourth and fifth, my thanks go to the reviewers for their guidance and assistance and to Blaise Donnelly, my acquiring editor at Sage Publications, for his encouragement and helpful suggestions. Sixth, to my friend and colleague, Professor Robert J. Waste of California State University, Chico, I give thanks for acting as a sounding board for some of my ideas and for his encouragement. I must thank my parents, Raymond and Helen Caves, for their love and encouragement in all of my endeavors. Finally, none of this manuscript would have been completed without the love and assistance of my wife, Carol J. Caves. While serving as an informal editor throughout the process, she put up with a lot of unsightly piles of paper around the house. I will always remember her encouraging words of "turn off the television and do some work." I dedicate this book to her.

—*Roger W. Caves*

O N E

Direct Democracy and Its Place in Democratic Theory

The issue of who governs and whether they govern wisely is a lengthy debate that shows no signs of being resolved (Cobb and Elder, 1983; Dahl, 1961; Dye, 1987; Hawley and Wirt, 1974; Ricci, 1971; Waste, 1987). Although a full discussion of the issues remains outside the scope of this book, a brief mention of the debate is needed. On one side of the debate are the pluralists (Dahl, 1961, 1982; Polsby, 1980; Waste, 1986, 1987). Pluralists argue that no one group dominates politics in a city. Instead, community power is distributed among various interest groups competing for influence. Interests, circumstances, and issues dictate which groups will exert power and influence. On the other side of the debate are the elitists (Domhoff, 1967; Dye, 1985; Hunter, 1953; Mills, 1956; Stone, 1989). Elitists feel power is concentrated in the hands of a small group of individuals. This elite group shapes community opinion and, in large part, determines key community decisions with the idea of furthering its particular interests. An important question facing both schools of thought is: What role do citizens play in the decision-making process?

CITIZEN PARTICIPATION

Citizen participation in deciding matters of public importance is an American tradition (Cole, 1974; Langton, 1979). The role and extent of citizen participation have been debated in the literature on democratic theory for many years (Cronin, 1989; Ford, 1924; Kelso, 1978; Magleby, 1984; Pateman, 1970; Pennock, 1979; Zimmerman, 1986). Should citizen participation be limited to simply electing officials to make the necessary public decisions, or should citizens be given the opportunity to have a larger role and decide matters of public importance? The answers to these and other questions depend, in part, on the model of democracy that an individual espouses.

Collective agreements over a number of aspects regarding citizen participation are rare. Reasons for citizen participation, the benefits and costs associated with participation, and the techniques used to encourage citizen participation are routinely debated in the existing literature. Even the definition of citizen participation varies from situation to situation. It might be defined as simply giving citizens a voice in the decision making process, or as Cunningham (1972, p. 595) defines it, "a process wherein the common amateurs of a community exercise power over decisions related to the general affairs of a community." Arnstein (1969) echoed this when she observed that the opportunity to exercise power differed according to specific situations. She developed a "ladder of participation," with eight rungs to illustrate the various degrees of participation that were potentially possible. These eight rungs could then be collapsed into the three general categories of non-participation, degrees of tokenism, and degrees of citizen power. As an individual progressed up the ladder, participation grew from simply being manipulated to being informed to ultimately possessing some power or control over an issue. In the end, Arnstein defined participation as:

The redistribution of power that enables the have-not citizens, presently excluded from the political and economic processes, to be deliberately included in the future . . . is the means by which they can induce significant social reform which enables them to share in the benefits of the affluent society. (p. 216)

The benefits accrued from citizen participation have been widely discussed in the literature (Austin, 1972; Burke, 1968; Morone, 1990; Pateman, 1970; Rousseau, 1953; Walker, 1966; Zimmerman, 1986). Much of the discussion centers around the belief that participation helps citizens develop to their full potential. Recognizing participation to be part of our democratic heritage, Rousseau (1953, p. 20) claimed that participation "could elevate men and turn them into moral and intelligent human beings." Kelso (1978, p. 8) reiterated this notion and commented that some individuals feel it encourages an individual's development and that since it does, participation "should be viewed as an end in and of itself and not as a means for the accomplishment of the substantive means." Moreover, Walker (1966) found it allowed citizens to broaden their own lives.

Others claim participation enables officials to hear a variety of opinions about an issue. This information ultimately results in the development of a policy with widespread community support.

Not everyone concurs with the need for and benefits associated with citizen participation. Some people complain that participation lengthens and tends to interfere with the traditional decision-making process. Opponents to participation have also claimed that citizens are concerned only with their own needs and ignore the community's needs. Furthermore, people have argued that citizen participation is costly and there is no guarantee the participants will understand the issue being discussed. Ultimately, Cunningham (1972, p. 600) lists the primary costs associated with participation:

> Amateurs are unqualified to decide many complex matters; citizen goals can be achieved more efficiently in other ways; it wastes resources; it opens the way to corruption; it sacrifices regional and long range to the local and immediate; it alienates the Establishment from the poor; it generates conflict; participants are often unrepresentative; the masses usually turn out to be reactionary and negative.

The role of citizen participation will undoubtedly continue to be debated among researchers and scholars.

REPRESENTATIVE DEMOCRACY

The most appropriate form of government for cities and states in the United States is routinely discussed in the literature. One school of thought has the people being separated from government by a representative system. The people would elect officials to decide matters of community importance. In turn, the elected representatives would conduct the act of governing. The idea, as Ford (1924, p. 3) saw it, was "that the people, while not in person present at the seat of government, are to be considered as present by proxy." However, it should be noted, as Thompson (1976) suggested, that the elected representatives control only the business of government. They are not to be considered the individuals who implement public policy.

Representative democracy enthusiasts included such early notables as John Stuart Mill, Alexander Hamilton, and James Madison, all of whom acknowledged that no form of government is perfect or free from defects in theory or application. However, when comparing representative democracy to direct democracy, the former was found to be superior.

An argument raised by Mill, which claimed that cities had grown too large for direct democracy, found many supporters. To him, theory and reality differed when faced with choosing the most appropriate form of government. As Mill (1873, p. 80) suggested:

> It is evident that the only government which can fully satisfy all the exigencies of the social state is one which the whole people participate; that any participation, even in the smallest public function, is useful; that the participation should everywhere be as great as the general degree of improvement of the community will allow; and that nothing less can be ultimately desirable than the admission of all to a share in the sovereign powers of the state. But since all can not, in a community exceeding a single small town, participate personally in any but some very minor portions of the public business, it follows that the ideal type of government must be representative.

He continued further by discussing the functions of a representative democracy:

> To watch and control the government; to throw the light of publicity on its acts; to compel a full exposition and justification of all of them which only one considers questionable; to censure them if found condemnable; and, if the men who compose the government abuse their trust, or fulfill it in a manner which conflicts with the deliberate sense of the nation, to expel them from office, and either expressly or virtually appoint their successors. (pp. 115-116).

His ideas are applicable to the lower levels of government.

The authors of *The Federalist Papers*—Alexander Hamilton, John Jay, and James Madison—wrote of the advantages of representative government. Called by Cronin (1989, p. 17) "the champion of representative government," Madison opposed widespread public participation because he felt it might cause instability in the government. In 1787, in *The Federalist* Number 10, Madison spoke of his concerns about factionalism. He believed there was a strong likelihood that one group would tend to dominate other groups and that the dominant group would continue to push for its own needs and desires at the expense of other groups. This domination would intensify when groups had opposing values. The solution to factionalism, according to Madison, was republicanism. Government would be better as it moved away from the people. The people would, in turn, be separated from the government by representatives, who became the voice of the public. Ultimately, representative government was superior to direct democracy.

Whereas Madison and others felt representative government was the superior form of government for the United States, a number of scholars have voiced reservations. Some point to the fact that representatives are, in fact, not really representative of the public they are to serve. Many representatives may simply be representing only the interests of a few individuals or groups and not the general public. Moreover, once in office, elected officials have been known to alter campaign pledges. As Wilcox (1912, p. 107) once observed: "Men who were supposed to be honest as private citizens, fall under a mysterious spell when they get into office. Time after time the people elect men who betray them. The result is discouragement and indifference." He went on to suggest that all representatives are not as equal as we might think:

> In fact, the fate of important legislation is often determined, not by the opinions of the majority of the legislators, but rather by the skill of the leaders of the assembly in manipulating the parliamentary procedure at critical

times so as to prevent a decisive vote or as to bring the
question to a vote in a form that is contrary to the wishes
of the majority. (p. 13)

Riker (1986) has also argued the same point.

Both the need for representative government and concerns
about the alternative to it continued to be addressed. There
were continued concerns that the issues to be decided were too
complex or technical for the voters. Ford (1924, p. 287) observed that direct democracy devices (i.e., initiative, referendum, or recall) "reduce the responsibilities of representative
bodies in a way that amounts to a division of the authority en-
trusted to them." Lucas (1976) wrote of why government
should be unenthusiastic about public participation. He noted
that public participation "clogs the system and submerges the
important messages with irrelevant noise" (p. 154). Overall,
Adrian and Press (1968, p. 108) observed that opponents to direct democracy, or the use of the initiative or referendum,
voiced the following complaints:

> It confused legislative responsibility, lengthened an al-
> ready overly long ballot, created a bad psychological effect
> upon the city council, expected more than was reasonable
> from an uninformed and uninterested electorate, would
> promote radicalism and a disrespect for property rights,
> was opposed to the best principles of Americanism (since
> the Constitution is based upon *representative*, and not *direct*,
> democracy), and would allow well-organized interest
> groups representing a minority of the population to exer-
> cise an inordinate advantage.

Nevertheless, there is a strong following for direct democracy.

DIRECT DEMOCRACY

Allowing citizens to vote directly on issues represents the antithesis to representative democracy. Tagged "legislation by popular vote" by Bowman and Kearney (1986, p. 114), direct democracy allows citizens, through various devices, and depending on the area, to decide a number of issues. Citizens, through the initiative, are allowed to propose legislation and to vote for its passage or defeat. Using the referendum, citizens are afforded the opportunity to vote on actions already taken by the legislative body before the actions become effective. And recall procedures, which are beyond the scope of this book, enable citizens to replace public officials or remove them from office. The literature on these topics has grown over the years (Baker, 1977; Berman, 1975; Cronin, 1989; Hyink, Brown, and Thacker, 1973; Magleby, 1984, 1986, 1988; Ranney, 1981; Schmidt, 1989; Tallian, 1977; Whitehill, 1985; Wilcox, 1912).

Reasons for the Initiative and Referendum

Should every issue to be decided go before the people for their approval or disapproval? The cost alone for elections should signal that the answer is no. Not every issue should go before the people (Magleby, 1984). For example, a vote on a national issue such as a declaration of war would be impossible. Furthermore, there is currently no provision in the U.S. Constitution for the proposal and enactment of laws by popular vote of the people of the United States. However, in 1977 there was a move to amend the U.S. Constitution in that manner. Leading the fight for the proposed amendment was U.S. Senator James Abourezk of South Dakota. In discussing why the amendment was needed, Abourezk (1977, p. 7) suggested:

It would make the legislative branch more accountable to the voters and it would allow for open educational debates on important issues . . . it would lessen the sense of alienation from Government to which millions of Americans now profess and would perfectly complement our representative form of government by enabling the average citizen to more effectively and directly communicate with the federal government.

Abourezk also chastised individuals critical of the proposed amendment for questioning the abilities of the people. Supporting the wisdom of the people, he proclaimed "what the critics ironically forget is that these very same 'untrustworthy and uneducated' people can be trusted and are educated enough to get politicians to office" (p. 7). The proposed amendment failed to win enough support.

The reasons citizens might turn to the initiative or referendum vary from situation to situation. In one case, an initiative or referendum may be used as a reaction against, and an alternative to, an unresponsive legislative body. Thus, the device acts, as Berman (1975, p. 66) suggests, as a "safety valve with which the voters can bypass legislative inaction, challenge governmental policies, and rid themselves of unsatisfactory elective officials." However, as Tallian (1977, p. 79) clearly points out, "It is an error to view the initiative as primarily a means of flogging reluctant lawmakers into action."

Many people also view the initiative or referendum as a means of avoiding the lengthy public policy process. Individuals advocating a specific policy are leery of a prolonged process, because the longer the process, the greater the likelihood that a proposed policy will be amended.

Finally, individuals may turn to the initiative or referendum to get an issue before the public eye. In many cases, it has become, as Magleby (1988, p. 604) notes, a "powerful agenda-setting tool." Calls for an initiative or referendum dramatize an issue and place it before the public. As the public becomes more

aware of the issue, officials may be forced to publicly address
that issue.

The Evolution of Direct Democracy
in the United States

The origins of direct democracy go back a long way (Cronin,
1989; Hyink, Brown, and Thacker, 1973; Magleby, 1984; Tallian,
1977; Wilcox, 1912). It is not a practice unique to the United
States. In fact, direct democracy can be traced as far back as
ancient cities in Greece, where, in addition to having public officials responsible for some functions, citizens decided many
public issues. And, as the years passed, voters in Switzerland,
Spain, Italy, France, and the United Kingdom have voted on
important issues facing their respective countries (Cronin,
1989; Magleby, 1984; Tallian, 1977). Cronin (1989) also found
that questions on boundary or border disputes have been
placed before the voters in several countries.

A number of individuals have contributed, directly or indirectly, to the development of direct democracy in the United
States. Jean Jacques Rousseau, called the "patron saint of government by the people" by Cronin (1989, p. 38), was an active
supporter of citizen participation. Opposing representative
government, Rousseau believed citizens should be able to both
make and execute the laws of the area. As Fralin (1978, p. 39)
has pointed out, Rousseau felt that "the moment people allow
themselves to be represented, they surrender their freedom."
However, Fralin (1978) also noted that Rousseau was actually
opposed to direct democracy. Other individuals shared
Rousseau's belief and faith in the wisdom of the people. Alexis
de Tocqueville and Thomas Jefferson professed confidence in
the people and advocated increased citizen roles in a democracy.

The town meeting represents perhaps one of the most visible
expressions of direct democracy. As early as the seventeenth

century, towns in New England and elsewhere practiced this form of government, wherein citizens debated issues and ultimately arrived at how best to deal with the issues (Zimmerman, 1986). This form of direct democracy has been widely applauded. To many individuals, it extols the virtues of direct citizen participation in deciding public affairs.

Not everyone holds town meetings in such high regard, and there have been suggestions that the institution is appropriate for small towns but not for larger towns and cities. In that same line of thought, as a city becomes larger, the number of issues that must be addressed and decided increases dramatically. The time it would take to have the issues heard and eventually decided would be prohibitive. In the interim, citizens might become frustrated and leave the town meetings. Finally, there is always the issue of how many people would attend such a meeting. Many oppose town meetings because the potential exists for so many people to not show up that final decisions on public issues would actually be made by only a small group.

The Populist and Progressive Movements

During the late 1800s and early 1900s, the American people had a sense of uneasiness and concern over government, which was due, in part, to their believing that government was being unduly influenced by certain individuals and groups, that is, being corrupted. The people felt that there was too much behind-the-scenes activity taking place and that powerful lobbyists were gaining control of state and local governments. Moreover, Mitau (1966, p. 86) indicated that government woes could be traced to "self-seeking political bosses and machines." In the end, the wishes of the citizens were being ignored in favor of the wishes of the powerful lobbyists.

Corruption in government was a recurring theme in the Populist and Progressive movements (Cronin, 1989; Magleby,

1984). Individuals in both movements acknowledged a loss of faith in public officials and called for investigations into the political deals taking place. They wanted to know just how powerful the lobbyists were in deciding matters of public importance. According to Jacobs and Sokolow (1970, p. 98), "the basic argument of the Progressives throughout the United States was that corruption could be removed from politics by turning a larger number of political decisions over to popular vote." Moreover, Magleby (1984, p. 21) added that "a central tenet of the Progressive ideology was that the vigor of democracy and democratic institutions could be restored only with the overthrow of bosses and machines, and that reforms should ensure that public officials remained accountable to the voters." The Progressives supported the direct democracy beliefs of the Populists and advocated the adoption of the initiative, referendum, and recall devices. Expanding opportunities for citizen participation became a central theme of the movement. Populists and Progressives alike believed direct democracy was preferable to representative democracy.

A number of notables championed the call for the initiative, referendum, and recall, including Theodore Roosevelt, Robert La Follette of Wisconsin, and Hiram Johnson of California. While it is beyond the scope of this book to discuss the activities of these and other influential advocates, we can briefly examine Johnson's role in California.

Governor Hiram Johnson was an early champion of direct democracy (Hyink, Brown, and Thacker, 1973; Jacobs and Sokolow, 1970). He, along with others, had grown tired of watching the Southern Pacific Railroad exert its power in California's state and local political processes. It was the state's largest landowner and so dominated state and local politics that any issue affecting Southern Pacific was generally decided in its favor.

Johnson campaigned strongly against the political dominance of the Southern Pacific Railroad. He wanted to return government to the people, at least partly through the adoption of the initiative, referendum, and recall devices. He was, however, realistic enough to acknowledge that these devices would not solve all of California's political problems. In 1911 his goal was realized when California's voters added the initiative, referendum, and recall to the California State Constitution. In addition to these devices, Johnson's "Progressive" measures included:

> the cross-filing system; county home rule; the extension of civil service through the state government; the revitalization of the State Railroad Commission, extending its power over all public utilities, and giving it to the people to fix rates and determine the character of services; the prohibition of child labor; workmen's compensation laws; and the inauguration of many flood control, reclamation, and conservation projects. (Hyink, Brown, and Thacker, 1973, p. 66)

Over the years, a number of states, through constitutional or statutory provisions, have allowed the initiative or referendum or both. Local charters may also authorize the use of the initiative or referendum. Table 1.1 lists the states that allow one or both of the devices. In 1898 South Dakota became the first state to adopt both measures. It should also be noted that both measures are available to voters in Washington, D.C. The ability of voters in other cities around the United States to develop an initiative or referendum varies from state to state (Schmidt, 1989).

Issues addressed by an initiative or referendum vary from state to state. There does not appear to be one dominant issue that has appeared in each state. As Table 1.2 shows, some of the issues that have been decided by initiative or referendum include government spending, political ethics, property taxes, toxic waste cleanup, and terms of elected officials.

Table 1.1 States Providing for the Initiative and Referendum

State	Initiative	Referendum
Alaska	x	x
Arizona	x	x
Arkansas	x	x
California	x	x
Colorado	x	x
Florida	x	
Idaho	x	x
Illinois	x	
Kentucky		x
Maine	x	x
Maryland		x
Massachusetts	x	x
Michigan	x	x
Missouri	x	x
Montana	x	x
Nebraska	x	x
Nevada	x	x
New Mexico		x
North Dakota	x	x
Ohio	x	x
Oklahoma	x	x
Oregon	x	x
South Dakota	x	x
Utah	x	x
Washington	x	x
Wyoming	x	x

SOURCE: Compiled by author

California appears to be the number one state in terms of the number of measures appearing on state ballots. One might say this shows the voters' extreme frustration over their elected officials' failure to make the necessary tough decisions. Someone else observing the situation might say the proliferation of ballot measures shows that Californians simply want to take a more active role in deciding issues that will affect them. Regardless of the reason for the measures, Californians are constantly confronted with a host of ballot measures. Table 1.3

Table 1.2 Sampling of Issues Addressed by Initiative or Referendum

Revenue sharing (state and local)	Employment
Deposits on plastic and glass containers	Limiting parole
English as an official language	Property taxes
Cigarette and tobacco tax	Redistricting
Terms of elected officials	Gambling
Toxic waste cleanup	Hand guns
Water supply systems	Death penalty
Government spending	Political ethics
Right to work	Nuclear power
Equal rights	Denturism
Mass transit	Abortion
School bonds	Fluoridation
Child labor	Job safety
Job pension	Road building

SOURCE: Compiled by author

Table 1.3 Selected Topics of State Ballot Initiative Measures in California, 1912-1982

Abolition of poll tax	Daylight Saving Time
Prize fights	Aged and Blind Act
Usury Law	Public housing projects
Alien Land Law	Television programs
Chiropractic	Death penalty
State Liquor Regulation	Coastal Zone Conservation Act
Intoxicating liquors	Nuclear weapons
State Civil Service	Gift and Inheritance Tax
Selection of judges	Income tax indexing
Fishing Control	Political Reform Act
Funds for elementary schools	Public schools
Railroad brakemen	City and county consolidation

SOURCE: Eu, 1988a

provides a sampling of some of the statewide issues Californians have had to decide via the ballot box. These include the death penalty, coastal zone preservation, property taxes, fishing control, and prize fighting.

The requirements for qualifying an initiative or referendum for a state ballot vary from state to state (Magleby, 1984). Differences may surface regarding the number of signatures required, subject limitations, the format of the measure, and the number of votes required for passage. For purposes of illustration, a general overview of the requirements in California will be discussed.

The California Elections Code sets out the requirements for preparing and qualifying a statewide initiative or referendum for the ballot (Eu, 1988b). The initial step in the process is to write the measure. If the idea for a measure has been signed by 25 or more voters, assistance in drafting the measure can be obtained from the Legislative Counsel. The draft measure is then submitted to the State Attorney General, who prepares a title and summary of the measure. A fee to prepare the title and summary is returned to the proponents if the measure qualifies for the ballot. Next, the title and summary are provided to the Secretary of State. Should the Secretary of State feel a fiscal analysis of the ballot measure is needed, the Department of Finance and Joint Legislative Budget Committee will be asked to prepare it. Requirements also exist for the format of the petition, the date the petition can be circulated, who can sign the petition, the number of signatures required to qualify the measure for the ballot, verification of the petition by election officials, and the date the measure becomes effective if approved by the electorate.

The requirements for placing a measure on a local ballot differ according to the type of city. In California, the requirements for general law cities can be found in the State Elections Code. Durkee, Jacobson, Wood, and Zischke (1990, p. 57) identified the following steps in the initiative process:

1. Submitting the proposed measure and petition;
2. Publishing and/or posting notice of intent to circulate the petitions;
3. Requesting a ballot title and summary;

4. Preparation of the ballot title and summary by the city attorney;
5. Circulating the petitions for signature;
6. Examination of signatures by the city clerk for possible qualification for the ballot;
7. Optional city report on the measure;
8. If there are enough signatures, then the city must either adopt the measure or place it on the ballot;
9. If the measure is placed on the ballot, an impartial analysis and ballot arguments are prepared; and
10. The campaign and the election.

Cities having a charter for their own government, consistent with and subject to the California Constitution, can have similar procedures. Durkee et al. (1990, p. 58) identified the following steps in the referendum process at the local level:

1. The city council enacts legislation;
2. Opponents circulate a referendum petition for signatures before the legislation becomes legally effective (usually 30 days);
3. The petitions do not need to be submitted to the city first and no notice needs to be published, but the petition must be in proper form;
4. Examination of signatures by the city for possible qualification for the ballot;
5. If there are enough signatures, the city council must either repeal the legislation itself or submit the measure to the voters;
6. If the measure is submitted to the voters, an impartial analysis and ballot arguments are prepared; and
7. The campaign and the election.

However, some of their requirements can vary from those of general law cities. For example, San Diego is a charter city that has enacted a set of requirements for getting a measure placed on the ballot. Section 27.2501 of the San Diego Municipal Code discusses the subject of an initiative:

Any proposed legislative act or proposed amendment or
repeal of an existing legislative act may be submitted to the
Council by an initiative petition filed in the office of the
Clerk. The Council may also submit to the people for vote
a proposed legislative act, or proposed amendment or repeal of an existing legislative act, without having first received a petition therefor.

The Municipal Code sets out the remainder of the requirements, such as the number of signatures required for submitting the measure to the Council (3%) or direct submission to the
voters (10%); notice of intention; contents of the petition; affi-
davit of authenticity; verification of the petition; notice of suf-
ficiency; notice of insufficiency; withdrawal of signatures;
action by council; special election to be called; effective date of
initiated legislative act; conflicting provisions in initiated legislative acts; amendment and repeal of initiated legislative acts;
initiative election not limited to one legislative act; initiative
election to conform to other elections; and amendment and repeal of the measure through action by council. A similar set of
requirements exists for placing a referendum on the ballot.

CITIZEN ATTITUDES TOWARD
DIRECT DEMOCRACY

A substantial amount of literature has examined how citizens
feel about direct democracy (Cronin, 1989), looking at such
areas as how well informed the citizens are about issues and
ballot measures, the complexity of the ballot measures, support
for direct democracy versus representative democracy, and improvements in the initiative process. Studies on these and other
issues can help shed some light on how well or how poorly
direct democracy is faring in the United States.

Table 1.4 Citizen Understanding of the Issues in San Diego
(*N*= 503) (in percents)

Issue	Agree	Disagree	Don't Know
The general public is not able to cast informed votes	23.5	74.3	2.2
The public is able to cast informed votes and deserves more of a say in government.	85.3	13.7	1.0

SOURCE: Caves, unpublished survey data.

Citizen Understanding of the Issues

The question of how well the voters understand the issues is constantly being debated. Opponents of direct democracy claim voters are not knowledgeable enough about the issues to make informed decisions. Conversely, direct democracy enthusiasts believe the voters are well versed in the issues and can be trusted to make informed decisions. Using a telephone survey undertaken for this book, Table 1.4 shows how a random sample of more than 500 San Diegans feel about their ability to make informed decisions on the issues. Table 1.4 illustrates that an overwhelming majority of the respondents disagreed with the claim that voters could not cast informed votes. Instead, they indicated a belief that they do cast informed votes. Thus, support does exist, in this respect, for direct democracy.

Complexity of the Issues and Ballot Measures

The issues placed before the voters vary in complexity, and this worries many scholars, who feel that citizens may fail to appreciate that complexity. Moreover, they feel the wording of the ballot measure with its "yes or no" decision is totally

Table 1.5 Citizen Perceptions on the Complexity of Issues and Ballot Measures in San Diego (N= 503) (in percents)

Issue	Agree	Disagree	Don't Know
Many issues are too complicated to be decided by a yes or no vote.	85.3	14.0	0.8
Initiative measures on the ballot are usually so complicated that one cannot understand them.	58.6	40.2	1.2
The wording of initiatives is too technical for most people to understand.	77.1	20.9	2.0
Most people who sign an initiative petition don't understand what the actual measure says or means.	72.2	24.8	3.0

SOURCE: Caves, unpublished survey data.

inappropriate. Table 1.5 lends support to this sentiment by showing that 85% of the respondents believed the issues put before them were too complicated to be decided by a simple "yes or no" answer. Furthermore, almost 60% of them acknowledged that initiative measures were also too complicated to understand, and more than 75% felt that the wording of the measures was too technical. To make problems even worse, almost 75% of the respondents indicated a belief that most people signing an initiative petition do not understand the actual meaning of the measure.

Support for Representative Democracy

The respondents repeatedly expressed the belief that both the issues and the ballot measures were complicated and technical. Does this mean that they would rather have their elected

Table 1.6 Citizen Support for Representative Democracy
(*N*=503) (in percents)

Issue	Agree	Disagree	Don't Know
Citizens should be able to vote directly on all issues.	72.0	25.8	2.2
The public should be allowed to decide an issue when public officials may have a conflict of interest with special interest groups.	86.3	10.2	3.6
The job of making laws should be left to locally elected representatives	44.7	48.7	6.6

SOURCE: Caves, unpublished survey data.

officials make the necessary public decisions? According to Table 1.6, the respondents were divided on this issue. More than 85% felt the public should be allowed to decide an issue when a public official has an apparent conflict of interest over that issue. Moreover, more than 70% of the respondents professed a desire to vote directly on all issues. This lends support to the belief that citizens possess enough intelligence to make informed decisions. However, there is divided support on whether the job of making laws should be left to the elected officials. Thus, the issue of who should decide public issues remains unresolved.

Changes in the Initiative Process

Although the respondents indicated a preference for allowing citizens to decide the issues via the initiative, Table 1.7 shows that more than 75% of the respondents felt significant changes were needed to make the process function better. Two specific recommendations received a great deal of support.

Table 1.7 Citizen Recommended Changes in the Initiative Process
(*N*= 503) (in percents)

Issue	Agree	Disagree	Don't Know
Significant changes are needed to make the initiative process more workable.	76.9	16.3	6.8
The number of initiatives that that can be placed on a ballot should be limited.	59.9	37.4	2.8
The number of signatures required in order to qualify an initiative for the ballot should be increased.	27.4	51.9	20.7
Using paid signature gatherers for collecting the required signatures for an initiative should be prohibited.	46.1	48.7	5.2
Stiff fines and penalties should be imposed for false or misleading advertising on initiatives.	95.6	2.2	2.2
Public meetings should be called to discuss the merits and drawbacks of a proposed initiative once it gets the necessary signatures.	91.0	6.6	2.4

SOURCE: Caves, unpublished survey data.

First, the respondents indicated a very strong desire (95%) to fine individuals or groups engaged in false advertising. Too many initiative campaigns have been plagued by advertising campaigns, slogans, and gimmicks that appear to be trying to either mislead or confuse the voters. On occasion, instead of rebutting the opposition campaign, an individual or group may have achieved the desired goal of defeating an initiative by simply confusing the voters. Second, 90% of the respondents would also like to see a public hearing convened to discuss the pros and cons of an initiative. A number of people may perceive this as a forum to eliminate frivolous initiatives and also an opportunity to get some first-hand information on the issue being addressed by a specific initiative.

Respondents made several recommendations for improving the system. Slightly less than 60% wanted to see a limit on the number of initiatives allowed on the ballot. Many people feel ballots have become too cluttered with initiatives, which eventually frustrates the voters. The final straw in this frustration is a failure to vote on the measures. Trying to limit the number of initiatives on the ballot would undoubtedly lead to a legal challenge. Interestingly enough, the respondents (51%) agreed that the number of signatures needed to qualify an initiative for the ballot was appropriate. This issue is constantly being discussed, with calls for increasing the number of required signatures in an effort to limit frivolous initiatives. Opponents see any increase as an improper impediment to direct democracy. Finally, the respondents were split on whether the use of paid signature gatherers should be prohibited. Forty-six percent of the respondents felt paid signature gatherers should be prohibited, whereas 48% felt it was legitimate to use them. The major complaint involving paid signature gatherers is that they are not well versed in the specifics of the measure; therefore, they are essentially unable to respond to questions they may be asked.

Overall Impressions About Ballot Measures

As the earlier sections of this chapter suggest, there is a wide range of opinions regarding direct democracy. In a 1989 survey, pollster Mervin Field asked Californians "what's good" and "what's bad" about statewide ballot proposition elections. The

Table 1.8 Citizen Perceptions About What's Good About Statewide
Ballot Proposition Elections in California (*N*= 1007) (in percents)

Reason	Percentage
Gives people a voice/a chance to give their opinions, to vote, to participate	48.4
Takes power out of the hands of a few, the Legislature/direct participation instead of indirect through Legislature	5.8
Voters can decide things Legislature is afraid, unable to/forces the issue. Voters can get things done	6.5
Allows concerned citizen groups to put things before the voters/allows for greater opportunities for change	7.0
It makes people read up on the issues, makes voters more aware, think more/ increases voter interest in political matters	5.6
Voter decisions benefit the state, everyone, is good politics	2.1
Enables citizens to get the attention of the legislature, political groups	2.6
Other	1.1
No answer/nothing specific	20.9

SOURCE: California Field Poll, No. 8901, January 23-31, 1989

responses echoed the opinions of earlier proponents and opponents of direct democracy.

Tables 1.8 and 1.9 indicate the positives and negatives of
statewide ballot proposition elections. In terms of what was
good about the elections, respondents noted the virtues of cit-

Table 1.9 Citizen Perceptions About What's Bad About Statewide
Ballot Proposition Elections in California (*N*= 1007) (in percents)

Reason	Percentage
Too confusing, complicated, misleading, wordy, legalistic/should be simpler, put in plain English	8.5
Too much to read, wasted my time, clutters the ballot, makes voting take too long	1.5
There are too many of them on the ballot/getting out of hand	7.1
Many Props are poorly thought out, not good law, unconstitutional/unintended effects	3.9
After some are voted into effect, nothing happens/laws are not enforced as written/no follow through after the election/too easily overturned by courts and special interests	6.2
Signature gathering is not always legitimate/people sign them without reading petitions/number of signatures needed is too low	1.5
Public is not knowledgeable enough to vote on them. Voters don't have all the information/can't really make an informed choice/people vote on things that don't affect them	7.5
Legislature should be deciding on most of them/elected officials are passing the buck, not doing their jobs	2.7
There are too many special interest group initiatives	5.9
Ads used in campaigns are misleading, distorted/no restrictions on funding	2.8
They are becoming too expensive, too many ads	4.1
Special interests can keep bringing them up again, even after they are voted down	0.4
Statewide initiatives are too broad, should be more regional/local	0.5
Not enough people vote/not a good reflection of the public's mind	1.1
Northern, rural voters don't count for much next to L.A.	0.4
Other	2.8
No answer/nothing specific	43.1

SOURCE: California Field Poll, No. 8901, January 23-31, 1989

izen participation. As Table 1.8 shows, slightly more than 48%
of the respondents liked statewide ballot proposition elections
because they afford citizens the opportunity to have their
voices heard and allow them to participate in government activities. Other positive reasons given for liking the elections included that they allow citizens the opportunity to place issues
on the public policy agenda, allow citizens to make decisions
when government officials fail to do so, and serve to increase
an individual's knowledge on important public issues.

The reasons why people feel ballot proposition elections are
bad, as shown in Table 1.9, vary a great deal. Most of the respondents did not select a specific reason; however, some respondents did say they felt that measures were too confusing
and too complicated to understand. Combined with a perceived belief that voters did not have enough information on
the issues, some of the respondents were concerned with
individuals' making uninformed decisions on important public policy issues. Other concerns over the elections included the
number of measures on the ballot, the lack of implementation
after a measure has been passed, the proliferation of special interest initiatives, and the cost of the election.

CONCLUDING COMMENTS

Chapter 1 has provided needed background information for
the remainder of the book, including a discussion of the origins
of direct democracy, the reasons for and against direct democracy, the role of citizen participation in government matters, and
citizen attitudes about the use of the initiative and referendum.

Existing research on direct democracy varies widely. Some
research extols its virtues and advocates its wider use. Other

research tries to criticize direct democracy by focusing on the complexity of the issues being addressed and on the lack of citizen awareness and education on the issues. Chapter 2 addresses how direct democracy has been applied to issues in the land use arena.

T W O

Ballot Box Planning
in the United States

Land use issues remain high on the public policy agendas in many cities across the United States. In some areas, citizens are frustrated over the continued growth and development of their areas and feel elected officials are ignoring their concerns. In other areas, citizens are taking proactive stances in trying to preserve open space and environmentally sensitive lands. We can turn to Beatley (1989) for reasons why land use decisions are important. He suggests they are important because "they influence the quality of life in communities, environmental amenities, and other social goods and services" (p. 27). In other words, one land use decision could potentially cause repercussions on a number of different levels.

Ballot box planning is the name commonly associated with the use of the initiative or referendum in deciding a land use matter (Orman, 1984). Whether citizens can turn to the initiative or referendum depends on the state in question. As noted in Chapter 1, some states have provisions for one or both of their uses in the state constitution. Other states may have provisions for one or both of their uses through state statutes or through home rule charters. Use of either tool is limited to legislative matters.

Potential topics for an initiative or referendum vary from state to state. While some states interpret their use broadly, other states may restrict their use to a few specific topics. In the latter case, the state is interpreting the power very narrowly. Ballot measures have dealt with such issues as the rezoning of a tract of land, adopting or rejecting a general plan, limiting the height of buildings in a certain area, allowing the construction of apartments, limiting development in an area to certain uses, creating a buffer zone, repealing a decision to create a street-paving program, adopting or rejecting a growth management plan, and allowing rental apartments in single-family zones. Readers are cautioned against generalizing these particular issues to all states. Once again, while one state may allow one of the aforementioned issues to be decided by a ballot, another state may prohibit the issue from being resolved in the same way. A legal interpretation of their use is examined in Chapter 3.

TRADITIONAL LAND USE CONTROL TECHNIQUES

All levels of government can directly or indirectly affect land use. However, land use planning powers were originally vested with the state governments. Through the years, local governments were given the power to regulate land use within their municipal boundaries. A variety of techniques are available to the local governments for this purpose (Branch, 1985; Brower, et al., 1976; Burrows, 1978; Clawson, 1973; Delafons, 1969; Gleeson, et al., 1975; Johnston, 1980; Patterson, 1988; Platt, 1976; Porter, 1986; Webster, 1958). It remains up to the individual municipalities to choose the most appropriate techniques to fit their particular needs.

Patterson (1988) notes that local governments possess four major powers that enable them to affect land use. First, they possess the police power, which enables them to promote and protect the public health, safety, and welfare. The states delegated this power to them via enabling legislation. Applications of the police power would include the use of zoning, subdivision regulations, and sanitation codes. Second, localities can use the power of eminent domain to acquire private property for a public purpose with payment of just compensation to the property owner. Third, localities have the taxing power, which allows them to raise revenue. Finally, they can spend the money raised from the taxing power on various public purposes, such as building schools, sewers, roads, parks, and libraries.

Zoning is far and away the most widely employed land use control technique today (Gleeson, et al., 1975; Nelson, 1980). According to Levy (1988, p. 106), the reason for its widespread popularity is quite simple:

> It has considerable power to achieve goals that the community favors, and it is free. More precisely, it is free to the community in that no compensation need be paid for the loss sustained by the property owner. In principle, the same could be achieved by exercise of the power of eminent domain or by the contract between municipality and property owner. But either of those courses would necessitate major expenditures by the municipality.

The issue of compensation must ultimately be decided on a case-by-case basis. Nevertheless, its application in controlling land use has evolved greatly over the years.

Conventional zoning has an area's land being divided into four general categories: agricultural, residential, commercial, and industrial. Of course, specific subcategories will differ from one city to another. Moreover, zoning will undoubtedly change as the city and its needs change. As such, zoning represents a volatile issue in many areas across the country, especially when land is rezoned to a higher intensive use (i.e., agricultural to residential, residential to commercial). Many citizens resent community change and actively resist it. They do not want to jeopardize their current quality of life.

While rezoning from a lower intensive use to a higher intensive use might draw the anger of some individuals, the same can be said of down-zoning. Down-zoning, currently being employed as a growth control technique, is the rezoning of property from a higher intensive use to a lower intensive use (i.e., commercial to residential, residential to agricultural). Lowering the intensity of development has been used to protect the public from "earthquake slide problems, erosion, watershed flooding, overburdening municipal services, and scenic damage" (Carter, Bert, and Nobert, 1974, p. 269). Property owners tend to resent down-zoning since it results in a reduction in the value of their property. Consequently, it is not unusual to hear a property owner claim that the value of the property has been reduced so much that the down-zoning constitutes a taking of private property without payment of just compensation (Caves, 1980). The extent of the reduction and whether the down-zoning is a taking of private property will be decided on a case-by-case basis.

Subdivision regulations constitute the second major tool that localities use to govern the development and use of land. According to Schultz and Kasen (1984, p. 388), subdivision regulations are intended "to facilitate the orderly conversion of vacant land to developed land and to ensure that the new developments are compatible with surrounding development." We can also add the intention that the new development will not be a financial burden or liability on the city and its existing residents. These regulations might define necessary street sizes, water pipe sizes, location of sewer outlets, grading and erosion control requirements, bicycle path dedications, parking requirements, and landscaping requirements.

Another related technique employed by cities to control land use is the dedication of land or public facilities. With most municipalities deeply concerned about additional capital outlays required for new residential, commercial, or industrial developments, developers are now required to share this burden with the city. For example, before an industrial development is approved, a municipality may require the developer to donate land for various public purposes. Furthermore, if no roads, water, or sewage lines are present in the proposed development area, the municipality may require the developer to install them. This can save the municipality a great deal of money. It also gives the area some leverage in determining how it will grow.

Municipalities can also control land use through the location of and access to public facilities. This technique has also been called everything from *development phasing* to *timed and sequential growth*. It recognizes that the location of and access to public facilities and services influence where growth occurs.

The location of public services and facilities acts as a significant land use planning tool designed to facilitate orderly growth (Clawson, 1972; Cooper, 1986; Council on Environmental Quality, 1976; National Academy of Sciences, 1972). In fact, it is often considered a no-growth weapon because without public services, nothing will be built, unless the developers construct the needed services and facilities.

Sewer moratoriums are occasionally employed by municipalities to ensure the adequacy of public services. Cities have instituted sewer moratoriums to alleviate possible environmental damages resulting from the operation of septic tanks. The moratoriums are temporary in nature and are relaxed when the services become available.

Municipalities have also sought to control land use by limiting the number of building permits that can be issued over a specific period of time. This is used for a given period of time so a municipality can literally "catch up" to the growth in terms of providing services. A number of legal battles have been waged over this technique.

Land-banking is also available to help prevent premature development and to promote more orderly development. With this technique, municipalities purchase the property instead of letting it be prematurely developed, thus avoiding the large capital outlays that would be needed to provide services and facilities to these areas. A major problem, although not insurmountable, to the creation of a land-banking program concerns the financing of the program. How will the necessary funds be raised to purchase the land? Raising a city's sales tax appears to be one option that was successful in Boulder, Colorado (Lewis, 1975).

There are numerous additional techniques at the disposal of municipalities for controlling land use. Depending on the location, municipalities might choose from various environmental controls, transfer or purchase of development rights, tax and fee systems, official maps, capital programming, developments of regional impact, and the development of a general or comprehensive plan (Carr and Duensing, 1983; DeGrove and deHaven-Smith, 1988; Gleeson, et al., 1975; Popper, 1981; Siemon, Larsen, and Fleming, 1988).

The selection of any land use control technique must be carefully thought out. Municipalities can no longer plan in isolation from their neighbors and the surrounding communities. They must take into consideration the effects of their actions on neighboring jurisdictions. After all, the land use actions of one municipality could result in serious extraterritorial repercussions. For example, if one municipality rezones the property along one of its borders from agricultural to a higher intensive use, and a neighboring municipality keeps its land in the affected area zoned for agricultural uses, the agricultural lands in the latter city could suffer from increased pollution. The result could be that the agricultural uses may be forced to leave the area. Overall, the idea of having cities consider the regional implications of their actions is important. As Brower (1980, p. 144) has observed, a city can no longer conceive of itself "as an island where planning choices caused as little effect as a ripple on an open sea."

The states have taken a more active role in controlling land use issues today, including the area of growth (Babcock, 1966; Bosselman and Callies, 1971; Council of State Governments, 1976; DeGrove, 1984, 1987; Healy and Rosenberg, 1979; New Jersey State Planning Commission, 1988; Popper, 1981, 1988; Reilly, 1973; Turner, 1990). We have witnessed increasing land use control and environmental regulation activities in such states as Hawaii, California, Oregon, Vermont, New Jersey, and Florida. As previously stated, although land use controls have been traditionally vested in the local governments, concerns over the inadequacies of local controls, environmental degradation, quality of life, and problems associated with local parochialism have prompted the states to assume a more active role in the land use arena. From time to time there have been calls for the creation of state agencies to review, and possibly override, local land use decisions (Babcock, 1966). Bosselman and Callies (1971, p. 3) acknowledge one of the major problems that led to more state activities in land use regulations:

> It has become increasingly apparent that the local zoning ordinance, virtually the sole means of land use control in the United States for over half a century, has proved woefully inadequate to combat a host of problems of statewide significance, social problems as well as problems involving environmental pollution and destruction of vital ecological systems, which threatens our very existence.
>
> It is this realization that local zoning is inadequate to cope with problems that are statewide or regionwide in scope that has fueled the quiet revolution in land use control.

Ten years later Popper (1981, p. 10) took an even stronger stance on the early problems of local actions when he stated:

> Most land-use plans, where they existed at all, consisted of little more than a record of good intentions. The plans were only advisory; they lacked the force of law. Zoning and subdivision regulations were supposed to be consistent with the plans, but a determined developer could almost always get around the intent of a plan by obtaining a variance, especially if he was willing to bribe or make campaign contributions to a few underpaid local government officials.

No one advocates taking away total land use control by the local governments and substituting it with state controls. The preponderance of land use control activity will ultimately remain in the hands of the local governments. Nevertheless, a closer working relationship between all levels of government and the private sector becomes imperative, and failure to establish it could bring dire consequences. This is especially true in the area of growth controls. Ron Rotella, the chairman of Florida's Governor's Task Force on Urban Growth Patterns (1989), predicted that, "If we fail to get a grip on our growth and do not begin planning for and implementing sound, concentrated urban growth patterns, incremental and ad hoc planning and permitting by citizen referendum may soon chart our path into the future." This prediction has already come true in some parts of the country.

THE POPULATION GROWTH DEBATE

There continue to be debates over the desirability or undesirability of population growth (Baldassare, 1981; Feagin, 1988; Logan and Molotch, 1987; Maraziti, 1987; Molotch, 1976; Vogel and Swanson, 1989). The adages, "growth is good" and "growth means progress," are no longer accepted at face value. The arrival of growth means different things to different people. A number of questions can be asked regarding the consequences of population growth. For example, what will happen to the area's quality of life? What will happen to the area's public services? Will the schools become overcrowded? What effects will the growth have on the area's open space and agricultural lands? How much will crime increase? Where will the area get additional water to meet the needs of a growing population? What will happen to the area's property values? What will happen to the area's neighborhoods? These are important questions that must be addressed by every city expected to increase in population. The issue of whether the advantages of growth outweigh the disadvantages depends on the individual city.

To many cities, population growth brings a number of positive attributes with it. For example, housing opportunities may increase with the influx of new residents. A growing population may also increase the likelihood of new and/or improved cultural facilities in the area. Furthermore, new industries may accompany the population increase, bringing the new jobs and increased tax revenue that are a definite plus to some cities. Providing that the existing infrastructure is not being used to capacity, increased population density could permit, depending on the particular service, a fuller exploitation of existing facilities. Ideally, this would then lead to lower per capita expenditures (economies of scale). Unfortunately, these economies of scale may turn into diseconomies of scale after an optimal population size has been reached and no improvements have been made in the facilities.

Population growth also has its associated costs. Agricultural lands or other types of open space may need to be sacrificed to meet the needs (i.e., housing, transportation, public services, and so on) of the growing population. If public facilities are being used at near or full capacity, and if the ability of the city to finance the improvement or construction of new facilities is limited, a number of negative effects may occur. For example, an influx of new people into an area may result in overcrowded schools and congested roads. In addition, air and water quality degradation are likely by-products of a growing population.

REASONS CITIZENS TURN
TO THE BALLOT BOX

Citizens are afforded a number of opportunities to participate in the land use planning process. They are able to voice their concerns by speaking at public hearings before the planning department, the planning commission, and the city council. Some citizens may also have the opportunity to serve on a citizen committee or subcommittee established to address a planning issue. The functions of such bodies differ by issue and purpose.

The timing of citizen participation is very important. In past years, citizen concerns had been generally heard after a government agency had decided a given course of action. This represented reaction to a given decision, not participation. However, as the years passed, citizen participation became a required component of many planning processes. It was required early in the process, not later. This led to the identification and resolution of many potential conflicts before a decision had been reached. On many occasions, this citizen participation helped influence decision makers and led to greater public support for the chosen course of action.

With the overwhelming majority of legislative decisions being made at the local level by city councils, and with provisions for citizen participation, why have citizens turned to the ballot box to decide various land use matters? Are they becoming discouraged with representative democracy? Do they want to take a more active role in governing themselves, or are they simply frustrated over one particular city council decision?

There is no one universal reason why either citizens or groups have ventured to the ballot box. The reasons for using the ballot box are site specific.

Many municipalities have taken a pro-growth attitude over the years. They have actively courted industries and companies to locate within their boundaries. These municipalities believe that the benefits associated with population growth (i.e., more jobs, more tax revenue, increased housing opportunities, increased cultural opportunities, and potential economies of scale regarding public infrastructure) outweigh the associated costs of growth. However, many of the municipalities may have experienced too much of a good thing. Their financial situations prevent them from adequately maintaining, repairing, or replacing the infrastructure. The added population may also have contributed to traffic congestion, overcrowded schools, and a general lessening of the area's quality of life. In response to a city's pro-growth stance, citizens have turned to the ballot box in an attempt to preserve the quality of life.

Molotch (1976) contends that cities are dominated by a land-based elite that he characterizes as a "growth machine." This idea has been examined on a number of occasions (Baldassare, 1981; DeLeon and Powell, 1989; Domhoff, 1986; Fleischmann and Feagin, 1987; Vogel and Swanson, 1989). According to growth machine theory, in this scenario, land is viewed as a commodity. Individuals and organizations comprising the growth machine include developers, real estate interests, lawyers, retailers, newspapers, and financial interests. According to Domhoff (1986, p. 59), "the central meeting points of the growth machine are most often banks, where executives from the utility companies and the department stores join with the largest landlords and developers, as members of the boards of directors." These individuals tend to dominate the political scene. They are in favor of actions that will benefit themselves and other members of the growth machine. They are all for anything that is in their best financial interest. Conversely, if an action is contrary to their best interests, they oppose it. Later Logan and Molotch (1987) suggested members of the growth machine tend "to oppose any intervention that might regulate development on behalf of use values." In addition, Logan and Molotch pointed out:

> They may quarrel among themselves over exactly how rents will be distributed among parcels, over how, that is, they will share the spoils of aggregate growth. But virtually all place entrepreneurs and their growth machine associates, regardless of geographical or social location, easily agree on the issue of growth itself. (p. 32)

Some cities continue to extol the virtues of local growth. Moreover, they are constantly promoting the city in direct and indirect ways. As Logan and Molotch also wrote:

> The celebration of local growth continues to be a theme in the culture of localities. Schoolchildren are taught to view local history as a series of breakthroughs in the expansion of the economic base of their city and region, celebrating its numerical leadership in one sort of production or another; more generally, increases in population tend to be equated with local progress. Civic organizations sponsor essay contests on the topic of local greatness. They encourage public celebrations and spectacles in which the locality name can be proudly advanced for the benefit of both locals and outsiders. They subsidize soapbox derbies, parade floats, and beauty contests to "spread around" the locality's name in the media and at distant competitive sites. (p. 61)

The idea of boosterism does not sit well with all members of the community. Many individuals do not share in the benefits of growth because they are not evenly distributed among the population. To these people, the only thing that growth means is that the rich get richer. In some cases, citizens may feel a need to turn to the ballot box as a response to the tremendous influence wielded by the growth machine. While the growth machine seeks to stimulate economic development to increase its financial interests in a city, other citizens might feel the ballot box represents the only place the growth machine can be stopped or even controlled.

Frustration over the failure of elected officials to enforce previously enacted land use plans and policies may represent another reason citizens have turned to the ballot box. For example, in a city that had previously adopted a city growth control plan, citizens may feel that the continued passing of growth-inducing projects is violating either the intent or the purpose of the previously adopted plan. In addition, citizens may feel utterly frustrated or even outraged over a city council's continued exempting of certain projects from the growth control plan. Sensing a lack of commitment on enforcing current policies, citizens have taken matters into their own hands and formulated growth control policies that allow the voters to decide whether new residential, commercial, or industrial projects will be approved.

Citizens may also resort to ballot box planning because of one particular land use issue. There is a group of activities needed in urban areas that are unpopular with the citizens. For instance, landfills represent a classic example of a "local unwanted land use" (LULU) or a "not in my back yard" (NIMBY) land use. The same opposition may occur if a city wants to put a new jail next to a residential area. In such situations, citizens may develop a ballot measure that gives them the right to approve or disapprove the location of that landfill or jail.

Ultimately, a list of reasons behind the increased use of ballot box planning would be endless. However, it can be stated that citizens are becoming increasingly upset with traffic congestion and land use changes that propose to either increase density or alter an area's quality of life. In the end, citizens will

turn to the ballot box if they feel the elected politicians are ignoring their opinions, or if they feel that some activity or activities will negatively impact their lives.

CALIFORNIA'S FASCINATION
WITH BALLOT BOX PLANNING

Article II, Section 11 of the California Constitution provides
that "initiative and referendum powers may be exercised by
the electors of each city and county under procedures that the
Legislature shall provide." Zoning and land use matters, subject to various limitations, are potential topics for an initiative
or referendum. The use of the initiative or referendum has
grown over the years. According to research reported by
Glickfeld, Graymer, and Morrison (1987, p. 113), there were 152
local land use ballot measures on the ballots from 1971 through
1986. More recent figures from the California Association of Realtors (1989) show that 357 land use planning measures (i.e.,
initiative, referendum, advisory measure, or council-sponsored
measure) could be found on local ballots from November 1971
to August 1989. Table 2.1 shows a breakdown of the measures
by specific years. It clearly shows that 1988 was, far and away,
the leading year for land use measures, with 109, or 30%, of the
total number of measures over the time period.

The topics or subjects of land use ballot measures vary by jurisdiction. Orman (1984, p. 2) noted the following land use actions
have been the subject of ballot measures around California:

1. Set limits on the annual rate or amount of allowed housing
   development;
2. Require a vote of the people to enlarge water or sewer service
   boundaries;
3. Set basic policy on key land-use issues;
4. Direct city council or county supervisors to prepare a plan in accordance with policies set forth in ballot measures;

Table 2.1 Frequency of Land Use Ballot Measures in California, 1971-1989

Year	Number of Measures
1971	1
1972	4
1973	3
1974	2
1975	0
1976	1
1977	3
1978	8
1979	15
1980	9
1981	10
1982	18
1983	5
1984	12
1985	17
1986	61
1987	58
1988	109
1989	21
Total	357

SOURCE: California Association of Realtors, 1989

   5. Set minimum lot sizes for residential building (especially in farm areas);
   6. Approve or disapprove development projects;
   7. Establish moratoria on land development or service delivery;
   8. Designate specific areas for development or conservation; and
   9. Require that changes in certain land uses be made only after an affirmative vote of the people.

Table 2.2 provides a sampling of how ballot box planning measures have been used in some jurisdictions.

No area in California is immune from a possible land use ballot measure. We have witnessed measures in small towns and large cities. The topics, as suggested above, vary from area to area. The likelihood of their passage or defeat depends on the specific circumstances of each area.

Concerns over rapid growth and its negative side effects prompted the City of Redlands to issue a moratorium on building permits. Although the city studied alternative ways to manage its growth, citizens became somewhat disenchanted when nothing came of the city's study. Feeling Redlands was losing its character as a result of the rapid growth, a group calling itself the Redlands Growth Initiative Committee developed Proposition R. This measure, an initiative, "set an annual limit of 450 building permits within the city limits and limited city service extensions to new units in the surrounding county to no more than 150 of the 450 permits" (California Office of Planning and Research, 1980, p. 21). The initiative was passed by the voters in November 1978.

As shown in Table 2.2, not all of the ballot measures have been passed by the voters. In 1978 citizens in El Dorado County tried, via Measure B, to place a limit on the number of building permits that could be issued in the unincorporated area of the county. The number of permits could be increased if the county's population increased. Proponents of Measure B believed the growth would outstrip the county's ability to provide needed services. Moreover, since services were already overburdened, the growth would exacerbate the problem. Conversely, instead of an initiative, opponents to Measure B called for careful planning that would preserve valuable open space. They felt the initiative was not needed and, if passed, would ultimately result in more problems. The measure was defeated in November 1978.

Two years later, in 1980, residents of Madera County sought to establish a growth-management system that would limit the county's growth to the percentage of California's yearly growth. While the measure's proponents focused on the negative externalities associated with population growth, opponents challenged the notion that Madera County was one of the

Table 2.2 Sampling of Land Use Planning Ballot Measures in
California, 1971-1989

Locality	Year	Title of Measure	Nature of Measure	Outcome
San Francisco	1971	Prop. T (I)	To ban buildings higher than 6 stories unless approved by voters	Failed
Livermore	1972	Measure B (I)	Impose moratorium on building permits pending resolution of deficiencies in public facilities	Passed
San Jose	1973	Measure B (I)	To limit zoning or rezoning of land to residential in areas where schools are impacted	Passed
Santa Barbara	1977	Measure A1 (A)	To amend the General Plan to limit population growth to 85,000	Passed
Belmont	1979	Measure B (C.S.)	To allow Council to establish limits on building permits	Failed
Bishop	1980	Measure B (I)	To limit housing construction and population growth	Failed
Simi Valley	1981	Measure A (R)	To confirm a rezoning to increase the density of a residential development	Failed
Fremont	1981	Measure A (I)	To protect hillsides and ridgetops from development	Passed
Monterey Park	1982	Prop. L (I)	To require voter approval on certain future zoning changes	Passed
Lodi	1983	Measure D (I)	To annex 52 acres to expand a subdivision	Failed
Hayward	1984	Measure M (I)	To limit hillside development	Failed
Modesto	1984	Measure F (C.S.)	To approve a sewer trunk extension	Passed

Table 2.2 Continued

Locality	Year	Title of Measure	Nature of Measure	Outcome
Victorville	1985	Measure Q (I)	To downzone 1,500 acres of commercial and R-3 properties to R-1	Passed
Tiburon	1986	Measure C (I)	To impose a building moratorium	Passed
Concord	1986	Measure A (I)	To restrict height of residential/ commerical development	Failed
Berkeley	1986	Measure P (I)	To restrict development of Berkeley waterfront	Failed
Pacific Grove	1986	Measure D (I)	To place all unclassified land in an open space category	Passed
San Mateo County	1987	Measure I (C.S.)	To repeal the park and open space program	Failed
Lewiston	1988	Measure B (A)	To advise the location of a solid waste disposal site in Lewiston	Failed
Danville	1989	Measure A (I)	To amend the circulation element to allow Camino Ramon to be extended as a through street	Passed
Tehama County	1989	Measure C (A)	Request for voter support for siting of a California State Prison in Tehama County	Failed
Davis	1989	Measure P (R)	To approve a pre-zoning agreement passed by the City Council allowing the Mace Ranch development	Passed

NOTE: I = Initiative; A = Advisory; C.S. = Council Sponsored; R = Referendum
SOURCE: California Association of Realtors, 1989

fastest-growing counties in California and predicted that the
county's economy would be harmed and the cost of housing
would increase. Voters rejected the measure on June 3, 1980.

The impacts of population growth have been a concern for
Walnut Creek residents for a number of years. Neither wanting
nor encouraging growth, Walnut Creek had the unenviable distinction of being located where several major highways
crossed. With no new roads being constructed, traffic congestion increased as the surrounding area grew. In addition to various local planning and land use actions that had been taken,
six land use measures had been placed on previous ballots. In
March 1985 residents voted on Measure A, which limited building heights to six stories and required voter approval for increasing the height of existing buildings—and Measure B,
which required voter approval for the rezoning of residential
land. The voters passed Measure A and defeated Measure B.
Eights months later, on November 1, 1985, the voters of Walnut
Creek went back to the ballot box and adopted Measure H,
which established a 2-year moratorium on new development
until traffic congestion at designated intersections was reduced
to specific levels.

In 1986 Walnut Creek voters returned to the ballot box to cast
their votes on Measures E and F. The former sought to exempt
a downtown project from the previously adopted Measure H,
while the latter asked to exempt specific projects from an already enacted growth control ordinance. Both measures were
defeated at the polls. Another ballot measure, Measure G, went
down to defeat in 1989. This measure would have required
voter approval for commercial development above a certain
square footage, and prohibited commercial development from
occurring until road improvements were under way.

The population of Carlsbad has been projected to increase
from 48,908 in 1986 to 106,323 in 2010 (San Diego Association
of Governments, 1987). In 1986 the issue of growth came to a
head. Two tandem measures, as they are called by Glickfeld,

Graymer, and Morrison (1987), were on the local ballot. The election pitted a council-backed measure against a citizen-initiated measure. Responding to the projected growth, Carlsbad's City Council proposed Proposition E—a measure designed to limit the number of residential units that could be built in the city. No development could be approved by the City Council unless public facility needs had been met. Furthermore, the City Council could not approve a residential development that would increase the number of units, as stated in the measure, without an affirmative vote of the people.

Competing against Proposition E was Proposition G—the Citizen's Slow Growth Initiative. The initiative sought to restrict the rate of construction of residential dwelling units to specified levels for a 10-year period. It was developed because citizens felt rapid growth was damaging Carlsbad's character and adversely affecting various public services and facilities.

Proponents of both measures did their jobs well. Both measures were passed by the voters. However, a so-called "killer clause" stipulated that, should both measures pass, only the one receiving the higher number of affirmative votes would become law. Much to the dismay of Proposition G supporters, Proposition E was adopted as part of Carlsbad's 1986 Growth Management Plan.

Oceanside represents another fast-growing city in San Diego County. It has been projected to grow from a 1986 population of 96,544 to a 172,017 in 2010—a 78.2% increase (San Diego Association of Governments, 1987). In 1987 voters saw two tandem land use measures on the same ballot. Proposition A, a citizen's group growth control measure, sought to establish a development control system. It would establish a maximum of dwelling units that could be constructed each year in the city, with a maximum limit of 1,000 units for the calendar year 1987 and a maximum of 800 dwelling units allowed for the calendar years 1988 through 1999. The measure also

called for the creation of a Residential Development Evaluation
Board to distribute the residential allotments.

Also on the ballot was Proposition B, a council-backed measure that would mandate voter approval of all General Plan
amendments to increase residential density. The measure
would also coordinate public facility availability with residential development and establish a neighborhood planning program throughout the city.

Proponents of Proposition A complained that developers had
created poorly planned developments in the city and that the
City Council had been unduly influenced by development interests. Moreover, they charged that Proposition B was only developed because Proposition A was already on the ballot.
Advocates of Proposition B claimed passage would reduce the
population of Oceanside by 35%. Passage would also mandate
voter approval of any land use changes that would increase the
number of residential units and would require that all necessary public facilities be in place before any development of the
property occurs.

On April 21, 1987, Oceanside's voters approved Proposition A by a 7,885 (57%) to 6,057 (43%) margin. Proposition B
was defeated by a 6,509 (47%) to 7,222 (53%) margin. Having
no choice but to implement the citizen initiative, Oceanside
has had to defend the initiative in litigation. As of November
1, 1990, more than $1.5 million in legal fees had been spent
by the City of Oceanside. The legality of the measure has yet
to be decided.

In June 1988 voters in Orange County were afforded the opportunity to decide the fate of Measure A, an initiative that
would have required that road improvements precede development in the unincorporated areas of Orange County. According to Prokop (1988, p. 446), the measure was "viewed as one
of the toughest slow-growth initiatives ever proposed." In the
end, the Measure A campaign was viewed as "a classic David
and Goliath struggle that pitted a relatively underfinanced

grassroots coalition against Southern California's wealthiest developers—who saw at stake nothing less than the future of their industry" (Prokop, 1988, p. 444). The well-financed, developer-oriented campaign won the battle, and Measure A was defeated.

Five months later, in November 1988, two land use ballot measures appeared on the Riverside County ballot. Measure B sought to limit growth by imposing an annual limit on residential units. The number of allowable housing units depended on the statewide growth rate for the previous year. Opponents of Measure B outspent the proponents, $1.7 million to $30,000 (" 'No' to No Growth," 1988, p. 3). Another ballot measure, Measure C, asked the voters not to apply any growth control ordinance or initiative in the unincorporated area of Riverside County. Both measures were defeated.

San Francisco has had a relatively long history of citizens turning to the ballot box to decide various land use issues. Since 1971 voters have cast their votes on at least 13 land use ballot measures. In 1971 voters defeated two measures that sought to limit building heights. A similar measure was defeated in 1979. Finally, in 1986 San Francisco's voters passed Proposition M, which, according to DeLeon and Powell (1989, p. 307), was "the most ambitious citizen-initiated growth control measure ever enacted in the United States." This initiative was designed to limit the height, size, and number of new buildings in a three-quarter square-mile downtown area (DeLeon and Powell, 1989; Lassar, 1987). It is interesting to note that the passage of Proposition M was the culmination of a 15-year battle over downtown office development.

The idea of growth control does not readily come to mind in discussions of Los Angeles. Yet in 1986, in a city "famous for its unmitigated sprawl and titanic expansion," voters did approve Proposition U, a measure that called for the amount of developable commercial floor space to be cut by 75% (Lassar, 1987, p. 26).

CITIZEN ATTITUDES
TOWARD BALLOT BOX PLANNING

What do citizens feel about using the initiative or referendum to decide a specific land use issue? Are their attitudes consistent with earlier studies? A survey by Calavita and Caves (1990) sheds some light on this issue. In an open-ended question at the end of the survey, the respondents, members of the general public and members of a local section of the American Planning Association, were afforded the opportunity to provide any additional comments regarding growth in the San Diego region. Many of the respondents addressed the use of the initiative and referendum. Among the comments offered by the public respondents were:

1. Recent initiatives are too complex for normal voters. People voted them down because they are too complicated.
2. Initiatives are the only tool we have if politicians don't perform during their term.

Members of the local American Planning Association section were vocal in their comments about using the initiative or referendum as a growth limitation device. Some of the comments given by the planning professionals were:

1. Government by initiatives from special interest groups is wrong. We need informed action by elected representatives who will be held accountable for their actions. The action otherwise tends to be one-sided and shallow.
2. Initiative and referenda planning issues, including location, design, infrastructure, economics, and so on, are much too complex for most people to understand based on limited advertising, mailers, and other politicized means of communicating.
3. Ballot measure information is so simplistic that voters believe they understand.

4. Initiative and referenda may not be the best, but are the prime available resource when planning issues are not addressed by public officials.

5. Initiatives and referendum ballot measures are a constitutional right granted to citizens and should be protected. However, it is not always a clear black-and-white issue that initiatives result because elected officials fail to respond to citizen concerns. Yes, local officials should decide on all local planning issues. But that doesn't mean that the initiative process should be compromised.

6. Controlling growth through the initiative process is a dangerous practice. In most cases the initiative is not thoroughly thought out and after adoption could lead to problems not anticipated, or the initiative may not be tailored for the community it serves.

7. Sometimes the initiative is the appropriate tool; but, in 20 years in California, I have yet to see an initiative that truly expresses what it is about.

8. Effective leadership to balance competing interests is required, but is currently lacking. Elected officials who should do this job, do not, leading to bickering factions and initiatives which represent extreme positions that are "sold to voters."

Overall, these comments are consistent with the literature on the debate over representative democracy versus direct democracy. The debate over whether an initiative or referendum should be employed to decide a land use issue will undoubtedly continue. Moreover, the passage of any ballot box planning measure will be subject to legal scrutiny. Possible legal considerations and challenges to the initiative or referendum in a planning context are discussed in Chapter 3.

THREE

Legal Considerations
in Ballot Box Planning

Any action restricting how property owners can use their property will certainly generate legal scrutiny. Land use ballot measures are no exception. Legal issues surrounding the use of the initiative or referendum in deciding a land use planning or policy issue have been examined by a host of legal scholars (Callies, Neuffer, and Caliboso, 1989; Chesley, 1984; Curtin and Jacobson, 1989; Durkee, Jacobson, Wood, and Zischke, 1990; Eastman, 1985; Eddins and Ono Hall, 1990; Fountaine, 1988; Freilich and Guemmer, 1989; Glenn, 1978; Goetz, 1987; Grossman, 1981; Gunn, 1981; Melious, 1988; Moore, 1987; Paris, 1977; Radar, 1983; Rosenberg, 1984; Salvato, 1986).

The courts are confronted with a variety of questions concerning the use of an initiative or referendum. They involve issues of both state and federal law. Among the questions that will be asked are the following:

1. Can cities, counties, and the residents use the initiative or referendum for land use issues?
2. Does their use conflict with any state enabling legislation?

3. Does their use violate any due process and equal protection guarantees?
4. Is the initiative or referendum being used to decide a legislative or administrative matter?

Ultimately, the courts will be faced with some tough questions. They are in an unenviable position. As Glenn (1978, p. 275) observed, "When faced with challenges to direct legislation, the courts must make the significant choice between the democratic values implicit in direct legislation and the goals of careful planning and individual fairness that are sought, if not always obtained, through the procedural and substantive requirements of zoning enabling legislation." The remainder of this chapter will attempt to answer the aforementioned questions. It is not intended to be an exhaustive examination of the issues facing the use of the initiative or referendum. It will simply illustrate some of the growing case law surrounding their use.

POWER TO USE THE INITIATIVE
OR REFERENDUM

A major question that must be answered is whether cities, counties, or the residents have the power to use the initiative or referendum to decide land use planning issues. In some states, they may have been prohibited from using them. In other states, cities, counties, and citizens may have been given the right to use them through state constitutions, statutes, or through home rule charters.

The initiative and referendum are probably used more in California than in any other state. In California, all political power is inherent in the people. By constitutional amendment in 1911, the people reserved to themselves the power of the initiative and referendum. State constitutions in other states such as Colorado and Oregon have also reserved the right of the initiative and referendum to the people.

Arizona courts have ruled separately regarding the use of the initiative and referendum. In *City of Scottsdale v. Superior Court*, 439 P.2d 290 (AZ 1968), the Supreme Court of Arizona held that the initiative process was not available to citizens as a mode for amending a comprehensive zoning plan. The case involved an ordinance rezoning property from single family residential use to neighborhood commercial. The Scottsdale City Council, believing it possessed the power to do so, voluntarily put the ordinance before the people for their vote. The Court disagreed and held that Scottsdale lacked the power to put the measure before the people. Moreover, since the Arizona legislature granted the power to zone to the governing body of the city, the city must act in accordance with the state mandate. The Court also ruled that the initiative was in conflict with the Fourteenth Amendment's due process clause.

Four years later, in *Queen Creek Land and Cattle Corporation v. Yavapai County Board of Supervisors*, 501 P.2d 391 (AZ 1972), the Supreme Court of Arizona had the opportunity to rule on the use of a referendum in a rezoning matter. Noting it had already decided an initiative could not be used to amend a comprehensive zoning plan, the Court noted the difference between an initiative and referendum:

> A referendum is distinguishable in effect from an initiative in zoning matters. The referendum stays the effect of the action of the law-making body until the electorate has had an opportunity to approve or reject it. It does not change zoning as an initiative would, and the notice and hearing process has been accomplished prior to the referendum. (*Queen Creek*, 501 P.2d 391, 394)

The Court held the referendum was proper and that "the traditional rule of noninterference with the legislative process should be observed" (*Queen Creek*, 501 P.2d 391, 394). Aggrieved parties could seek judicial review once the legislative process had been completed.

CONFLICT WITH STATE ENABLING LEGISLATION

The authority to plan and zone can be found in enabling legislation from the state. More specifically, the basis for planning and zoning for most states can be found in the Standard City Planning Enabling Act and the Standard Zoning Enabling Act. These authorities allow localities to plan and zone, actions they were previously unable to do. They set various procedures (i.e., notice, hearings, and so on) that must be followed. The question then becomes whether the procedures mandated by the enabling legislation apply to the use of the initiative or referendum.

A number of cases have considered whether the use of the initiative or referendum conflicts with state enabling legislation. In 1929 the Supreme Court of California held that an initiative was incompatible with its Zoning Act of 1917 in *Hurst v. City of Burlingame*, 277 P. 308 (CA 1929).

In 1923 the voters of Burlingame, through the initiative process, approved a zoning ordinance that regulated and established the location of residences, apartments, trades, and industries, and established zones for the various uses. The plaintiff was engaged in the selling of various building materials. The ordinance placed Hurst's property in a residential zone, thereby prohibiting any commercial activities. Accordingly, Hurst claimed that the passage of the initiative failed to comply with the 1917 Zoning Act, which represented a general law of the state. The Act also set out the requirements for enacting a zoning ordinance in a city such as Burlingame.

The Supreme Court of California held that since Burlingame was organized under general law, it was subject to the provisions of general law of California. It ruled that adoption of the

ordinance through the initiative process violated the Zoning
Act, which required notice and hearing:

> The requirement of notice and hearing provided by the
> statute may not be treated lightly or at all disregarded.
> When the statute requires notice and hearing as to the pos-
> sible effect of a zoning law upon property rights the action
> of the legislative body becomes quasi judicial in character,
> and the statutory notice and hearing then becomes neces-
> sary in order to satisfy the requirements of due process and
> may not be dispensed with. (*Hurst*, 277 P. 308, 311)

In the end, the Supreme Court noted a major problem between
initiative law and the 1917 Zoning Act:

> The initiative law and the zoning law are hopelessly incon-
> sistent and in conflict as to the manner of the preparation
> and adoption of a zoning ordinance. The Zoning Act is a
> special statute dealing with a particular subject and must
> be deemed to be controlling over the initiative, which is
> general in its scope. (*Hurst*, 277 P. 308, 311)

The decision would prohibit zoning by initiative in California
for almost half a century.

The Supreme Court of Utah had the opportunity to decide
whether a residential rezoning ordinance conflicted with state
law in *Dewey v. Doxey-Layton Realty Co.*, 277 P.2d 805 (UT 1954).
There was no disputing the fact that citizens of any legal subdivision of Utah possessed the power to initiate legislation.
However, the state legislature had also delegated the power to
zone to the legislative bodies of Utah's municipalities and
towns. The enabling legislation also contained a provision for
notice and public hearing. In the end, the Court ruled the ap-
pellants failed to comply with the state zoning statute.

In 1976, *Hurst* was overruled by *Associated Home Builders v.
City of Livermore*, 557 P.2d 473 (CA 1976). At issue in this case

was an ordinance enacted by initiative that prohibited the issuance of any additional residential building permits until various public facility standards were met. The question facing the Supreme Court of California was whether the initiative exceeded municipal authority under the police power.

In its ruling, the Court held that *Hurst* had been incorrectly decided. While the Supreme Court in *Hurst* noted that the requirements of notice and hearing were applicable to initiatives, the Supreme Court in *Livermore* ruled that the procedural requirements of notice and hearing were applicable only to council actions, not to initiatives. Moreover, it was noted that the right of the initiative was guaranteed by a 1911 amendment to the California Constitution. Ultimately, it was held that zoning ordinances enacted by initiative did not have to apply to the procedural requirements of the 1917 Zoning Act.

Justice Clark disagreed with the Court's decision and issued a dissenting opinion. He felt there was a conflict between the initiative provisions and the zoning provisions to general law cities. In one respect, Justice Clark noted, "The zoning statutes contemplate that to achieve orderly and wise land use regulation any change in zoning ordinances is not to be made until the experts in the field have had an opportunity to evaluate the effects of the change after noticed hearing and report" (*Livermore*, 557 P.2d 473, 491). This is not accomplished through the initiative process. Moreover, he suggests the presence of additional conflicts:

> There is no assurance that interests of nearby residents will be considered by the electorate, although such consideration is required. There is no procedure under the initiative law for determining compliance with the general plan as required by statute. . . . There are potential conflicts between the initiative law's requirement that amendment be by the voters and the zoning law's provision for variances, and between the majority vote of the

initiative and the zoning law's specific requirements for interim zoning. (Livermore, 557 P.2d 473, 492)

He would have enjoined the enforcement of the initiative and would not have overruled *Hurst*.

A potential conflict with state law was also an issue in *Gumprecht v. City of Coeur D'Alene*, 661 P.2d 1214 (ID 1983). In this case, Coeur D'Alene wanted to amend its municipal code, via an initiative, to prohibit the construction of new buildings beyond a certain size and to prohibit the issuance of building permits at a specific location in the city. The Court ruled that the Idaho Constitution authorized its municipalities and counties to zone, but that the Local Planning Act of 1975 required notice and hearing for zoning acts. As such, in rejecting the initiative because it conflicted with state law, the Court noted, "The comprehensiveness of zoning legislation in Idaho leaves no room for direct legislation by electors through an initiative election" (*Gumprecht*, 661 P.2d 1214, 1217).

Justice Bistline disagreed with the Court's decision. In his dissenting opinion, he failed to see why direct democracy could not coexist with the required procedures of the Local Planning Act of 1975. He reasoned that "since zoning is a proper subject for municipal legislation, and since the initiative statute provides for 'direct legislation' through the initiative process, it would appear that zoning is within the initiative authority originally granted in 1911" (*Gumprecht*, 661 P.2d 1214, 1221).

VIOLATION OF DUE PROCESS AND EQUAL PROTECTION

The Fifth Amendment to the United States Constitution provides that "nor [shall any person] be deprived of life, liberty, or property, without due process of law." Although it is only applicable to the actions of the federal government, the adoption of the Fourteenth Amendment made it applicable to the states. Section 1 of the Fourteenth Amendment reads that "Nor shall any State deprive any person of life, liberty, or property, without due process of law." The phrase can be broken down into two areas: substantive due process and procedural due process. The former requires "all legislation be in furtherance of a legitimate governmental objective" while the latter guarantees "procedural fairness where the government would deprive one of his property or liberty" (Giftis, 1984, pp. 145-146).

The Fourteenth Amendment also avows that "no State shall . . . deny to any person within its jurisdiction the equal protection of laws." This issue has been acknowledged and addressed in a number of decisions regarding the use of the initiative or referendum. Gunn (1981, pp. 136, 137) has argued "the primary defect of direct democracy lies in its failure to protect the interests of numerous minority groups." Goetz (1987, pp. 806, 814) has also suggested that using the initiative and referendum "risk allowing the majority to overwhelm minorities" and that the major deficiency of their use is "the ability of the populace to use the direct vote to oppress minorities."

Several cases stand out in a discussion of this issue. In *Bi-Metallic Investment Company v. State Board of Equalization*, 36 S.Ct. 141 (1915), the U.S. Supreme Court was confronted with a decision by the Tax Board of Colorado to increase the value of all taxable property in Denver by 40%. The Bi-Metallic Investment Company owned property in Denver and claimed that the Tax Board's decision violated its due process rights because it was not provided the opportunity to be heard. According to Justice Holmes, who delivered the Court's opinion, the issue was whether "all individuals have a constitutional right to be heard before a matter can be decided which all are equally concerned" (*Bi-Metallic*, 36 S.Ct. 141, 142). The answer to the question was no. The Court's reasoning was as follows:

Where a rule of conduct applies to more than a few people, it is impracticable that everyone should have a direct voice in its adoption. The Constitution does not require all public acts to be done in town meeting or an assembly of the whole. General statutes within the state power are passed that affect the person or property of individuals, sometimes to the point of ruin, without giving them a chance to be heard. (*Bi-Metallic*, 36 S.Ct. 141, 142)

One of the first significant equal protection challenges to the use of an initiative or referendum occurred in *Reitman v. Mulkey*, 87 S.Ct. 1627 (1967). This case involved California's Proposition 14, a state constitutional amendment adopted by the voters that prohibited the state government from interfering with a residential property owner's right to sell, lease, or rent to anyone. The U.S. Supreme Court struck down the amendment for violating the Fourteenth Amendment. The Court ruled it encouraged racial discrimination, and the fact that the discrimination was part of the California constitution exacerbated the problem.

Two years later, another possible violation of equal protection was the issue in *Hunter v. Erickson*, 89 S.Ct. 557 (1969). In *Hunter*, a Negro citizen challenged an Akron, Ohio, city charter amendment to a fair housing ordinance that had been passed by a majority vote in 1964. The amendment was framed in the following language:

Any ordinance enacted by the Council of the City of Akron which regulates the use, sale advertisement, transfer, listing assignment, lease, sublease or financing of real property of any kind or any interest therein on the basis of race, color, religion, national origin or ancestry must first be approved by a majority of the electors voting on the question at a regular or general election before said ordinance shall be effective.

The U.S. Supreme Court struck down the ordinance because it discriminated against minorities since the mandatory referendum applied only to racial housing regulations. Nonracial housing regulations were subject to a permissive referendum. Furthermore, as Justice Harlan (with Justice Stewart joining) added in a concurring opinion, "We have a provision that has the clear purpose of making it more difficult for certain racial and religious minorities to achieve legislation that is in their interest" (*Hunter*, 89 S.Ct. 557, 563). As such, the amendment imposed an unfair burden on racial minorities and was held unconstitutional.

The constitutionality of California's Article 34 was the issue in *James v. Valtierra*, 91 S.Ct. 1331 (1971). Article 34, approved by California's voters, stated that "no low-rent housing project should be developed, constructed, or acquired in any manner by a state public body until the project was approved by a majority of those voting at a community election." The dispute in this case arose when San Jose and localities in San Mateo County were prevented from applying for federal funds due to the defeat of low-cost housing proposals at referendum elections. The question before the Court was whether a mandatory public housing referendum violated the equal protection clause of the Fourteenth Amendment because it discriminated against people on the basis of their wealth.

The U.S. Supreme Court upheld the constitutionality of Article 34. Encouraging the use of direct democracy and noting the initiative and referendum had been used on numerous occasions, the Court noted that "provisions for referendums demonstrate devotion to democracy, not to bias, discrimination, or prejudice" (*Valtierra*, 91 S.Ct. 1331, 1334). Moreover, in lauding their use, the Court also added:

> This procedure ensures that all the people of a community will have a voice in a decision which may lead to large expenditures of local governmental funds for increased public services and to lower tax revenues. It gives them a voice

in decisions that will affect the future development of their own community. This procedure for democratic decision making does not violate the constitutional command that no State shall deny to any person "the equal protection of the laws."

Justice Marshall (with Justices Brennan and Blackmun joining) in a dissenting opinion indicated the referendum did discriminate against low-income people. Discrimination could take other forms. According to Justice Marshall, "singling out the poor to bear a burden not placed on any other class of citizens tramples the values that the Fourteenth Amendment was designed to protect" (*Valtierra*, 91 S.Ct. 1331, 1335). He felt Article 34 constituted "invidious discrimination," which is prohibited by the Fourteenth Amendment (*Valtierra*, 91 S.Ct. 1331, 1335).

Claims that an individual's procedural due process rights had been violated was an issue in *City of Fort Collins v. Dooney*, 496 P.2d 316 (CO 1972). In this case, a piece of property had been rezoned by the city. The property owner wanted a referendum on the city's action. The City Council rejected the idea of a referendum on the ground that a referendum was not applicable to an ordinance amending the zoning map. After examining Fort Collins' City Charter, the court held the amendment was subject to a referendum. The only exceptions, as noted in the City Charter, were making the tax levy, making the annual appropriation, and ordering improvement initiative by petition (*Fort Collins*, 496 P.2d 316, 318). Since they were the only exceptions noted, the court's hands were tied. It could not place another exception in the City Charter.

The court was also not persuaded by Dooney's complaint over lack of due process. Noting that the presence of debate throughout the campaign acts as an alternative to the public hearing, the court ruled:

The due process provisions of notice and hearing alluded to in the Council's resolution are proper and must be followed when amending the zoning map by council action. . . . The fact that due process requirements may be met in one manner when the change is by council action does not preclude other procedures from meeting due process requirements under the referendum. (*Fort Collins*, 496 P.2d 316, 318-319)

An initiative establishing a 30-foot height limit for buildings in San Diego's coastal zone was at issue in *San Diego Building Contractors Association v. City Council of San Diego*, 529 P.2d 570 (CA 1974). Plaintiffs claimed the initiative violated San Diego's City Charter and violated the due process clause for lack of notice and hearing. The Supreme Court of California ruled against the Building Contractors Association, holding that the City Charter established the right of citizens to use the initiative on all legislative matters. In this instance, zoning was a legitimate topic for an initiative. Moreover, the Court held that notice and hearing was required in quasi-judicial or adjudicatory settings but not in the adoption of general legislation. It was not persuaded by the plaintiff's due process arguments. Noting the initiative dealt with legislative matter, the Court ruled that "from the inception of this nation's legal system, statutes of general application have regularly been enacted without affording each potentially affected individual notice and hearing" (*San Diego*, 529 P.2d 570, 573).

In 1976 the U.S. Supreme Court ruled in *Eastlake v. Forest City Enterprises*, 96 S. Ct 2358 (1976) that a real estate developer's due process rights were not violated by a provision in the Eastlake City Charter requiring that any land use change agreed to by the city council be approved by a 55% vote in a mandatory referendum. Earlier, the developer had applied for a zoning change to build a high-rise apartment building. With the application pending, the City Charter was amended in the aforementioned way. The developer felt the referendum was an unconstitutional delegation of power to the people. The Court noted it was not a delegation of power and that the Ohio Constitution reserved to the people the power of the referendum to decide matters that the municipality can control by legislation. In addition, no due process violations would occur provided the decision was not arbitrary or unreasonable. Therefore, a delegation of power to the legislature had not occurred.

Justice Powell, in a dissenting opinion, spoke of the importance of procedural safeguards. While not disputing the applicability of zoning as the subject of a referendum, he observed:

> The only issue concerned the status of a single small parcel owned by a "single" person. This procedure, affording no realistic opportunity to the affected person to be heard, even by the electorate, is fundamentally unfair. The "spot" referendum technique appears to open disquieting opportunities for local government bodies to bypass normal protective procedures for resolving issues affecting individual rights. (*Eastlake*, 96 S.Ct. 2358, 1365)

In another dissenting opinion, Justice Stevens (with Justice Brennan joining) wrote of an individual's right to have fair procedures in consideration of an application for a zoning change. Noting the potential for abuse when procedural safeguards are inadequate, Justice Stevens went on to note that "the essence of fair procedure is that the interested parties be given a reasonable opportunity to have their dispute resolved on the merits by reference to articulable rules" (*Eastlake*, 96 S.Ct. 2358, 2371).

The Court's decision in *Eastlake* was greeted rudely by the planning and legal communities. Goetz (1987, p. 803) noted that commentators saw the case as "one of a number of 1970's Supreme Court zoning decisions which indicated a hands-off approach to zoning controversies." Callies (1976) was concerned that cities with the mandatory referendum process could overturn land use decisions by rejecting them at the polls. According to Callies (p.82), the situation is unfair to the landowner:

Having won his case on merit before the planning commission and the city council, the landowner then stands to lose his recently won right to develop his property—to lose it in a process subject to no standards and no guidelines, the referendum. He had little if no opportunity to try his case before the voters, most of whom have only a remote interest in his particular parcel of land.

Moreover, he criticized the Court's analogy between a town meeting and the referendum:

The analogy between the referendum and the town meeting, of which the Supreme Court majority is so enamored, may be appropriate for the few communities that can fit all their electors into the town hall. But to apply the analogy to the average city or its suburbs demonstrates a naivete about local government processes and land use decision making that is frightening. (p.83)

Others joined in criticizing the Court's decision. Hartzer (1976) and Babcock (1976) spoke of the decision's being a predictable one since the Court rarely hears zoning cases. Babcock (1976, p. 4) also suggested that a moral to the case was that "advocates of reform in the zoning process should stay out of the federal courts." Bair (1976, p. 5) warned of the "Eastlake Solution" spreading to "exclusionary suburbs and no-growth enclaves" and to its "loading the dice against desirable change." Finally, Meck (1976, p. 8) characterized the Court's decision as a reminder of its "regrettably myopic perception of the zoning process."

The *Eastlake* decision was also criticized for something it did not do. Although it mentioned them in a dissenting opinion, the Court did not pursue the exclusionary impacts of the referendum. Goetz (1987, p. 801) criticized the decision as one "remarkable for its non-decision on the issue of exclusion through direct democracy." Meck (1976, p. 8) even characterized the case as being "about a bad law hiding behind a facade of propriety, with an areawide exclusionary impact." By not addressing the exclusionary impacts of the referendum, the case certainly did not help the cause of minority rights. The decision continues to be discussed in debates on the use of the initiative and referendum to resolve zoning issues (Callies and Curtin, 1990; McClendon, 1990).

LEGISLATIVE/ADMINISTRATIVE DISTINCTION

It has been widely held that legislative acts are proper subjects for an initiative or referendum. The issue then becomes defining the term legislative act. Is approving a tentative map, adopting a specific plan or general plan, granting a variance or conditional use permit, or approving a rezoning application considered a legislative act or an administrative, quasi-judicial, or adjudicative act (Callies, Neuffer, and Caliboso, 1989; Freilich and Guemmer, 1989; Mandelker, 1988)? The way the various acts are considered or interpreted vary by state. Overall, an initiative or referendum can only do as much as the local government can do in its legislative capacity. The initiative or referendum can do no more.

There is no clear-cut distinction between a legislative or nonlegislative act. Callies, Neuffer, and Caliboso (1989, p. 41) suggest the difference might be when "the people as a whole have no legally protected interest in the application of policy and law to an individual or an individual situation, as compared with a broad policy decision that affects everyone." It has even been suggested that the distinction between a legislative and nonlegislative act is more difficult in zoning enactments since they "involve an unending variety of factual circumstances and relate to peculiarly local matters" (Kemper, 1976, p. 1035). To help settle the issue, Kemper suggests that the following test may help:

The courts have generally attempted to apply the test of whether the enactment in question could reasonably be said to originate a permanent law or lay down a rule of conduct or course of policy, in which case it would be legislative, or whether it simply put into effect, or executed, some previously adopted law or policy, and was therefore administrative. (p. 1035).

The issue continues to be addressed by the courts.

The legislative/administrative distinction goes as far back as the U.S. Supreme Court decision in *Bi-Metallic*, 36 S.Ct. 141 (1915). In this case, Justice Holmes noted that there were different types of zoning issues and spoke of the number of people affected by a particular zoning decision. The Court held that since more than a few people are affected by a legislative decision, procedural due process was not applicable. However, with only a few people being affected by an adjudicative decision, procedural due process was required.

In 1964 the Supreme Court of Utah, in *Bird v. Sorenson*, 394 P.2d 808 (UT 1964), held that a city ordinance rezoning property from residential to commercial uses was not subject to a referendum. In reaching its decision, the Court discussed potential problems of implementing the city's master plan. The Court ruled "if each change in a zoning classification were to be submitted to a vote of the city's electors, any master plan would be rendered inoperative" (*Bird*, 394 P.2d 808).

Nine years later the Oregon Supreme Court, in *Fasano v. Board of County Commissioners of Washington County*, 507 P.2d 23 (OR 1973), had to decide whether a map amendment should be considered a legislative act. If it was found to be a legislative act, it would be entitled to presumptive validity. However, the Court noted it "would be ignoring reality to rigidly view all zoning decisions by local governing bodies as legislative acts" (*Fasano*, 507 P.2d 23, 26).

The *Fasano* Court noted the important difference between developing general zoning policy and the rezoning of a specific piece of property. In other words, it was important to determine how many people would be affected by the land-use decision. As the Court noted:

> Ordinances laying down general policies without regard to a specific piece of property are usually an exercise of legitimate authority, are subject to limited review, and may only be attacked upon constitutional grounds for an arbitrary abuse of authority. On the other hand, a determination whether the permissive use of a specific piece of property should be charged is usually an exercise of judicial authority and its propriety is subject to an altogether different test. (*Fasano*, 507 P.2d 23, 26)

The test to determine in what authority the city is acting involves:

> the determination of whether action produces a general rule or policy which is applicable to an open class of individuals, interests or situations, or whether it entails the application of a general rule or policy to specific individuals, interests or situations. If the former determination is satisfied, there is legislative action, if the latter determination is satisfied, the action is judicial. (*Fasano*, 507 P.2d 23, 27)

In this particular instance, the map amendment was held to be a quasi-judicial act.

Three years later, in *Leonard v. City of Bothell*, 557 P.2d 1306 (WA 1976), the Washington Supreme Court had to rule on whether an ordinance, which rezoned property from agricultural to community business and modified the city's comprehensive plan to allow for a regional shopping center, was subject to a referendum. Noting that referendums can be held on matters judged to be legislative in nature, the Court ruled that the rezoning was a means of implementing the zoning code and municipal plan and, therefore, not subject to a referendum. Moreover, the Court acknowledged the importance of expertise in making land use decisions, stating that "amendments to the zoning code and rezone decisions require an informed and intelligent choice by individuals who possess the expertise to consider the total economic, social, and physical characteristics of the community" (Leonard, 557 P.2d 1306, 1311).

California Courts have traditionally been very supportive of the use of the initiative and referendum. They have interpreted their use very broadly. In *Arnel Development Co. v. City of Costa Mesa*, 620 P.2d 565 (CA 1980), the California Supreme Court ruled an initiative that rezoned property from mixed use single-family and apartments to single family only was a legitimate subject of an initiative. However, it did not rule that all planning topics are legislative actions. While zoning ordinances in California have been held on numerous occasions to be considered as legislative actions, other issues such as variances and subdivision approvals have been considered adjudicatory actions.

The Court in *Arnel* was not persuaded by the argument that the rezoning should be considered an adjudicatory action since it would only affect three landowners and a relatively small area of land. Claiming this logic was somewhat faulty, the Court held:

> This is a very myopic view of the matter; the proposed construction of housing for thousands of people affects the prospective tenants, the housing market, the residents living nearby, and the future character of the community. The number of landowners whose property is actually rezoned is as unsuitable a test as the size of the property rezoned. (*Arnel*, 620 P.2d 565, 572)

Justice Richardson, in a dissenting opinion, felt the rezone was an adjudicatory action. While recognizing there was no precise definitions for an adjudicative matter and a legislative matter, he did feel that the small number of voters approving the measure were being allowed to "abort the construction of a carefully considered moderate income housing project without giving appellant owners any prior opportunity to express their opposition at a full public hearing" (*Arnel*, 620 P.2d 565, 574). To him, due process was not afforded to the landowners.

In 1982 the Supreme Court of Utah, in *Wilson v. Manning*, 657 P.2d 251 (UT 1982) had the opportunity to overrule *Bird*. The action in question in *Wilson* was a rezoning from residential to commercial, the same kind of rezoning found in *Bird*. The Court acknowledged its frequently held position that "the enactment of zoning laws and ordinances is the exercise of a legislative function" (*Wilson*, 657 P.2d 251, 253). However, in this particular case, the rezoning was not considered an enactment of a zoning law and ordinance. On the contrary, the Court held that "ordinances implementing the basic zoning enactment, such as by exceptions and variances, would generally be administrative acts not subject to referendum" (*Wilson*, 657 P.2d 251, 253). Ultimately, the rezoning was found to be an improper subject of a referendum.

CONCLUDING COMMENTS

This chapter has examined some of the legal issues that will surface whenever the initiative or referendum either is being considered or has been used to decide a land use matter. There are certainly additional issues that will need to be addressed on a state-by-state basis. For example, where a general plan is required, a number of new issues may surface. Courts will need to decide whether a land use regulation enacted by initiative or referendum is consistent with the general plan. Moreover, where a growth control element has been added to the general plan via the initiative process, the courts will need to decide whether the element is consistent with the remainder of the general plan. Overall, as the desire to use the initiative and referendum grows in various states, the courts will be there to decide whether they can be used.

Barnstable County, Massachusetts: Managing Growth at the Regional Level

Barnstable County, Massachusetts, perhaps better known to the rest of the country as Cape Cod, is an area that elicits different views or responses from its two main populations— tourists and residents. Visitors are immediately struck by its rustic charm and scenic beauty. Many tourists view it as "the place" to vacation in the summer months. Permanent residents are also struck by its charm and beauty; however, they also see a different picture of Cape Cod. They see increasing traffic congestion, a shrinking water supply, and strains on public facilities and services, as the area experiences major population growth in both summer tourists and permanent residents.

This chapter explores Cape Cod's recent experience with ballot box planning. As residents of the 15 towns that comprise Cape Cod (as shown in Figure 4.1), voters in Barnstable County were given the opportunity to share their opinions on consid-

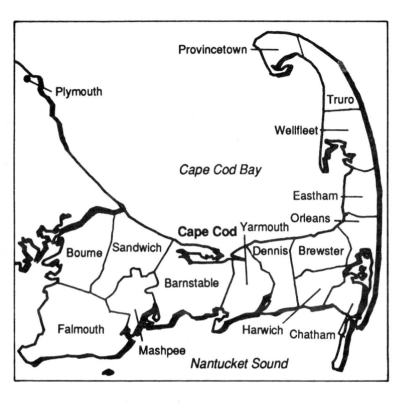

Figure 4.1. Barnstable County, Massachusetts

ering a moratorium on Cape development as well as creating a regional land use planning and regulatory control agency. These measures were initiated by the voters and represented nonbinding public policy referendum questions. In other words, both measures were advisory and designed to gauge public support for the two proposals.

Table 4.1 Barnstable County Population, 1980-2000

Year	Population	
	Year-round	Summer
1980	147,925	441,003
1985	167,743	494,864
1990	189,985	536,274
1995	213,605	576,660
2000	230,038	604,449
Year-round population increase		
1980-1985	13%	
1980-1990	28%	
1980-2000	55%	

NOTE: Summer population represents peak population in July and includes year-round population as well as estimates of summer residents and visitors, based on overnight accommodations; day-trippers are not included, but are estimated to approximate 15,000 daily.
SOURCE: U.S. Census of Population, 1980 (1980 year-round population); estimates of Cape Cod Planning and Economic Development Commission (1980 summer population; year-round and summer population, 1985-2000). Compiled by Cape Cod Planning and Economic Development Commission.

BACKGROUND

Both the number of people residing permanently on the Cape and the number of people residing there for either the summer months or part of the summer had ballooned over recent years. The resident population in 1920 was estimated at 26,670 and had expanded to 170,600 in 1986—a dramatic 540% increase (Cape Cod Planning and Economic Development Commission, 1988). Moreover, as Table 4.1 indicates, the year-round population on the Cape is projected to grow by 55% over the period from 1980 to 2000. The summer population is projected to grow by 37% over the same period. This growth will place additional pressure on the various public facilities and services, many of which are already being strained.

The Cape's growth ranks high in comparison to that of other areas in both Massachusetts and New England. Of

Table 4.2 Estimated Population Growth in New England Counties, 1980-1987

Numerical Growth		Percentage Growth	
1. Hillsborough, NH	46,100	1. Dukes, MA	25.8
2. Rockingham, NH	38,100	2. Nantucket, MA	22.7
3. Hartford, CT	28,800	3. Rockingham, NH	20.0
4. Barnstable, MA	25,900	4. Carroll, NH	17.9
		5. Barnstable, MA	17.5

SOURCE: Cape Cod Planning and Economic Development Commission, 1989.

Massachusetts' 14 counties, it ranked number one by adding 25,900 residents from 1980 through 1987. The growth rate during that period was more than nine times that of Massachusetts. Moreover, only four counties in New England, two in Massachusetts and two in New Hampshire, grew at a faster rate. Table 4.2 shows the estimated population in New England counties from 1980 through 1987.

Indicative of the Cape's growth, the number of housing units has skyrocketed. In fact, the number of units has increased from 65,676 in 1970 to an estimated 131,660 in 1989—a 100% increase (Cape Cod Planning and Economic Development Commission, 1989). Table 4.3 shows the number of building permits authorized for additional housing from 1970 through 1988. As the table indicates, the housing growth has occurred in a sporadic fashion.

Many of the ideas and thoughts contained in the remainder of this chapter can be traced to an innovative type of goal-setting project called Prospect: Cape Cod. B. Jean Thomas, chairman of the Cape Cod Planning and Economic Development Commission (CCPEDC) termed the project "the start of a visionary movement for Cape Cod as a whole" (Holmes, 1986, p. 1).

Initiated by the CCPEDC in 1986, Prospect: Cape Cod sought to not only examine regional solutions to various problems but

Table 4.3 Housing Units Authorized for Construction by Building
Permits Issued in Barnstable County, 1970-1988

Year	Housing Units Authorized	Percent Change
1970	2,970	—
1971	4,657	+56.8
1972	4,677	+0.4
1973	4,818	+3.0
1974	2,305	-52.2
1975	1,647	-28.5
1976	2,295	+39.3
1977	2,963	+29.1
1978	2,853	-3.7
1979	2,962	+3.8
1980	2,585	-12.7
1981	2,855	+10.4
1982	2,618	-8.3
1983	3,893	+48.7
1984	4,877	+25.3
1985	4,807	-1.4
1986	4,503	-6.3
1987	2,888	-35.9
1988	2,710	-6.2

SOURCE: Town Building Inspectors' Reports, compiled by Cape Cod Planning and Economic Development Commission, n.d.

also set goals for actions to be taken. The project took approximately 8 months to complete, with a budget of $122,700. Funding for the project was obtained through grants awarded by the federal and state governments and also through donations from the private sector.

Prospect: Cape Cod involved a great many people from around the Cape. Three task forces made up of citizens, government officials, and business leaders, examined a host of regional issues ranging from economic development, environmental quality, housing, health services, and support services to land use. Each of the issues was affected, directly or indirectly, by concerns over population growth. In the end, the project gave impetus to transforming the CCPEDC into a regional land use planning and regulatory body for Barnstable County.

THE BUILDING MORATORIUM AND CAPE COD COMMISSION DEBATES

The rapid growth of the towns on the Cape has transformed them into a regional community with problems that do not respect town boundaries. Problems such as traffic congestion, waste disposal, and groundwater pollution have spilled over town boundaries and are plaguing the entire Cape. To many people, the problems are of such magnitude that they deserve regional attention. The groundwater pollution problem becomes even more acute when you consider that the Cape's drinking water supply is provided by aquifer. Continued leakage from septic tanks jeopardizes the water supply. This, combined with developers submitting new residential and commercial project proposals, makes it appear that the time has come for the problems to be handled on a regional basis.

Considering a Cape-Wide Building Moratorium

In 1987, after the state's environmental operations had been criticized, a Special Commission on Environmental Operations was created. Composed of 23 members, the Special Commission was charged with reviewing the state's environmental agencies and making the Department of Environmental Affairs more efficient. The Special Commission was to play a major role in the building moratorium debate.

The chair of the Special Commission was former U.S. Senator Paul Tsongas, a part-time resident of the Cape. He was apparently concerned over the growth of the Cape and the effect this growth had on the Cape's source of drinking water. This concern became clear in one sentence of the Special Commission's report in Appendix A—Environmental Directives— where it stated that "the Commonwealth should explore the feasibility of a moratorium on development on Cape Cod until such time as we know the condition and viability of the Cape Cod aquifer." The possibility of a moratorium represented only one of several alternatives under consideration by the Special Commission. It was, however, not the first time a moratorium had been proposed on the Cape. Some towns had adopted temporary moratoriums in earlier years.

Tsongas acknowledged that a moratorium would not solve the Cape's problems; however, it would send Cape officials a message that citizens were concerned over the pace of development on the Cape. Reaction to the Tsongas moratorium proposal was quick. Some individuals praised the proposal, saying something had to be done about the pace of development on the Cape before it was too late. Some even wrote Tsongas to offer their assistance in getting the moratorium passed. Others were equally quick in criticizing him. Recognizing that he was a part-time resident of the Cape, some people suggested that if he did not like what was happening on the Cape, he could always go back to his other home. Others commented that a moratorium would be disastrous for the Cape since many of the area's jobs were construction-related. If a moratorium passed, he would have played an instrumental role in increasing the area's unemployment.

There was widespread support from individuals and groups for the moratorium. A belief that the Cape was approaching an overbuilt status led many people to support the moratorium. Others were attracted to the idea because they felt it was needed to protect the Cape's drinking water supply. Still others argued for it on the grounds that some towns had caved in to pressure from developers and approved their development proposals rather hastily.

The most visible group supporting the moratorium was the Association for the Preservation of Cape Cod (APCC). With more than 2,000 members from all over the Cape, the APCC serves to educate the public on environmental issues and conducts scientific research projects on the environment. The APCC was quick to lend its support to the moratorium and called for it to be put to the people in an election. Susan Nickerson, APCC Executive Director, pointed out why a moratorium was needed:

A look at the growth facts for Cape Cod tells the story. Between 1981 and 1986, 14,600 acres of land were developed on Cape Cod, the 3rd fastest rate of development in New England's 67 counties. The majority of major roads on Cape Cod exceed their rated capacity to handle traffic. Sixty-six million gallons of septage are generated every year, most of which is dumped, untreated, into open pits at our landfills. Two and a half billion pounds of trash are generated every year on Cape Cod. Six thousand acres of shellfish beds are currently closed due to pollution. These problems are directly related to the rapid and inadequately controlled growth that has occurred in the absence of planning. In many respects, Cape Cod has exceeded its environmental carrying capacity (Nickerson, 1988, p. 3).

The president of the APCC, Herbert S. Elins, calling the Tsongas idea "a catalyst for action," praised Tsongas for providing "the environmental community of Cape Cod with a unique opportunity to spur public servants into organized and effective regional action to control growth" (APCC, 1988, p. 1). This group, along with the Cape Cod Alliance for Preservation, would play a major role in getting the moratorium qualified for the ballot.

To place on the ballot a nonbinding public policy question such as the moratorium, a number of procedural requirements had to be followed. Special forms for starting the public policy question had to be obtained from the Office of the Secretary of the Commonwealth. A specific number of signatures from voters registered in Massachusetts also had to be obtained and later verified or certified by either local registrars of voters or election commissioners in the appropriate cities and towns. Signatures from 200 voters in a state representative district, and 1,200 in a state senatorial district, are required to put the question on the ballot. The Cape had five state representative districts and one state senatorial district. In the present case, the petitions had to be filed with the appropriate body for certification by July 6, 1988. Furthermore, petitions containing the required number of signatures had to be filed with the Secretary of the Commonwealth by August 3, 1988. If all the requirements were met, the Secretary and Attorney General would then draft the public policy question's final form as it would appear on the November 8, 1988 ballot.

On June 17, 1988, the APCC board of directors announced its unanimous support for the building moratorium. In reiterating the importance of the moratorium and the widespread support it had generated, the APCC also announced its desire to organize a Cape Cod Environmental Council with members coming from other environmental organizations on the Cape. This group would push for the moratorium's passage.

Early in July 1988 the APCC proclaimed it had collected far more than the required 1,000 signatures needed to qualify the public policy question for the ballot. On July 28, 1988, their goal was realized when more than 3,800 signatures were delivered to the Secretary of the Commonwealth's office.

In an August 4, 1988 letter, Secretary of the Commonwealth Michael Joseph Connolly requested Attorney General James M. Shannon's opinion on whether a number of proposed ballot questions, including the moratorium and Cape Cod Commission questions, were appropriate ones of public policy. Recognizing that other residents of the state visit and enjoy the Cape's natural resources, and that the Cape Cod National Seashore was recognized in 1961, Attorney General Shannon, in a September 2, 1988 letter to Secretary of the Commonwealth Connolly, held that "both [moratorium and Cape Cod Commission] implicate the broad subject of controlling growth and establishing a comprehensive environmental policy for the Massachusetts coastline." His letter continued by observing that "it is clear that issues affecting the environment are not simply of local concern, but rather are of interest to every citizen in the Commonwealth." The two questions were found to be legitimate questions of public policy.

Having qualified the questions for the November ballot, the pro-moratorium campaign moved forward. On October 18, 1988, a major cooperative effort between the APCC and the Massachusetts Audubon Society to promote the moratorium commenced. The support of the latter group may have surprised some individuals since the group tended to not support any building moratorium. However, the widespread public support it had elicited and concerns over growth were contributing factors to the group lending its support.

Mounting what was called the "Just Say Yes" campaign, the groups urged voters to vote yes for all of the public policy questions on the ballot—ratifying a home rule charter for Barnstable County, passing the moratorium, and creating a Cape Cod Regional Commission. The two groups attempted to raise approximately $12,000 to cover the costs of advertising, direct mailings, and other campaign expenses. According to one supporter, the Massachusetts Audubon Society contributed $5,000 toward the goal. Support for the campaign also came from the Environmental Lobby of Massachusetts, which agreed that it was necessary to send a message to officials saying that new land use controls were needed. Additional support for the moratorium and the other public policy questions came from the Massachusetts League of Environmental Voters, a nonprofit organization dedicated to the preservation and protection of Massachusetts' environment. This support was predicated on the belief that more control over the timing and direction of growth and development was needed. Concomitantly, better protection of the environment in the face of continued growth was needed.

A federal official also supported the moratorium. Acknowledging that a moratorium could harm property owners and developers, regional director of the federal Environmental Protection Agency Michael R. Deland felt the moratorium would allow Cape officials the necessary time to develop ways to control future growth and development. He even suggested that "the values that have made the Cape . . . the place it is are being eroded, if not destroyed" (Holmes, 1988c, p. 14). Ultimately, protection of the Cape's environment is important for environmental reasons as well as public health concerns since the Cape relies on groundwater for its drinking water.

The pro-moratorium campaign represented a strong grassroots effort between individuals and various interest groups. Although a small amount of funding was raised to offset campaign expenditures, the campaign relied on volunteers to get signatures for the moratorium petition, stuff envelopes, and give talks on the need for the moratorium.

One might expect that a building moratorium would not sit well with some property owners and various business concerns. This was the case on Cape Cod. Primary opposition to it came from the business community in general and the building trades and real estate interests in particular. Their reasons for opposing the moratorium were varied; however, a major reason commonly shared was that a moratorium simply does not work. Their argument was that it would be counterproductive to impose a moratorium when the housing industry is experiencing an economic slowdown. Supporters of the moratorium countered that these slowdowns are generally followed by economic upswings, and they had to be prepared for such an event.

The potential consequences of a building moratorium greatly concerned a number of individuals. To many people, the consequences of a moratorium would be devastating. In fact, one opponent predicted a moratorium would result in an "unmitigated economic disaster" to the Cape (Castrodale, 1988, p. 1). Among the impacts of the moratorium would be temporary layoffs and possibly permanent layoffs. According to the opponents, young and low-income individuals and families would suffer the most.

The development industry was particularly concerned about the impact of the moratorium on small development firms. Acknowledging that a large number of the developers could be classified as small development firms, many thought they would be driven out of business. On the other hand, the large developers would not suffer as much. These firms had the enviable option of going to another area and then possibly returning to the Cape when the moratorium was lifted. Unfortunately, it would not be feasible for the small developers to simply pick up and go to "greener pastures."

Opponents were also leery of trying to solve the growth dilemma by means of ballot box planning. To them, ballot box planning was ineffective because it ignored the principles of land use planning. Furthermore, such measures would give rise to legal challenges from people claiming they had been deprived of their property without payment of just compensation.

It has become somewhat fashionable in many parts of the country to blame developers and other real estate interests for the ills associated with population growth. The Cape Cod experience was no different. Judging by various citizen commentaries and letters to the newspapers, the development industry appeared to be the main culprit in the minds of many people. The industry responded by noting that the fault was wrongly placed on it. Instead, the industry felt that responsibility for the growth problems should be directed to the various government entities because it was the governments that allowed or approved the growth to occur.

Responding to repeated charges from all directions that they were responsible for the growth problems facing the Cape concerned members of the opposition. On one occasion, an opponent claimed that Tsongas was portraying members of the building, real-estate, and associated industries as "evil, greedy parasites thriving on the Cape's ruination" (Holmes, 1988b, p. 1). They appeared to believe that they had been placed in a "them or us" situation. The debate had polarized the community into two distinct camps. Repairing any perceived damage that may have been caused by statements such as the above consumed many of the opponents.

The anti-moratorium campaign waged by the development industry and others appears to have centered around fliers, informative talks before various audiences, and position statements on the moratorium. At a hearing of the Special Commission on Environmental Operations, opponents turned out in large numbers and carried signs dramatizing how they felt about the moratorium. On that same occasion, some individuals attempted to shout down supporters of the moratorium, including Paul Tsongas. A petition signed by several thousand individuals opposed to the moratorium was also presented at the hearing.

The opposition sensed throughout the campaign that citizens were supporting the measure without really asking any tough questions about it. Calling the moratorium "short-sighted," the Home Builders Association of Massachusetts suggested citizens demand answers to such questions as:

1. Would owners of businesses and homes that have been destroyed by fires, storms, etc., be barred from repairing or rebuilding their property while the moratorium remains in effect?

2. How many construction-related jobs would be eliminated during a moratorium?
3. What effect would a moratorium have on sales tax revenue generated from the building industry?
4. What are the potential costs to local, state, and regional governments to defend legal actions which will be brought by property owners injured by the proposed building moratorium?
5. How would a moratorium affect communities which abut the Cape? (Home Builders Association of Massachusetts, 1988)

They reasoned that if citizens asked specific questions, such as the above, about the moratorium and listened to the responses, many of them might reverse their stances on the moratorium.

A couple of months after the Home Builders Association of Massachusetts suggested that citizens ask questions about the moratorium, the Home Builders Association of Cape Cod (1988) issued a position on "The 'M' Word." Strongly opposing the moratorium, the group compared it to a pneumonia patient with two doctors:

> Cape Cod is like the pneumonia patient with two doctors trying to administer treatment. One treatment is passive. It calls for putting the patient to bed and having him rest. The other is active. It proposes medication. A moratorium is like bed rest. Our fear is that the patient receiving only such treatment may still die. (p. 1)

The moratorium was just not the answer to the Cape's growth problems. The problems were too complex to be solved by a simple moratorium.

All of the moratorium's opponents knew that developing and implementing solutions to the problems would be costly. However, traffic problems could be fixed, as could leaky onsite septic tanks. What was needed were strong public officials willing to tackle the problems. The importance of strong leadership echoed throughout the campaign. As the Home Builders Association of Cape Cod (1988, p. 5) observed:

> We must have leaders who are not afraid to stand up and say that zoning a town all 1 and 2 acre lots and concentrating commercial uses leads to urban sprawl not rural charm: that clustering housing and allowing small commercial areas near housing clusters need not increase overall density or poison our water.

Instead of sitting idly by and waiting for something to happen, the Home Builders Association took the offensive and came up with a list of proposals which, as they mentioned, "can help to clean the collective nest we have all been inadvertently fouling over time" (Home Builders Association of Cape Cod, 1988, p. 3). Some of their proposals included:

1. Permitting of Community Septic Systems and small Wastewater Treatment Plants for older existing developments in coastal areas of small lots;
2. Required upgrading of non-complying septic systems and municipal drainage structures;
3. Building permit caps to control runaway growth;
4. Growth phasing; promotion of long-term phasing and negotiated development;
5. Regional planning, both environmental and economic, with special assistance for smaller towns;
6. Traffic planning, roadway improvements construction, and promotion of alternative transportation mechanisms;
7. Development of innovative infrastructure funding mechanisms including legally consistent impact fees; and
8. Planning for affordable housing. (pp. 3-5)

In an effort to get their points across to the public officials, they mailed their position paper to town officials throughout the Cape. The effort was apparently not that successful. A member of the Home Builders Association recalled that the paper was not well received and essentially fell on deaf ears.

Supporters of the moratorium were not always the opponents' only foe. There were also occasional complaints of biased media coverage. On several occasions, opponents noted the media's coverage was one of emotionalism. They claimed they wanted to deal with the issues and facts involved in the campaign, but usually had to respond to the emotionalism. However, after the alternative proposals to the moratorium had been released, some people applauded the Home Builders Association's efforts. The task was now for all of the various groups involved to work together.

As stated previously, development interests were not the sole opponents of the proposed moratorium. The Barnstable County Selectmen's Association criticized the moratorium because the threat of a moratorium would result in a run on building permits. In other words, people would try to get their building permits as quickly as possible before the moratorium took effect. Furthermore, they objected to not having been contacted by Tsongas earlier in the campaign. They would later vote not to support the proposed moratorium. Moreover, the Association was somewhat annoyed over Tsongas's earlier criticism of Cape Selectmen. Earlier in the campaign, Tsongas had remarked, "In my whole political life I've never seen such a strong dichotomy between voters and their elected officials" (Holmes, 1988a, p. 14). Some of them may have wondered whether he was implying they were out of touch with their constituents.

Anti-moratorium sentiment also surfaced in the town of Falmouth, where some individuals felt the moratorium would create too many problems and could possibly fail to pass any legal challenges to it. They also felt that a moratorium should not arbitrarily be placed on them, because Falmouth was a leader on the Cape in planning and zoning matters. Essentially, the belief was that Falmouth was taking care of its own business and did not need additional help. To some in Falmouth, if citizens and other towns on the Cape wanted to know how to control growth, all they had to do was to examine what Falmouth was doing.

The moratorium public policy question was controversial. Some individuals saw it necessary to protect the Cape's residents' quality of life and to prevent additional environmental damage to the water supply and other resources. The proposed creation of a regional land use planning and regulatory body for Cape Cod was not as controversial or divisive; however, the idea did cause various individuals and organizations to oppose its creation.

Creating a Regional Land Use Planning and Regulatory Body

As previously stated, the problems facing towns on the Cape had evolved from primarily local problems to problems that were regional in nature. As such, a regional approach to their solution was envisioned that was patterned after the Martha's Vineyard Commission Act. Growing out of the earlier Prospect: Cape Cod project, a proposal was drafted to change the CCPEDC into a regional land use planning and regulatory body called the Cape Cod Commission (CCC).

At the time the proposal was developed, the CCPEDC served in an advisory capacity to the Cape's 15 towns on land use planning and environmental issues. It comprised selectmen or designated alternates from each of the towns, the three county commissioners, and a minority representative. The new agency would absorb the old agency and replace the planning commission. Thus, the old agency would be transformed and strengthened by adding new land use regulatory powers. A primary responsibility of the proposed agency was to develop a regional growth plan while protecting ecologically sensitive areas on the Cape. Towns could also prepare comprehensive plans and goals that would be consistent with the regional plan. The new agency also had the authority to review projects having potential impacts on the surrounding regional community. Overall, the proposed commission represented the first time that there would be regional control over growth, where previously planning for growth had been conducted in a town-by-town piecemeal approach.

Any discussion of the public policy question concerning the creation of the CCC has to be divided into two parts. Part one of the discussion revolves around whether the voters would instruct the State Representative from the district to vote in favor of creating the CCC at the state level. If they did, the CCC bill would then go to the State Legislature for its approval. Should the bill be approved at the state level, it would then return to the voters for final ratification.

The lengthy proposal, more than 40 pages long, to create the CCC garnered widespread support from the public, interest groups, and various public officials. Many of those supporting the proposed CCC also supported the moratorium. The APCC, along with the Massachusetts Audubon Society, the Environmental League of Massachusetts, and the Massachusetts League of Environmental Voters participated in the "Just Say Yes" campaign for all three public policy questions. Other individuals and newspapers, wishing it had been proposed at an earlier date, argued for the creation of the CCC. Still others, who had opposed the moratorium, turned and supported the idea of a regional commission. For example, the endorsement by the Barnstable County Selectmen's Association came slowly because some members were concerned that their towns were being told what to do. Its membership voted later to support the commission.

There did not appear to be a great deal of criticism concerning the proposed regional commission. People did, of course, have questions regarding its creation. Some individuals were skeptical over how much power the new agency would possess. What would happen to the town's existing powers? Would the commission take over a town's existing powers?

The complexity of the CCC bill worried many people. They claimed the bill was so technical that many people would not be able to understand it. They urged voters not to rush into something and then later regret it. After all, if the public policy question was approved, the bill would, in all likelihood, undergo numerous changes in the coming months.

Election Day

On November 8, 1988, the voters of Cape Cod went to the polls to decide the fate of the three public policy questions. Question #5 (the Barnstable County Charter question) concerned the creation of a regional government for Barnstable County with "home rule" to deal with problems that were Cape-wide in nature. The measure was passed 69,604 (71.2%) to 28,142 (28.8%). Its passage was expected by all parties. It was the least controversial of the public policy questions on the ballot.

Question #6 (#7 in the town of Barnstable), the Cape Cod Commission Act, asked the voters whether a regional land use authority should be created on the Cape. The question was worded in the following manner:

Shall the Representative from this district be instructed to vote in favor of legislation establishing the Cape Cod Commission, a regional land use planning agency and regulatory body with authority to: prepare a regional policy plan; regulate developments of regional impact; designate districts of critical planning concern, including fragile environmental areas; regulate, in conjunction with the towns, developments within such districts; and foster the preparation, adoption, and implementation of local comprehensive plans consistent with the regional policy plan?

The question passed by a substantial margin—66,992 (76.4%) to 20,714 (23.6%). Its passage was not that surprising, but the wide margin may have surprised a number of people. Supporters of the question felt that a strong message or mandate had been sent to public officials. The message was that the citizens were upset with the lack of effective management and control of growth. They wanted something done that would help preserve the quality of life on the Cape.

Perhaps the most controversial question on the ballot was Question #7 (#8 in the town of Barnstable), asking whether a temporary moratorium on development on Cape Cod should be approved. It was worded as follows:

Shall the Representative from this district be instructed to vote in favor of legislation that would impose a temporary moratorium on development on Cape Cod, suspending the approval, endorsement, or recoding of land division plans creating additional lots, and suspending the issuance of building permits for construction or improvement of owner-occupied single-family dwellings on single approved lots and other exemptions to be determined by municipal regulatory authorities for public projects and affordable housing; this moratorium to continue for a period of one year or until municipal, county, or state legislation and regulations have been adopted for controlling development and preserving Cape Cod's environment?

In a bitterly fought and divisive campaign, the moratorium question was approved by the voters—67,446 (68.4%) to 31,124 (31.6%). Once again, the voters had sent a message to public officials, alerting them that they were upset with uncontrolled growth. Advocates of the moratorium decided not to pursue a statutory moratorium if the towns worked to effectively control growth.

THE BATTLE MOVES INTO ROUND TWO

Citizen approval of the public policy question advocating the creation of the CCC was only the first step in the process. The battle would now proceed to the state level. Nevertheless, the groups that participated in the first campaign continued to advance their respective positions. All of the parties recognized that getting the CCC bill passed at the state level would be difficult. Acknowledging the strong possibility that the bill would be changed, both sides braced themselves for a long, tough fight.

The first hurdle the CCC bill would face at the state level was getting through the State Legislature's Local Affairs Committee. The Committee's co-chairmen had worked hard to have the bill placed in their committee (Hamilton, 1989). The chairmen expected both sides to exert pressure in the form of amendments strengthening or weakening their respective positions. In addition, other communities and politicians around the state would be watching the progress of the bill in case a similar bill were to be contemplated in their areas. Members of the committee would eventually travel to the Cape to get a first-hand view of the Cape's situation.

A coalition of environmental groups, calling itself the Coalition for the Cape Cod Commission Act, played a key role in urging the CCC's creation. A number of groups, including the APCC, Massachusetts Audubon Society, Cape Cod Museum of Natural History, Berkshire Natural Resources Council, Environmental Lobby of Massachusetts, Trout Unlimited/Cape Cod Chapter, League of Women Voters chapters in Falmouth and Lower Cape, and the Barnstable Conservation Foundation, participated in the Coalition. Members were active in fund-raising activities, testifying at public hearings, and sending out campaign fliers. Among the more interesting campaign activities were using buttons with "76" on them, to show the public that 76% of the voters approved the November 8, 1988 public policy question, and starting a fund-raising drive with the slogan "a bill for the bill." The goal was to raise approximately $50,000 to cover campaign costs.

The Coalition's opponents were, once again, primarily real estate and other development interests. Real estate interests were concerned that the bill would negatively affect the Cape's economy and urged the bill be altered to reflect their many concerns. They were quick to note, however, that while they agreed growth should be better guided, the proposed bill was not the answer. Local bankers also questioned the potential impact of the CCC. Noting the uncertainty attached to the bill, one banker noted that "the commission's unknown impact is contributing to banks' unwillingness to lend money in an already sluggish market" (Milton, 1989a, p. 1). Once again, just like the real estate interests, various banks supported the objectives of the bill but questioned the bill as being the needed solution.

Perhaps the most visible opponent to the bill was Paul Doane, a former state senator. His involvement appears to have clouded the issue so much that he essentially became an issue. In fact, one person commented that Doane was unnecessarily crucified for his role in the campaign.

Doane's participation infuriated many people. They wondered where he was when the bill was being written. Why did he wait so long to voice his concerns? Others supporting the bill suggested he was lobbying against the bill and that such lobbying violated state ethics laws. The laws prevented former politicians from promoting or opposing legislation for a given period of time. Doane disputed the allegation and noted that he was not getting paid for his work. Nevertheless, an opinion from the State Ethics Commission indicated his activities did not pose a conflict of interest with state laws.

In May 1989 a group of about 80 members, calling itself CAPE (Citizens Advocating Planning Excellence), was formed to oppose the bill. CAPE opponents jokingly said the initials actually stood for Citizens Against Planning Excellence. The group was composed of realtors, real estate developers, business owners, and other individuals. Serving as CAPE spokesman, Doane indicated the group was simply trying to educate the public on the complexities of the bill. Contrary to public opinion, he suggested the group was not trying to kill the bill. In fact, he claimed CAPE members agreed with the concept but had questions that needed answering. To help advance its position, CAPE hoped to raise $100,000. The group also hired a firm to act as its lobbyist on Beacon Hill.

Two months later CAPE surprised everyone by announcing it was disbanding. The group announced it had done its job by getting people to question the specifics of the bill. Opponents speculated that CAPE disbanded over its failure to raise the $100,000.

As the campaign progressed, the bill gained the backing or endorsement of various groups. On June 8, 1989, it won the support of the Barnstable County Assembly of Delegates in a 93-to-0 vote. Two members voted "present" during the voting—an allowable vote under Assembly rules. The bill had earlier received the support of other groups, including the Barnstable County Selectmen's Association and the Barnstable County Commission.

Everyone expected the bill to be subject to revisions, considering the importance and magnitude of the issue being considered. No one was disappointed. Early revisions regarding an individual's property rights, determining the commission's jurisdiction, establishing possible exemptions from commission review, and determining the time frame for reviewing projects were supported by a number of parties. The Cape Cod legislative delegation even asked the Joint Committee to adopt the amendments. To many of the bill's proponents, progress was being made. All of the necessary support was falling into place.

Individuals applauded the Cape Cod legislative delegation's work on crafting the bill. All interested parties were working together, and not working against each other. Unfortunately, the momentum would soon be lost. At the end of June, the Joint Committee on Local Affairs voted to postpone action on the bill until September so that its members could study the bill in greater detail.

Both sides of the campaign used the time to advance their positions. The side opposing the bill continued its plea for citizens to question various aspects of the bill before it was finalized. However, their position had been weakened when CAPE left the fight and disbanded.

Proponents took the time to have a fund-raising dance, sell woodcut prints to raise campaign funds, and start the previously mentioned "a bill for the bill" fund-raising campaign. A "Save Cape Cod" bus trip to Beacon Hill was also organized to show support for the bill. Organizers had hoped to get 1,000 people to attend the rally, but had to settle for nearly 500. Those in attendance listened to a number of speakers, including members of the Cape legislative delegation and Governor Michael Dukakis, urging passage of the bill.

There was continued fighting over the bill's wording, and new amendments were proposed and hotly debated. Many of the amendments were viewed as attempts to weaken the agency's proposed powers. Some of the proposed amendments dealt with such topics as a hardship clause, limiting the commission's jurisdiction, allowing town selectmen to overrule the commission, and protecting subdivisions approved by a certain date from review by the commission. The first two proposed amendments were adopted while the latter two were rejected.

On October 3, 1989, proponents of the bill were glad to see the bill gain unanimous approval by the Legislature's Local Affairs Committee. However, another amendment was accepted by the committee before its vote. The amendment "would allow the county to bill the Cape's 15 towns, through their property taxes, for the commission's operating budget" (Milton, 1989b, p. 7). Although the committee's approval was important, additional debate was expected on the bill as it went through the legislative process.

The bill would now go to the busy House Ways and Means Committee. Additional amendments were anticipated by the bill's supporters. Delays were also anticipated by the supporters. Unfortunately, much to the chagrin of the supporters, delays became commonplace and were jeopardizing the likelihood of the bill's getting out of the Legislature and eventually being signed by the governor.

Disagreements over amending the bill became controversial. Supporters of the bill, including the Assembly of Delegates and Barnstable County Commissioners, were upset over wording about who would control the CCC. Conversely, the real estate lobby continued its quest to have the bill amended, ostensibly to make it a better and more workable bill.

As the bill remained in the Ways and Means Committee, supporters became increasingly frustrated. One of the local newspapers even encouraged voters to telephone committee members and urge them to vote in favor of the bill, even going as far as providing the names and telephone numbers of the committee's members. Apparently not completely satisfied with the amount of voter response to its plea, the newspaper repeated the list 2 days later and, once again, urged voters to either write or telephone the members.

Time was running out for enacting the bill. It needed to be passed by the House and Senate. If not, the process would start over the following year. The bill, having successfully gone through the House Local Affairs Committee, Counties

Committee, and Ways and Means Committee was ultimately passed by the entire House on November 1, 1989 by an overwhelming 145-2 vote. The large turnout, demonstrating the strong support for the bill, was recorded as a show of strength. On the Senate side, the bill was addressed by the Counties Committee and the Ways and Means Committee. The bill's supporters grew restless on occasion when the Senate Counties Committee questioned the extent of minority representation on the proposed commission. Nevertheless, with amendment, the Senate passed the bill, in a voice vote, on January 2, 1990. The voice vote was not considered unusual for a noncontroversial item. On that same date, the House, in another voice vote, agreed to the Senate amendment.

On January 12, 1990, Governor Michael Dukakis signed the Cape Cod Commission Act into law, as Chapter 716 of the Acts of 1989. In his transmittal letter to the Secretary of the Commonwealth Joseph Connolly, Governor Dukakis added that, in his opinion, "protecting the fragile environment and the character of communities in Barnstable County requires that this Act's terms take effect immediately." Nearly 2 years had passed since voters on Cape Cod endorsed the idea of a regional commission through a nonbinding public policy question.

Acknowledging the importance of protecting and enhancing the many values (i.e., natural, scientific, archaeological, cultural, and so on) on the Cape, citizens finally achieved one of their goals—the creation of a regional planning and land use commission for Barnstable County. The purpose of the Commission, as stated in Section 1(c) is to further:

> The conservation and preservation of natural undeveloped areas, wildlife, flora and habitats for endangered species; the preservation of coastal resources including aquaculture; the protection of groundwater, surface water and ocean water quality, as well as the other natural resources of Cape Cod; balance economic growth; the

provision of adequate capital facilities, including transportation, water supply, and solid, sanitary and hazardous waste
disposal facilities; the coordination of the provision of adequate capital facilities with the achievement of other
goals; the development of an adequate supply of fair affordable housing; and the preservation of historical, cultural, archaeological, architectural, and recreational
values.

In addition, the Commission, as noted in Section 1(d) shall:

Anticipate, guide and coordinate the rate and location of
development with the capital facilities necessary to support such development; review developments which will
have impacts beyond their local community and determine the comparative benefits and detriments of those
projects and their constituency with the regional policy
plan and local comparative plans and goals; identify and
protect areas whose characteristics make them particularly
vulnerable to adverse effects of development; preserve the
social diversity of Cape Cod by promoting fair affordable
housing for low-income and moderate-income persons;
promote the expansion of employment opportunities; and
implement a balanced and sustainable economic development strategy for Cape Cod capable of absorbing the effects of seasonal fluctuations in economic activity.

As it was created, the Commission would be an agency
within the governmental structure of Barnstable County, comprising 19 members: 15 members of which would be from the
Cape's 15 municipalities and appointed by the appropriate
board of selectmen, one county commissioner appointed by the
board of county commissioners, one Native American appointed by the board of county commissioners, one minority
appointed by the board of county supervisors, and one minority appointed by the governor. Except for the governor-
appointed minority member, each of the members would have

one vote. The minority member appointed by the governor would vote only in case of a tie. To be considered for appointment to the Commission, individuals must be residents of one of the towns of Barnstable County and registered to vote. The remainder of the legislation dealt with such issues as its powers, public notice of public hearing, process of proposing regulations, process of developing a regional policy plan, designation of areas of critical concerns, and standards and criteria for developments of regional impacts. The issue of grandfathering was also decided. State zoning law protects developments from a zoning change for 8 years if a plan has been submitted for approval. According to some town officials on the Cape, grandfathering hindered a town's ability to control its development. The Act indicated that some development would be grandfathered, while the 8-year grandfathering provisions of the state law would not apply to DRIs or districts of critical planning concern. The Act would now go back to the voters for final ratification.

THE FINAL ELECTION

On March 27, 1990, in a special election, voters in Barnstable County went to the polls to ratify the Cape Cod Commission Act. The public policy question appeared on the ballot in the following form:

Shall the provisions of Chapter 716 of the Acts of 1989 which would authorize (1) the establishment of the Cape Cod Commission which will be funded by the Barnstable County Assembly of Delegates, in accordance with Barnstable County administrative and budgetary procedures; and (2) the possible assessment by the County Assembly of Delegates of up to but not more than $2 million per year, which amount shall be placed into an account to be known as "The Cape Cod Environmental Protection Fund" to be used only to fund the approved budget of the Cape Cod Commission and which amount would, at most, result in an increase in the property tax rate in the municipality of_____(name of municipality to be inserted) of no more than_____(amount to be inserted), be accepted in Barnstable County?

The Cape Cod Commission Act was ratified by a margin of 30,549 (53%) to 27,284 (47%) in a 50% turnout of the registered voters. Voters in all but 5 of the Cape's 15 towns approved the measure—Truro, Wellfleet, Eastham, Orleans, and Bourne did not. The first four towns are located on the outer Cape and are more rural in nature. They have large amounts of land already protected from development because they are in the Cape Cod National Seashore. The towns supporting the measure were the ones experiencing the most growth.

Reasons for opposing the measures were somewhat predictable. The reasons had been voiced on many previous occasions. Some people argued against the measure because it would simply create another agency and lead to more bureaucracy. Others opposed it because the Cape was in the midst of some bad economic times, and controlling growth would result in jobs being lost. Other objections concerned unanswered questions over its broad powers, "home rule" reasons, questions over property rights, and its impact on tax bills.

A number of actions have taken place since the CCC was created. An executive director and complete staff have been hired and are busily working on creating the numerous ordinances that have to be in place before any project work can be started. Since its inaugural meeting on April 25, 1990, more than 100 DRI projects have been screened. The CCC staff does not have the luxury of time. It has to meet the time deadlines stated in the Act itself. Currently, the CCC meets every 2 weeks. Work on developing administrative regulations and developing the regional policy plan is carried out in CCC subcommittees.

No one expected the CCC to function without problems. Disputes were expected to arise over CCC powers. One dispute concerned the issue of an ordinance defining a DRI. The CCC proposed a definition for a DRI to the Barnstable County Assembly of Delegates. The Assembly attempted to amend the ordinance by approving it. However, according to Section 6(a) of Chapter 716 of the Acts of 1989:

> The commission shall prepare proposed regulations of general application to enable it to fulfill its duties under this act, including, but not limited to . . . the review of developments of regional impact. . . . The commission shall submit these proposed regulations for adoption by ordinance to the assembly of delegates. The assembly of delegates shall either adopt the proposed regulations by ordinance or return the proposed regulations to the commission for restudy and redrafting. In the event the assembly of delegates has objections to the proposed regulations, the assembly shall return the proposed regulations to the commission, together with a written report identifying the elements to which the assembly has objections and a request for changes. After such restudy and redrafting, the commission shall again submit the proposed regulations to the assembly in accordance with the provision of this section.

As such, the Assembly was not following the proper procedures. Ultimately, the CCC told the Assembly to send its concerns to them, as stated in the Act. The CCC amended the definition and sent it back to the Assembly, which later approved the amended definition.

All eyes are on the CCC, which knows it is being watched carefully by a number of individuals and groups to see how it functions during the state's economic woes. Senator Michael

Barrett, co-chairman of the Legislature's Local Affairs Committee, stated it best when he commented, "The Cape Cod Commission will be the pearl of interest in regional government in the '80s and '90s, if it is enacted" (Hamilton, 1989, p. 1). The CCC is currently functioning, but only time will tell if it will be successful.

FIVE

Portland, Maine:
Preserving the Working Waterfront

Residents of Portland, Maine are justifiably proud of their city's waterfront heritage and understandably concerned with its future. Throughout its history, the waterfront has experienced alternating periods of prosperity and decline (The American City Corporation, 1982). Moreover, the waterfront appears to have been a continual topic of inquiry. Task forces have been created on various occasions to study a vast array of waterfront issues. Harbor pollution has been studied on a number of occasions. Debates continue to be heard over the future of the waterfront. This chapter examines one of those debates. More specifically, it examines a debate over whether Portland should maintain a "working waterfront" or allow a "mixed use waterfront." A major part of this debate centered around the development of an initiative that asked voters to "secure the Portland waterfront for marine uses." Readers should be advised that while the media and some individuals associated with the initiative campaign occasionally refer to the initiative using the more popular term *referendum*, the measure is, in a legal sense, an initiative. Although the initiative was decided

on May 5, 1987, the debate over the future of Portland's waterfront continues to be a major topic of discussion.

THE AMERICAN CITY CORPORATION STUDY
AND THE REACTION TO IT

A great deal of the controversy over whether Portland should
maintain its working waterfront can be traced back to 1981. In
that year the City of Portland hired the American City Corporation (ACC), a Columbia, Maryland firm and affiliate of the
Rouse Company, to propose a waterfront development program for the city. More specifically, it was asked to do the following tasks:

1. to conduct a market analysis of the future potential of
   the waterfront;
2. to provide the city with a land use report dealing with
   general zoning principles designed to guide the future
   of the waterfront; and
3. to set forth specific development projects which they
   felt were financially achievable in a relatively short period of time. (City of Portland, 1982, p. 2)

The ACC is the planning division of the Rouse Company, a
firm known for its waterfront regeneration work in Baltimore,
Boston, and other cities in the United States.

Various sources of funding were found to meet the $95,000
cost of the ACC study. For example, federal and state grants
were obtained to fund a portion of the study. Moreover, private
contributions from local businesses, such as banking interests,
construction interests, a broadcasting company, a petroleum
company, and a baking company, were obtained to help offset
the cost of the study.

The ACC issued its study to Portland in March 1982. It noted that the purpose of the report was "to provide the City of Portland with a realistic and attainable development program for revitalization of the waterfront—Commercial Street area" (ACC, 1982, p. 4). The study acknowledged the importance of the city's waterfront. In fact, it noted that "one of Portland's most valuable resources is its deep water port and harbor related economic activities" (ACC, 1982, p. 5). These related economic activities could be broken down into water-dependent uses and waterfront-enhanced uses. Examples of the former were fish harvesting, lobstering, fish processing, cargo shipping or waterfront access, while examples of the latter were chandlering, marine suppliers, waste rendering, storage and wholesaling, and a trucking area that serves the waterfront uses (ACC, 1982, p. 5).

A controversial conclusion of the ACC study was that multiuse or mixed-use projects of the waterfront could occur without damaging the working waterfront. To support its claim, the ACC pointed out that working waterfronts and non-maritime mixed-use developments in such areas as Boston, Baltimore, Oakland, and San Francisco have worked. Apparently, the authors of the study felt that if such a mix could work in other areas, then it could also work in Portland.

The ACC study pointed out that the potential existed for other desirable land uses in addition to preserving the city's working waterfront. It noted a strong potential for residential development along the Commercial Street waterfront. This residential development would take the form of both condominiums for sale and the rehabilitation of existing warehouses for rental units. Moreover, the potential for office space existed on the eastern portion of Commercial Street. In addition, retail shops and parking garages were envisioned for the waterfront area. Finally, the study recommended the addition of a major hotel, complete with convention facilities, which would be a focal point for additional commercial activities.

Table 5.1 ACC Recommended Program

Development Component	1982	1983	Year 1984	1985	1986	Total
Residential (Dwelling Units)	50	100	150	150	150	6,000
Garden Apts. (Condo)						
Garden Apts. (Rental)						
Townhouses						
Office (sq. ft.)	—	—	100k	150k	150k	400k
Hotel (rooms)*				275		275

* Assumes inclusion of conference facilities
SOURCE: American City Corporation, 1982, p. 15

The development program recommended by the ACC for the waterfront can be found in Table 5.1. To attain the recommended program goals over the 1982-1986 period would cost approximately $64 million—$53 million in private investment and $11 million in public investment.

Public reaction to the ACC study quickly surfaced. One congressional candidate claimed that "the American City Corporation plan, if implemented in anything like its present form, would ultimately destroy the Portland waterfront as we know it," while the owner of a ship chandlery and general marine supplier saw "a collision course coming with what they have planned" (Ferland, 1982a, p. 1). Concerns over what would happen to the working waterfront were paramount. Some individuals felt that if the ACC study's recommendations were to materialize, the existing fishing and maritime uses would be pushed off the waterfront. Opponents felt the city was embarking on the wrong course. Several opponents preferred to see funding go toward improving existing property, a viewpoint shared by many.

What started off with a small group of residents complaining about the ACC study soon blossomed into debate featuring various interest groups. On March 8, 1982, businessman

Robert W. Roffler announced the formation of a group called the Waterfront Preservation Association (WPA) to oppose the ACC study. At a March 11, 1982 organizational meeting of the WPA, a number of individuals expressed their displeasure with the study. One individual, apparently alluding to Rouse Company's past waterfront regeneration work across the country, expressed the following sentiment: "Clearly this is our waterfront. . . . It's not Boston. It's not Baltimore. It belongs to the people of Portland and the people of Maine" (Ferland, 1982c, p. 12).

The WPA would later criticize the ACC study by saying that the "plan looks more like a repackaged Quincy Market [in Boston] than a proposal to protect the working waterfront" (Ferland, 1982e, p. 14). Although the WPA did not oppose mixed-use projects on the landward side of Commercial Street, it felt that introducing condominiums and the other recommended uses to the waterfront area would ultimately destroy Portland's working waterfront. The WPA continued to gain the support of other residents, including a number of waterfront business leaders, in its effort to oppose the ACC study.

Another argument voiced by some citizens was that the ACC did not consult with enough people. In fact, some waterfront businessmen and property owners complained that although the ACC recommendations would affect them, they had not been contacted by the ACC. This issue would later be addressed by Portland officials and a representative of the ACC.

City officials responded to citizen uneasiness about the ACC study. Mayor Pamela P. Plumb, not wanting a confrontation with the citizens, responded to the criticism by saying the ACC study acted as a catalyst to get individuals talking about the waterfront and welcomed citizen input into its planning. Furthermore, Mayor Plumb felt that the citizens failed to understand the city's intentions about waterfront development. As she indicated:

Nobody is going to say to the landowners, "Do this with your land." What we're trying to do is to develop a consensus of how this community wants the waterfront to develop. The waterfront will grow, change and evolve— that's a given. The issue is whether we, as a collective city, have input into that happening or will we let things develop as they might. (Ferland, 1982b, p. 1)

City Manager Tim Honey also responded to various citizen concerns about the ACC study. The ACC's task was to use its expertise to study the waterfront area and provide a possible course of action, not to talk to everyone interested in the study. Talking with the public and getting their opinions was a task for city officials. He also echoed Mayor Plumb's remark that the city was willing to hear any citizen concerns.

The ACC was not surprised by citizen criticism or disagreement with its study. Dennis J. Connolly, vice-president of ACC, expected disagreement. However, the misunderstanding of the ACC proposal was unexpected. Contrary to public opinion, Connolly claimed the ACC proposal would not take away berthing spaces. Instead, he felt existing berthing spaces were to remain, where possible, and even expand to other areas. Responding to a concern that fishermen, residents, and other businesses cannot coexist because of the smells and other disamenities associated with the fishing industry, Connolly believed that people who wanted to live on a waterfront would have taken such disamenities into consideration before moving to the waterfront. He also denied that the ACC plan would eliminate Portland's working waterfront. He felt the plan was appropriate because "if development occurs independently, the fishing and marine industries will suffer" (Ferland, 1982d, p. 1). Finally, Connolly acknowledged that they could not and did not talk with everyone on the waterfront. All ACC was trying to do was to determine what uses were located in the waterfront area and what uses people wanted to see in the waterfront area, investigate the market potential of the area, and ultimately see how everything could fit together on the available land.

The WPA continued to object to the ACC study. Interestingly enough, the ACC proposals were acceptable to the WPA if they remained on the land side of Commercial Street. The WPA would later reach a compromise with city officials regarding waterfront development after city officials agreed to help existing marine industries grow, not displace them. In addition, officials removed several of ACC's proposals from the study. Consequently, a modified version of the ACC study was to be prepared.

On April 26, 1982, City Manager Honey presented the City Council with a 144-page waterfront development plan titled "Strategies for the Development and Revitalization of the Portland Waterfront." It represented an amended version of the ACC study, which would later be shelved, and incorporated comments from the public and city staff. Overall, the report made clear that "the Portland Waterfront should continue to prosper as a 'working waterfront'—that its principle function is to provide jobs and economic activity that are uniquely related to and dependent upon a waterfront location" (City of Portland, 1982, p. 2). The following are among the recommendations contained in the report:

1. Establish zoning protection for fishing and other marine businesses;
2 Increase berthing;
3. Help people who own property in the proposed mixed-use zone;
4. Build a public landing at the end of the Portland pier;
5. Make improvements at the International Ferry Terminal;
6. Build a parking garage;
7. Participate through federal grants or other financing programs in housing conversion projects for the upper

stories of vacant and underused buildings on the land side of Commercial Street. ("Waterfront Proposals," 1982, p. 8)

The report also recommended some zoning changes for the 250-acre waterfront. At that time, the waterfront was zoned W-1 (Waterfront Zone), I2b (Industrial Zone), B-3 (Business Zone), R-6 (Residential Zone), and I3b (Industrial Zone). The W-1 zone represented the major source of concern. One of the problems with the zone was that it was not open to a variety of uses and was "too liberal and does not provide adequate protection for uses which are dependent upon a waterfront location" (City of Portland, 1982, p. 20).

The report made several recommendations regarding the waterfront zoning. It called for the creation of a W-2 (Waterfront Zone), which was designed for the needs of waterfront-dependent uses. It also called for a text change and a boundary change in the existing W-1 (Waterfront Zone) that would allow for mixed uses and for the uses allowed in the W-2 zone.

On April 25, 1983, the new W-1 and W-2 zones were adopted. The purpose of the W-1 zone, as noted in the Portland Land Use Code, Division 18, Section 14-306, was:

1. To provide an area for the compatible mixture of waterfront dependent uses such as marine shipping and fishing-related activities, and waterfront enhanced uses such as traditional commercial, industrial and residential uses.
2. To encourage adaptive reuse of existing structures.
3. To encourage more intensive uses of land and buildings.

The purpose of the W-2 zone, as found in Division 18.5, Section 14-313, was:

1. To reserve a substantial portion of the waterfront for uses which are waterfront dependent such as marine and fishing-related activities.
2. To protect water dependent uses from other competing but incompatible uses.

Shortly after City Manager Honey issued the "Strategies" report, the WPA decided against backing the waterfront development plan. It felt the plan was long and difficult to comprehend and that the public needed time to assimilate the information and respond to it. In addition, there were still concerns by some waterfront businesses that the plan would thwart possible future expansion and that some businesses would ultimately be displaced because of the mixed-use zone.

THREATS TO THE WORKING WATERFRONT

The waterfront zoning changes that were adopted in 1983 came under fire in early 1986. Some waterfront property owners urged a change in the zoning that would allow temporary nonmarine use on the working waterfront area. Accordingly, Portland's Planning Board, on January 14, 1986, voted 6-1 to recommend that the City Council amend the text of the W-2 zone to allow the following: (a) Professional business or general offices, but only above the first floor and (b) No such use after December 31, 1990, except lawful uses existing on April 25, 1983, when new waterfront zoning went into effect (McNulty, 1986, p. 23).

Not everyone was in favor of the Planning Board's recommendations. Some citizens questioned the need for the changes and wondered whether additional changes would be forthcoming. Karen Sanford, who was actively opposed to the change, claimed the change would be the first step to "dissemble

piecemeal" [*sic*] the city's commitment to a working waterfront (McNulty, 1986, p. 23).

Concerns over a possible condominium build-up on the waterfront prompted a coalition called Keep the Port in Portland
to become more active in not only opposing waterfront condominium development but also urging city officials to enforce
the W-2 zone. Karen Sanford, one of its leaders, indicated that
the group became angered when a Boston concern wanted to
build a condominium development on Cumberland Wharf. Although this development was not built, Keep the Port in Portland felt the condominium threat was real and growing.
According to Sanford, the feeling was that the fishing industry
would be forced off the waterfront by other land uses. The condominium threat became more real when additional property
owners in an industrial zone were contacted to see if they
would be interested in selling their property for a 330-unit residential development.

In October 1986 members of three citizens groups—Portland
West Neighborhood Planning Council, Keep the Port in Portland, and Save the Hill—called for a moratorium on waterfron
development. In a letter to City Manager Robert Ganley, they
declared their intention to meet with city officials to discuss
their concerns over waterfront development and see whether
city officials shared their concerns. If the groups' concerns were
not shared by city officials, other steps would be taken in an
attempt to curb the pressures in favor of waterfront development

The three groups did not meet with city officials because
Mayor Ronald Dorler refused to meet with their representatives. In a *Portland Evening Express* Opinion, the newspaper attributed Mayor Dorler's lack of interest in meeting the group
to the fact "he doesn't like the way the groups asked for the
meeting" ("Dorler," 1986, p. 10). Claiming the groups made a
major issue of asking for a private meeting, Dorler might have
met with the groups if they had approached him first instead

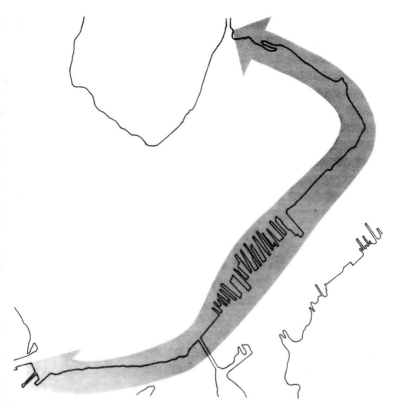

Figure 5.1. Areas Covered by the Waterfront Initiative

of going to the city manager. It appears Dorler was upset with the groups' publicizing the issues and their concerns without first discussing them with him—a matter of proper protocol. The groups decided to take the issue and their concerns directly to the people.

Table 5.2 Organizations Within the Working Waterfront Coalition

---

Don't Kill the Hill
Portland West Neighborhood Planning Council
Greater Portland Central Labor Council (AFL-CIO)
Keep the Port in Portland
Neighborhood Action Coalition
Casco Bay Island Development Association
Maine Fishermans Cooperative Association
Maine Lobstermans Association
Local 6 of the Industrial Union of Marine and Shipbuilding
National Maritime Union
Riverton Community Group
Deering Citizen's Group for the Working Waterfront
Munjoy Hill Neighborhood Organization

SOURCE: Working Waterfront Coalition, 1987

On December 22, 1986, the Working Waterfront Coalition (WWC), a group formed earlier in 1986, filed a petition for a citizen initiative that would amend the City land use code to secure the waterfront for marine purposes. A listing of the groups in the WWC can be found in Table 5.2. As shown in Figure 5.1, the proposed initiative would expand the W-2 zone from Tukey's Bridge to the north to Veteran's Memorial Bridge in the south. Existing non-marine waterfront uses would be grandfathered under the initiative. Among the uses advanced for the area were berthing for boats; fish processing, storage, marketing, and transportation; chandlery (marine supplies and support services); tourist boats, cruise ship, and ferry facilities; public facilities serving educational or recreational purposes (aquarium, marine park, or marine museum); and ground-level parking and loading space incidental to the above water-related uses (WWC, 1987a, p. 9). To get the measure on the ballot, petitioners had to get the petition signed by 10 city voters and get 750 voters to sign the petition in City Hall within a period of 45 working days. A public hearing would be scheduled by the city once the signatures had been obtained. The final step in the process would be to schedule a vote on the initiative. Ultimately, more than 1,300 signatures were obtained.

Proponents of the waterfront initiative pointed to a multitude of reasons why it was needed. To some, the current means employed to revitalize the waterfront were not enough. Others wondered whether city officials were not too pro-development. Furthermore, the WWC claimed that much of the development occurring on the waterfront did not need a waterfront location. To them, "shoreline development for land uses which do not require a shoreside location, or do not provide goods and services to water-dependent uses, threaten to limit severely or eliminate the availability of this resource for marine uses" (WWC, 1987a, p. 2). Waterfront condominiums would represent a land-use not requiring a shoreside location. As Thom Ennen, the executive director of the Boston Harbor Associates, has said regarding industry and upscale development, "Don't be fooled into thinking that you can put these kinds of uses together and they'll marry" (WWC, 1987a, p. 3). It was an issue of compatible versus noncompatible uses, where it was felt that noncompatible uses not requiring a waterfront location were forcing the water-dependent uses off the waterfront. In the end, the WWC (1987a, p. 9) hoped to advance the following values:

1. Broad, diverse water-related uses of the working waterfront;
2. Stable investment climate for existing and future waterfront uses;
3. Creation of good-paying, long-term jobs;
4. Neighborhood preservation and community development;
5. Continuation of Portland as an historic seaport city;

6. Protection of public trust rights of access to shoreline; and
7. Local self-determination for Portland residents.

The stage was now set for a classic debate.

THE WATERFRONT DEBATE

The debate over the future of Portland's waterfront involved a variety of individuals, politicians, groups, and organizations. Among the parties participating were the WWC, City Council, Chamber of Commerce, Concerned Citizens for Portland's Waterfront, local newspapers, and other members of the public. These parties used debates, leaflets, radio ads, yard signs, and posters to get their respective messages across. In addition to attracting people who volunteered their time and labor, the proponents and opponents of the initiative raised approximately $36,000 for each side by obtaining campaign funds from individuals as well as firms.

Arguments Against the Initiative

Opponents to the waterfront initiative raised a host of arguments against it. Some individuals were opposed to it in principal, while others felt it would hurt the economic development of the waterfront, thereby preventing its revitalization. Still others were satisfied with the existing W-2 zone. They felt that it should be left alone and that any attempt to alter it was a bad idea. Roger Hale, president of General Marine Construction Company, indicated it was "a bad idea whose time has not come" (McNulty, 1987b, 3). He continued:

This is just further swords and pins in the back of the waterfront. There is too much pie-in-the-sky talk about bringing the working waterfront back to what it once was. That is a fallacy. We cannot bring back the working waterfront of 50 and 75 years ago. (McNulty, 1987b, p. 3)

Later, he would call the ban on the non-marine uses on the waterfront, "socialism in its highest degree: restricting property, making it useless through zoning" (Murphy, 1987a, p. 14).

The debate over representative democracy and participatory democracy also became evident. Some people felt zoning decisions should be made through the traditional planning process with appropriate provisions for citizen participation and public debate. Hale went on to suggest that "it would be bad government for the city to zone by referendum because the average citizen isn't well-acquainted with the complexity of city zoning ordinances" (Bradbury, 1987, p. 34). This argument has been raised on numerous occasions by opponents of initiatives or referendums dealing with land use matters.

The Portland Community Chamber of Commerce was a major organization opposing the waterfront initiative. Analyzing a waterfront inventory that it had commissioned, the Chamber noted that a high vacancy rate existed in the W-2 zone. Acknowledging concern over the initiative, the Chamber president observed that the study suggested that "after more than three years with maritime-only restrictions in the W-2 zone, ground-level space—not upper stories—is the primary need of maritime and marine-related businesses" (McNulty, 1987a, p. 16). To the Chamber, the waterfront initiative, if passed by the voters, would not be able to change the high vacancy rates.

On March 16, 1987, the Chamber of Commerce formally announced its opposition to the waterfront initiative. In a prepared statement, the Chamber (1987, p. 1) proclaimed its support of "thoughtful, planned development that preserves and enhances the quality of life in Portland and that enables marine related users to find the facilities they need at prices they can afford." The Chamber also indicated that if the measure passed, it "would tie the hands of the City Council on questions of land use and essentially be a vote of no confidence in the Council and in the established system" (Portland Chamber of Commerce, 1987, p. 1). It urged voters to defeat the measure.

A majority of the Portland City Council, seven out of nine, also opposed the waterfront initiative. Their lack of support was not unexpected by initiative supporters. Although declaring support for some of the initiative's major goals, Mayor Ronald Dorler was concerned that it would tie the hands of some existing businesses on the waterfront. Other members objected to it because they felt that zoning by initiative was simply not the way to proceed, an opinion voiced by a number of people.

Perhaps the most vocal and visible group opposing the waterfront initiative was Concerned Citizens for Portland's Waterfront. In announcing the group's formation on April 2, 1987, the chairman of its steering committee, a former Portland mayor and Maine Senate president, acknowledged that the city was changing and that other ways to preserve the waterfront should be examined. According to this group, the waterfront initiative was not the way to proceed. Other members of the group's steering committee included a city councilor, businessmen, and other individuals.

Concerned Citizens for Portland's Waterfront employed a variety of means to get its messages across. Members participated in debates, gave informational talks, and distributed fliers explaining their position. A major point they tried to get across to the public was that most people did not realize the ramifications associated with passage of the initiative. In urging voters to vote no on the initiative, the group offered the following reasons:

1. **The referendum is not condos vs. marine use.**
   It is not simply a "condo ban." The referendum would stop all other nonmarine commercial and industrial development from Tukey's Bridge to Veterans Memorial Bridge. Many existing businesses would be prevented from expanding.
2. **Marine uses are protected.**
   Our waterfront has 17 piers, four of which have been set aside for mixed use. Those four wharves represent about 5% of the land area addressed by the referendum. The rest of the waterfront is already zoned for marine and industrial uses only.
3. **There are better solutions.**
   Zoning by referendum is not the way to protect our waterfront. Better solutions can be found by identifying specific areas of concern and working together to address them. The city enacted a "master plan" three years ago to protect and preserve our working waterfront. Any change to that plan can and should be done through the normal municipal process.
4. **This referendum affects all Portland citizens.**
   We cannot afford to limit our options. Over 22 million public dollars have been spent to promote and preserve jobs on the waterfront. Restricting the entire waterfront to only one use will severely limit the private investment necessary to keep the waterfront working. (Concerned Citizens for Portland's Waterfront, n.d.)

Developers of Eastern Point—a $50-million project including condominiums, marine, and retail shops—also opposed the waterfront initiative. This project had already been approved by the Portland Planning Board but not by the City Council. It represented perhaps the ultimate insult to those opposed to condominium and office developments along the waterfront. Passage of the waterfront initiative could stop the project.

The developers of the Eastern Point project claimed they were exempt from the initiative. Noting the project had features the public would like, Joel Russ, one of the developers, called the initiative "an ill-conceived idea" and said that it was unrealistic and irresponsible for Portland's land use policy to be developed in that way (Murphy, 1987c, p. 14). Moreover, doing so might ultimately end up hurting the area instead of helping it.

Portland's newspapers covered the waterfront initiative debate extensively. One newspaper, the *Portland Evening Express*, recognized the right of citizens to be concerned about the growth and development of the waterfront. However, it felt the waterfront initiative represented the wrong approach and that prohibiting any nonmarine activities on the waterfront "is to jeopardize the harbor's future as a place to live and play—as well as work" ("Harbor," 1987b, p. 16). Instead, the newspaper advocated a balanced approach to harbor development, including allowing mixed uses that were compatible with marine activities. To the newspaper, marine activities could be housed on the ground floors and nonmarine uses could be accommodated on the upper floors—an idea previously advanced by other groups.

A number of citizens wrote to the newspapers and expressed their displeasure over the waterfront initiative. Many of them complained that the measure was too restrictive and was not the answer to the waterfront problems. They felt allowing mixed uses would enhance the working waterfront, not hurt it. One individual agreed with what was happening on the waterfront and was concerned that passage of the measure would negate what had already been done ("Readers Write," 1987a). Others commented that the passage of the measure would hurt the existing property owners and that the power of eminent domain should be considered to compensate them ("Readers Write," 1987b).

Arguments in Favor of the Initiative

Supporters of the waterfront initiative were not surprised by opposition to the measure. On the contrary, they expected it. As Karen Sanford indicated, "We didn't expect the Chamber of Commerce to be interested in a no-condo referendum, and judging from some of the decisions coming out of City Hall, we're not surprised that the council is coming out against it" (Murphy, 1987b, p. 12).

A major point initiative supporters wanted to get across to the public was that they were not against waterfront development. They supported the idea of marketing the waterfront for marine uses. To them, nonmarine uses threatened the working waterfront and could be accommodated on non-waterfront locations.

The WWC tried to garner support for the initiative on numerous occasions. On one occasion it sent a letter to supporters, requesting their monetary support for a newspaper advertisement that would be a statement of support for the measure followed by the names of supporters. In another flier to voters, the WWC informed voters why they should vote for the initiative: "A vote FOR this initiative will stop condo development on the waterfront and secure the waterfront for marine related uses. It will give the city five years to promote *rational* marine development of the waterfront. We need this time to determine Portland's future as a seaport city" (WWC "Campaign," n.d.). In another letter requesting supporters to sponsor a radio ad, the WWC challenged their opponents actions and statements:

As you know, the recent building boom has placed immense speculative real estate pressures, especially from condominium development, on our waterfront. Condos threaten to change the working waterfront into an exclusive residential neighborhood.

The real estate speculators and the developers say they want a "mixed use" waterfront. Don't be fooled. "Mixed use" zoning has failed in every port in the country that it has been tried.

Unfortunately, our city officials have succumbed to the temptation to sacrifice the long-term viability of the marine economy for the short-term profit-taking of the coastal real estate boom.

That's what this election is all about.

Who will decide the future of Portland? The people of Portland or the developers and the speculators? (WWC, 1987b)

Unlike Portland's City Council, the majority of Portland's state legislative delegation supported the waterfront initiative. In fact, seven out of nine members supported it. Their reasons for supporting it differed from member to member. Some predicted doom if the initiative failed. Senator Thomas H. Andrews spoke of the initiative's importance to the state. In noting that the eyes of the state would be on Portland on election day, Andrews proclaimed, "This could be one of the most critical battles in the statewide war to preserve our natural resources" (Perry, 1987, p. 1). Representative Laurence E. Connolly, Jr., echoed a sentiment shared by many residents when he said: "Passage of the referendum will give the city sufficient controls to protect the waterfront from the insatiable thirst of a handful of developers and speculators who want to acquire waterfront property and turn a quick profit by developing condos" (Perry, 1987, p. 10).

Support for the initiative also came from businessmen, shipbuilders, and fishermen on the Portland waterfront. These individuals were opposed to mixed uses on the waterfront and called for marine uses only. They felt their livelihoods were being jeopardized by the entrance of nonmarine uses.

Ed Blackmore, president of the Maine Lobstermen's Association, commented that "there is a strong conviction among the Board of Directors that unless the waterfront uses (fishermen) join the WWC, the lobstermen of Portland will in a very short time be denied all access to the Portland waterfront" (WWC, 1987c, p. 2). Concomitantly, Willie Spear, vice-president of the Maine Fishermen's Cooperative Association, was concerned over uncontrolled development and advocated getting "control over short-sighted development and plan for long-term development of the working waterfront" (WWC, 1987c, p. 2).

As was the case with the opposition, a number of individuals wrote to local newspapers expressing their support for the waterfront initiative. Their reasons for supporting the measure generally coincided with the reasons already mentioned. They were concerned that marine uses and nonmarine uses could not coexist. Moreover, they perceived waterfront development as being out of control and believed passage of the initiative would give the city time to find solutions to the waterfront problems. Finally, one individual criticized the opposition's belief that zoning by referendum is wrong:

> It's true that zoning by referendum is not the way things are usually done, but anyone who has been following recent waterfront development proposals and ongoing condominium construction can see that what we have now is zoning by developers. Is this representative government? Maybe our councilors are really perturbed by the fact that at least 1,300 Portlanders don't trust them or their appointed Planning Board to make decisions about who will or will not be on the waterfront. ("Readers Write," 1987b, 10)

While not giving zoning by referendum blanket acceptance, this individual felt it was appropriate in this case.

Debates on the Initiative

The use of debates represented an excellent medium for the various parties to get their respective messages across to the general public. Each party was able to state its position on the topic and respond to points made by the other side.

On April 21, 1987, the University of Southern Maine's Public Policy and Management Program sponsored a debate on the waterfront initiative, featuring Representative Anne Rand and University of Maine law professor Orlando Delogu speaking in favor of the initiative, and Jean Gilpatrick, regional sales manager for Guilford Transportation Industries, and Ed Bradley, Jr., maritime attorney and former chairman of the Portland Planning Board, speaking against the measure. Rand and Delogu argued that the city needed to do a better job of marketing the waterfront. They continued to point out that mixed uses do not work with marine uses. There were better locations for the various mixed uses. Gilpatrick and Bradley countered the arguments in favor of the initiative by claiming the city had kept condominiums out of the W-2 zone for 4 years and that the city was doing a good job for the waterfront. Gilpatrick also argued that the initiative was interfering with the traditional planning process and that citizens had the right to ask for a zoning change (Sleeper, 1987).

Some 4 days later, another debate took place at a Munjoy Hill Neighborhood Organization meeting. Once again Rand and Delogu spoke in favor of the measure and called for the city to support the waterfront. Two different individuals, Jack Humeniuk, chairman of the Portland Planning Board, and James Salisbury, general manager of the Portland Fish Exchange, spoke against the measure. Humeniuk disagreed with Rand and Delogu over whether the city was marketing or supporting the waterfront. He commented that: "The city has thrown its fiscal support behind major marine and cargo projects, but office building and condominium projects, and other nonmarine business, are necessary to subsidize them" (Gardner, 1987, p. 26). To Humeniuk, "the success of one will guarantee the success of the other" (Gardner, 1987, p. 26).

The Ballot Wording Controversy

On April 6, 1987, the Portland City Council, in an 8-1 vote, approved the wording of the waterfront initiative for the May 5, 1987 ballot. The approved wording was: "Shall the Ordinance Entitled: 'Land Use Code Amendment to be Enacted by Initiative' be adopted?" The question would then be followed by an "Explanatory Statement of City Council" and then by a larger "Explanatory Statement of Petitioners."

The initiative's proponents criticized the City Council's action. They claimed the Council was "manipulating the ballot box" (McNulty, 1987c, p. 1). Instead of the approved wording on the ballot, they wanted their version, which read as follows: "Shall the Ordinance Entitled: 'Land Use Code Amendment to be Enacted by Initiative,' whose purpose is to secure the Portland waterfront for marine uses, be enacted?" The statement would be followed first by their explanatory statement of 197 words and then by a City Council statement.

According to the proponents, the problem was that the wording of the ballot question would confuse the voters. More specifically, Representative Laurence Connolly claimed voters would be confused by the wording and that the voters would associate the negative City Council statement, since it is given first, with the first box on the ballot. The City Attorney disagreed with Connolly and suggested that since the Council was neutral, its statement should go before the petitioners' statement. He went on to claim the individuals that drafted the original initiative were partially to blame because "they chose the title" (McNulty, 1987c, p. 1). The *Portland Evening Express* agreed with Lourie and said the City Council was not manipulating the ballot box. As it noted in an April 8, 1987 editorial: "Portlanders don't live in caves. Virtually everyone knows that a "yes" vote would bar any nonmaritime activity anywhere on the waterfront ("Harbor," 1987b, p. 6).

As the days passed, the WWC filed suit against the city claiming the ballot question was unconstitutional in its present form. It wanted both explanatory statements removed from the ballot. The WWC lawyer, R. John Wuestoff, indicated the WWC wanted the initiative title expanded or to keep the existing title and print the ordinance on the ballot. City Attorney Lourie wanted the ballot to be left alone. It is interesting to note here that the WWC filed its suit after a Portland resident, David L. Koplow, found a 1951 case, *Lafleur v. Frost*, 80 A.2d 407 (1951), where the Maine Supreme Court ruled that explanatory statements should not accompany a proposed initiative referendum.

On April 23, 1987, Superior Court Justice G. Arthur Brennan ruled that the City had to replace the explanatory wording with the text of the waterfront initiative. City Attorney Lourie, displeased over the ruling, felt citizens would be more confused by the actual ordinance than by the statements of the City Council and WWC. The WWC attorney was pleased with the ruling and suggested that the judge and the WWC did not underestimate the intelligence of the Portland electorate. A complete copy of the measure that appeared on the May 5, 1987 ballot can be found in the Appendix.

THE PUSH TO THE ELECTION

As election day approached, both sides stepped up their campaigns. Their messages continued to stress their earlier arguments. The side favoring the initiative wanted to preserve the working waterfront and claimed the entrance of mixed uses would lead to the working waterfront's becoming a thing of the past. On the other side, opponents felt the initiative would be very damaging to the city because it would hinder continued economic development. Each side predicted doom if it lost the election.

Controversy also centered around what would happen to existing land uses on the waterfront. Proponents claimed existing businesses would not be harmed by passage of the initiative. In other words, they would be grandfathered under the measure (Weir, 1987). Conversely, the Concerned Citizens for Portland's Waterfront was of the opinion that the measure would prevent existing businesses from expanding, altering, or modifying their operations in any way (Weir, 1987, p. 12). The answer to this issue would only be determined if the measure passed.

The overall campaign was clearly divisive. Waterfront workers were split over the issue. One newspaper columnist proclaimed the campaign as the battle of "Yuppies vs. Haddock" (Rawson, 1987, p. 6). Another newspaper article noted the campaign pitted "protectionists against developers and businesses—and against City Hall" (Lovell, 1987, p. 1).

The newspapers continued to run extensive coverage of the campaign. In addition to encouraging voters to vote against the waterfront initiative, the *Portland Evening Express* criticized the wording of ballot measures in general and this measure in particular. It felt simplicity was needed in the wording. As noted in one of its editorials:

> All referendum questions should be simply worded to elicit a "yes" vote from those who favor the action proposed and a "no" from those who oppose it. Never mind what the referendum proposal is. A "yes" vote would give it a green light, a "no" would stop it on red. And it would be that way on every referendum question year after year.
> Granted, voters have a responsibility to understand what they're doing before they mark their ballots. But the

system should support them in that process, not confront them with mushy words and tricky questions. ("Ballot," 1987, p. 6).

This sentiment has been acknowledged by a number of parties before.

ELECTION DAY AND THE AFTERMATH

On May 5, 1987, Portland's voters overwhelmingly approved the waterfront initiative by almost a 2-1 margin—8,965 votes to 4,510 votes (Portland City Clerk's Office, 1989). It won in all 28 of the city's precincts. One proponent of the measure noted the voter turnout was one of their highest.

Passage of the initiative meant different things to different people. To Karen Sanford, a leading advocate of the measure, its passage represented "a step to stabilize the waterfront so we could then move together and promote and market the waterfront" (Bradley, 1987, p. 13). Conversely, opponents felt passage of the measure would lower property values and force off the waterfront some businesses that wanted to expand. Regardless of the particular points of view, the tasks at hand were to enforce the measure and to make the working waterfront work.

Gauging what has happened since the measure was passed is tenuous at best. How soon should the impacts be measured? Who is measuring the impacts? These and other questions will confront any individual trying to assess what has happened since the measure's passage.

Some 9 months after its passage, impacts of the measure were still being disputed. To some individuals, it was too early to gauge any effects. To others, slow private investment on the waterfront and difficulty in attracting tenants to the upper floors of buildings were directly attributable to the initiative. Later, individuals were to offer suggestions on how to make some progress on the waterfront, ranging from better marketing of the waterfront to pursuing all available state and federal waterfront funds. These and other suggestions were apparently welcomed by a number of individuals.

On March 28, 1988, an interesting issue was raised at a City Council meeting. On that night, City Councilor Joseph D. Casale proposed that a referendum be held that would allow voters to decide whether nonmaritime restrictions of Portland's waterfront zoning could be eased. Claiming the 1987 waterfront measure was too restrictive, Casale advocated allowing office buildings and other commercial developments on the waterfront. In essence, his proposal would delete most of the prohibitions mentioned in the 1987 measure.

A number of parties took exception to Casale's proposal. Frank Kadi, chairman of WWC, expressed his dismay by suggesting, "What we are witnessing is an attempt to say to the people of Portland: 'No matter how exhaustive the public debate, we will not respect your wishes' " (WWC "Statement," n.d.). Others thought Casale's proposal was ill-conceived and out of touch with current government activities regarding growth management and environmental protection in Maine.

The Portland City Council, in a 6-3 vote, defeated Councilor Casale's proposal. A general sentiment among the councilors was that ways were being discussed to correct any problems that had been created by the measure. Progress was being made, and interrupting the progress would be a mistake. Instead, one councilor suggested that the City Council should be concerned with issues affecting the waterfront zone and not with the referendum's wording.

An issue debated throughout the campaign and after was whether the initiative was retroactive. According to its advocates, the measure was retroactive to December 22, 1986—the date the petition was filed. The developers of one particular project, the Fisherman's Wharf office-retail project, claimed they had secured vested rights and would therefore not be

subject to the initiative. They claimed the retroactivity statement in the initiative was unconstitutional. The Maine Supreme
Court unanimously decided the issue by ruling that the developers had not acquired vested rights.

In April 1988 the City Council's Community Development
Committee recommended a new set of 24 waterfront policies
and policy options for the City to pursue. The policies were
adopted by a 5-4 vote on May 2, 1988. To oversee the policies,
Mayor Dorler appointed a 12-member Waterfront Task Force.

The appointments to the task force, much to the surprise of
Mayor Dorler, generated a bit of controversy. Councilor Pamela
Plumb, chair of the task force, strongly criticized the appointments. Arguing for more appointees without a direct stake or
interest on the waterfront, Plumb claimed that what "the committee put forward does not reflect the concerns" she expressed
to Dorler (Murphy, 1988, p. 12). Karen Sanford, another appoin-
tee to the task force, initially resigned from it because she felt it
had been set up to undermine the referendum:

> First, it has as one of its goals the questioning of the refer-
> endum zoning itself. We say the case is closed. The people
> have spoken! When will some of our elected officials get
> the message? Second, the taskforce membership is stacked
> against the referendum. Appointing this taskforce to im-
> plement the referendum is like, after the American Revolu-
> tion, appointing the British to write our Constitution!
> (Sanford, 1988)

She would later rethink the situation and remain a member of
the task force.

A number of people were anxiously awaiting word on the
status of the 24 waterfront policies that had been adopted in
May 1988. Had they been implemented? Were they just sitting
there? The results were mixed. Several of the goals, such as
soliciting cruise ship business and improving the Interna-

tional Marine Terminal, had been achieved. Other goals, such as the coordination of local harbor management activities and acquiring certain properties, were in progress. No progress had been made regarding an aquarium on the waterfront.

Another interesting event occurred on March 8, 1990. On this date, City Attorney Lourie sent a memorandum to City Manager Ganley, proposing an amendment to Chapter 9, Article III of the Portland City Code, which would repeal and replace the Initiative and Referendum Ordinance. Among the proposed revisions were:

1. Adopting signature requirement of the 20% of votes in the last gubernatorial election from the statutory scheme on charter amendments,
2. Providing for a petition procedure that is substantially the same as charter amendments,
3. Shortening the period of time during which the Council is bound by the vote of the people from five to three years, and
4. Adopting the 30% requirement for voter turnout as in the case of charter amendments. (Lourie, 1990)

According to City Attorney Lourie, these and other changes were necessitated by the actions of the last Maine Legislature.

The proposed changes generated a backlash of criticism. To some individuals the proposed changes were simply unnecessary. State Senator Thomas Andrews suggested that the proposal "conflicts with the essential purpose of that law—to make citizen initiated referendums in cities and towns more accessible to Maine people" (Andrews, 1990). In urging the City Council to reject the proposed changes, Andrews wrote:

A 600% increase in the required number of signatures is unreasonable and unfair. The outright ban on retroactivity would leave voters powerless to address some pressing public concerns, as we saw demonstrated with the

Table 5.3 Sampling of Recommendations Contained in the Waterfront Task Force Report

Berthing Recommendations

1. New recreational berthing should be encouraged outside the central harbor.
2. Existing marinas within the central harbor should be allowed to expand within the limits of their current premises.
3. Recreational berthing should not displace commercial vessels.
4. The permitting process should be streamlined.
5. There needs to be increased police power in the harbor.

Marketing Recommendations

1. In the short term the Department of Transportation and Waterfront should be renamed the Port of Portland.
2. A favorable image of the port should be developed and promoted.
3. The City, region, and state should jointly develop a port impact study.
4. The competitive position of the port should be monitored continually.
5. Waterfront signage should be provided with tourism information for pedestrians and parking information for motorists.

Economic Impact of Land Use Regulations

1. Portland should start a zoning review process to create a waterfront land use plan and to consolidate layers of zoning.
2. South Portland should develop a waterfront plan designed to protect marine related businesses and services.
3. The Planning Departments, Planning Boards and Councils of Portland and South Portland should coordinate their waterfront planning and zoning processes.
4. The cities of Portland and South Portland should ask the State to fund a study of the economic impact of marine business.
5. A variety of mechanisms for economic assistance for wharf owners should be made available.

SOURCE: Waterfront Task Force Recommendations, April 1990.

waterfront referendum of a few years ago. And, the reduction in time a referendum-initiated ordinance could stand on the books is a major step backward for our citizens. (Andrews, 1990)

Others criticized the proposed changes as an attack on their rights to participate in democracy and as a measure designed to thwart the public. In the end, the changes were rejected.

The Waterfront Task Force finally issued its report on April 6, 1990—2 years after its creation. The purpose of the report was to analyze three points—berthing, marketing, and economic impact of land use regulations—in greater detail and to make recommendations to the City Councils of Portland and South Portland. A total of 42 policies and initiatives in the three areas were recommended to be taken by the appropriate parties. Table 5.3 illustrates some of the recommendations given in the report. On April 10, 1990, a public hearing was held at Portland's City Hall so that the public could comment on the report. A small group of about 20 individuals attended the meeting. The report would later be presented to the City Council for its action.

CONTINUING CONCERNS

In May 1987 the voters of Portland had approved the waterfront initiative. It was the culmination of a battle over waterfront growth and the need to preserve the working waterfront. Citizens had become tired and frustrated over the development pressures facing the waterfront and were alarmed over the "creeping condominiumism" of the waterfront (WWC 1987a).

The waterfront initiative campaign became highly politicized. On the one hand, advocates of the initiative stressed that the 1983 zoning did not go far enough and that mixed uses would destroy Portland's working waterfront. They felt it was imperative that something stronger be done to protect the waterfront. On the other hand, its opponents wondered whether the initiative would overprotect the waterfront and eventually lead to its demise. Both sides featured the participation of interest groups, politicians, and members of the general public.

In the end, the waterfront initiative essentially places an overlay zone on the existing zoning and allows only fishing or maritime activities, functionally water-dependent uses, or authorized public uses over the affected waterfront area. It is not a moratorium in a strict legal sense. It is simply a change in zoning. After the 5-year period, as covered in the initiative, the City of Portland has a number of avenues it can take. It could make needed changes without going to the public. It could revert back to the earlier 1983 zoning, or it could decide to do nothing. In the interim, the citizens of Portland have spoken. They want to keep the city's working waterfront and are waiting for the city to develop and market the working waterfront

S I X

San Diego, California: Preventing the Los Angelization of San Diego

Called "America's Finest City" by its residents and politicians, San Diego has been experiencing growth pains for many years. Today, it is the nation's sixth most-populated city. This growth can be attributed to a number of factors—natural causes, continued economic growth, tourism, increases in military presence, defense spending, and retirement migration. Table 6.1 shows the extent to which San Diego has grown since 1900.

Concerns over population growth and its various side effects have become highly emotional and politicized issues that remain high on the local public policy agenda. Virtually not a day goes by without some discussion of population growth and growth management. For every reason given for imposing growth controls, there is an opposing argument for why growth controls should not be implemented. And, for the time being, there is no indication that the growth debates will ever be resolved.

Table 6.1 Population Growth, City of San Diego, 1900-1990

Year	Population
1900	17,700
1910	39,578
1920	74,361
1930	147,995
1940	203,341
1950	334,387
1960	573,224
1970	697,027
1980	875,504
1990	1,118,300

SOURCES: U.S. Census, Population Estimate by California Department of Finance, Estimate as of January 1, 1990

EARLY ACTIVITIES CONCERNING GROWTH

Concerns over population growth in San Diego have been voiced for many years. In 1967 the City's Progress Guide and General Plan laid the groundwork for future activities regarding the management and control of growth. Among the objectives stated in the document were:

1. Creation of a strong central core;
2. Development of a more compact city;
3. Prevention of sprawl;
4. Encouragement of greater variety and choice in the living environment;
5. Promotion of a more handsome environment;
6. Recognition of the importance of San Diego's harbor; and
7. Preservation of the open space system. (City of San Diego, 1967)

The seeds of managing the city's growth had been planted.

In the early 1970s San Diegans again questioned whether the city should continue growing at a rapid rate. Citizens were concerned about the rising costs of public services and facilities, the environmental damage associated with growth, and other spillover effects of growth. The Sierra Club even tried to place an initiative on the ballot that would have limited San Diego's growth to its "fair share" of the national growth rate (City of San Diego Planning Department, 1986). The initiative failed to gain a place on the ballot due to a lack of signatures.

An increase in the number of suburban communities continued to plague San Diego as well. Officials started questioning the adequacy of the city's public facilities and its ability to meet the increasing service needs of these communities. In 1975 two noteworthy events occurred. First, Mayor Pete Wilson, with the approval of the City Council, called for the City Planning Department to develop a Growth Management Plan, which would then be consolidated into an updated Progress Guide and General Plan. Second, a "pay as you grow" philosophy was adopted by the City Council as a means of managing growth. This philosophy held that the public facilities needed for a new community would be developed concurrent with the community's development. Moreover, the facilities would be funded with the revenues generated from the new community, not out of the City's general fund.

An updated Progress Guide and General Plan, which included the City's Growth Management Plan, was adopted on February 26, 1979. In terms of guiding growth, the Plan recommended the city be divided into three planning areas or tiers: Urbanized, Planned Urbanizing, and Future Urbanizing (City of San Diego, 1979). These areas are shown in Figure 6.1.

The Urbanized Area represents the central portion and older sections of the city and is expected to function as a regional center. The goals of the area are to attract the most intensive and varied land use, including office-administrative, financial, residential, and entertainment, and strengthen the viability of the central areas through renewal, redevelopment, and new construction (City of San Diego, 1979). The conservation and rehabilitation of deteriorating neighborhoods would be emphasized in the other older communities of San Diego.

Newly developing communities comprise the second planning area—the Planned Urbanizing Area. The goals in this area include supporting the additional public investment necessary to complete development and allowing the growth of communities already served by capital facilities. It would be opened gradually for urbanization through the orderly extension of public facilities and the provision of housing for various income levels.

The final planning area is the Future Urbanizing Area—also referred to as the urban reserve. This area includes land presently vacant and for the most part zoned for agriculture. The land is held in reserve for future development and will be released in 1995. However, the land in this area could be opened for development, provided that the planned communities were built out or as opportunities to implement the city's balanced housing or land use goals arose. By doing this, San Diego was attempting to prevent development and possible environmental damage.

In 1984 Mayor Roger Hedgecock and the City Council established a task force charged with the duty of checking on whether the goals and objectives of the 1979 Progress Guide and General Plan were being realized. Recommendations on how to improve the Growth Management Plan were to be made to the City Council. Among the conclusions reached by the task force were that new land would be needed for development; service levels were satisfactory in the Planned Urbanizing Area; and services and facilities had failed to keep up with the needs of the population and had failed to meet General Plan standards (City of San Diego Growth Management Review Task Force, 1984).

SAN DIEGO GENERAL PLAN, 1979

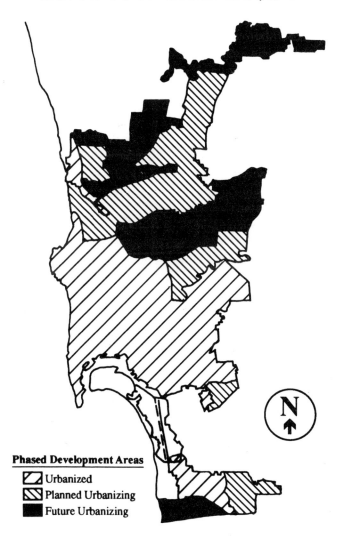

Figure 6.1. Phased Development Areas of the 1979 San Diego General Plan

RATIONALE FOR PROPOSITION A:
THE MANAGED GROWTH INITIATIVE

As noted in the previous section, the 1979 Progress Guide and General Plan divided the city into the Urbanized Area, Planned Urbanizing Area, and Future Urbanizing Area. The latter area contained approximately 29,100 acres. The designations for the various categories of land were not etched in stone. Change could occur in designated areas. Any change would occur only after the Planning Department and Planning Commission examined a proposed project and a majority of the City Council felt there was a need to open land in the Future Urbanizing Area for development.

The ability of the City Council to approve an area being changed from one category to another concerned a number of San Diegans. They felt that too many requests for changing designations had been approved and that the goals of the 1979 Progress Guide and General Plan were not being realized. For example, in 1982 the City Council approved the Fairbanks Country Club project, an exchange of 785 acres of future developed lands for 616 acres of open space. The project would contain a number of houses, a golf course, and a country club. Its developers emphasized that the exchange would help further the city's open space goals as stated in the General Plan. One year later the City Council approved another shift of 600 acres for a Sorrento Hills project, which included an industrial area, specialized commercial area, residential units, and some open space. Getting the city to amend the Growth Management Plan was becoming somewhat routine. Mayor Roger Hedgecock even acknowledged that "the exceptions to the rule are now greater than the rule" (Smolens, 1983, p. A-4). In 1984 the City Council approved another shift of 93 acres in the North City West area.

The La Jolla Valley project represented the final insult to some citizens—the "straw that broke the camel's back." This project would require shifting some 5,100 acres from the Future Urbanizing Area to the Planned Urbanizing Area—a significant portion of the city's urban reserve. The project was slated to include a variety of land uses, including some 1,000 acres for a Christian University with a projected enrollment of 10,000 students, an industrial park on 400 to 600 acres, an east-west road, and a later addition of some 15,000 housing units. The developers must have thought there would be no problems obtaining the necessary approvals. They spent a great deal of money on studies and other tasks before any construction activities had started. La Jolla Valley essentially represented a city within a city. Its developers even claimed the project would further city goals in a number of areas and would contribute up to $1 million a year in property taxes.

Two prominent politicians came out in opposition to the La Jolla Valley. Councilman Mike Gotch questioned the need to open up land in the Future Urbanizing Area. He suggested, "My initial impression is that there is sufficient land within the Planned Urbanizing Area to accommodate commercial, industrial, and residential needs of this city well into the 1990s" (Weintraub, 1983, p. II-8). Mayor Hedgecock was even more adamant in his opposition. He proclaimed:

> I have already told them it [La Jolla Valley] is not going to happen. They are going to have to get around me to make it happen. It may be one of the best-planned communities in the world, but it's in the wrong place at the wrong time. (Weintraub, 1983, p. II-8)

Mayor Hedgecock was clearly upset over the project and what he perceived it was doing to the city's Growth Management Plan, and he sought to make some reforms in the city's growth management policies. His idea was to have strict adherence to the Growth Management Plan and to restrict development on the city's hillsides and canyons. La Jolla Valley remained a thorn in his side. Its developers felt that since they had already expended large sums of money on the project, they should be exempt from a threshold determination—the first step to determine whether projects in this area could continue through the planning and development processes. Mayor Hedgecock's reform package was unanimously approved by the City Council on December 13, 1983. However, for the overall passage, he agreed to a compromise that allowed La Jolla Valley to proceed in its planning process.

On January 27, 1983, the City Planning Department recommended that the La Jolla Valley project be rejected. Its objections centered around the points that the project would strain existing city services and that there were enough available residential and industrial lands to meet the city's needs to the year 2000.

On February 2, 1984, the San Diego Planning Commission voted against changing the land from a Future Urbanizing Area designation to a Planned Urbanizing designation by a 4-3 vote. It agreed with the City Planning Department's recommendation to not approve the shift.

The La Jolla Valley developers appealed the Planning Commission's decision to the City Council. To help plead their case, they scaled down their proposal to include only the Christian University and the industrial park. The other proposed land uses would be postponed until 1995. Evidently, the City Council was sufficiently persuaded by the new version of the project, because it approved the project by a 5-4 vote on September 12, 1984.

A number of individuals and groups took an interest in the managed growth issue, which would ultimately become highly spirited and politicized. Many participants limited their participation to getting signatures needed to qualify the initiative for the ballot, while others published various informational pieces supporting or opposing the measure. In addition, there were a number of lively debates featuring proponents and opponents of the measure.

The most visible in the debate was a group called Citizens for Managed Growth. This group was made up of individuals, college professors, attorneys, members of local planning groups, and other organizations concerned with the negative effects of growth in San Diego. The group felt the City Council was violating the Growth Management Plan. To them, the Council was simply caving in to developer pressures to open up lands in the Future Urbanizing Area, which was encouraging the premature development of land. Ultimately, the group reasoned that the City Council could not be trusted to implement the Growth Management Plan.

On January 21, 1985, San Diegans for Managed Growth published in a local newspaper their notice of intent to circulate an initiative petition. If passed by the voters, this initiative petition would be added to the San Diego Progress Guide and General Plan. Section 1 of the initiative stated:

> No property shall be changed from the "future urbanizing" land use designation in the Progress Guide and General Plan to any other land use designation and the provisions restricting development in the future urbanizing area shall not be amended except by majority vote of the people voting on the change or amendment at a citywide election thereon.

The initiative would be retroactive to August 1, 1984. Overall, the initiative provided for voter ratification of City Council approval of land development in the Future Urbanizing Area. It would put the land use decision in the hands of the voters.

On January 28, 1985, Dave Kreitzer, chairman of San Diegans for Managed Growth, announced that the group would formally file, on that date, its intention to circulate a Managed Growth Initiative petition and seek to qualify it for

the November 1985 ballot (Kreitzer, 1985). Kreitzer offered the
following reasons for the group's actions:

> We are taking this step because recent actions by the city
> council have seriously compromised the integrity of our
> city's growth management plan.
> By prematurely shifting land out of the urban reserve the
> council has abdicated its responsibility for orderly growth.
> In its rush to accommodate development, the council is
> ignoring the wishes of its constituents as expressed in the
> growth management plan: a decent quality of life without
> smog, traffic jams and pressures on public services.

In addition to San Diegans for Managed Growth, a number of
individuals and groups came out in support of the initiative,
later referred to as Proposition A. One of its biggest supporters
was Mayor Roger Hedgecock. His support centered around the
belief that "the City Council has failed to enforce the Growth
Management Plan adopted by the Council in 1979 after many
years of work and millions of dollars of expense" (Hedgecock
1985, p. 2). He also added that, "In fact, support for Proposition
A is support for the planning process itself. The Proposition A
battle is a test of whether our development decisions will be
guided by that planning process or whether they will be hos-
tage to narrow development and expedient political interests"
(Hedgecock, 1985, p. 2).

Another proponent of Proposition A was a group called Citizens Coordinate for Century III (C-3)—an interest group with
broad membership committed to proper planning and citizen
involvement in the planning process. Its reasons for supporting
Proposition A were similar to those of Mayor Hedgecock. C-3
felt the City Council was ignoring the already adopted Growth
Management Plan and that it was of paramount importance to
keep the integrity of the plan intact. The group contributed to
the campaign by publishing information on why the measure
was needed.

The San Diego League of Women Voters also supported Proposition A because it was fed up with the City Council's continual removal of land from the urban reserve. To show support for the measure, the League circulated petitions to help get the measure on the ballot and provided educational information in its newsletters.

The San Diego Chapter of the Sierra Club represented a visible proponent of the initiative. It circulated petitions, ran articles in its *Hi Sierran* newspaper, manned phone banks, sat at shopping centers with information supporting the initiative and even had a signature-collecting contest to see who could get the most signatures for the measure (San Diego Chapter of the Sierra Club, 1985).

A formidable list of individuals and organizations opposed Proposition A. A group called Citizens for Community Planning—a coalition of real estate interests, politicians, and others—raised a substantial amount of campaign funds and played a major role in opposing the initiative. In total, opponents spent more than $700,000 in an attempt to defeat the initiative—out-spending proponents by more than a 10-to-1 margin.

A sampling of some of the major contributors can be found in Table 6.2. A main argument used by the opponents was that the City Council was doing a good job of managing the city's growth and that we should simply let them do their job. To the opponents, this initiative would complicate matters.

A leading member of the Building Industry Association, Mike Madigan, complained that the initiative was not the answer. It did not further the cause of managing growth. Instead, Madigan believed:

> So, rather than managing growth, Proposition A shuffles growth. The financial costs of this misbegotten policy will have to be borne by those who are crowded into old established neighborhoods and currently urbanizing areas.

Table 6.2 Sampling of Contributors Opposing Proposition A

Group Name	$ Amount Contributed
Pardee Construction	$220,000
University Development, Inc.	77,099
Home Federal Savings and Loan Assoc.	7,500
Building Industry Association—President's Council	5,000
Golden Eagle Political Action Committee	3,000
R. E. Hazard Contracting Co.	2,000
John Burnham and Co.	2,000
Hawthorne Machinery	1,250
Daley Corp.	1,000
McMillin Development, Inc.	1,000

SOURCE: San Diego City Clerk's Office, 1990

> Selfish irresponsibility as public policy is not good for planners, taxpayers and—yes—even environmentalists. The give and take of flexible planning makes the system work. Rather than violating the plan, that is the plan. (Madigan, 1985, p. 21)

Opposition to Proposition A was not confined to development and building interests. A former chairperson of the San Diego Planning Commission opposed the initiative because "new growth will be forced into existing neighborhoods, whether they are ready for it or not" (Leonard, 1985, p. 2) Even a city councilman who was an early leader of the anti-Proposition A campaign expressed alarm over the adequacy of public facilities in the urbanized communities. Finally, a former member of one of the San Diego's many community-planning groups even claimed that many past and present chairpersons of community-planning groups in the City of San Diego opposed the measure (Bradley, 1985). Overall, San Diego was primed for a major battle over the future of the city.

The San Diego Municipal Code stipulates that before an initiative can qualify for the ballot, it must first obtain a required number of signatures from registered voters—52,000 in this case. The proponents were confident of getting the required signatures because they knew San Diegans were getting frustrated over the negative impacts of growth and were concerned about maintaining their quality of life.

In a June 12, 1985 press conference, San Diegans for Managed Growth announced they had obtained more than 75,000 signatures from registered voters in San Diego. To apparently dramatize their effort, they took the signed petitions to the City Clerk's office in a shiny wheelbarrow. Opponents to the initiative were not surprised over the ease with which San Diegans for Managed Growth had obtained the signatures. Councilman Uvaldo Martinez, a leading opponent of the initiative, claimed that the signatures were obtained so easily because "they've only been telling half the story" (Smolens, 1985a, p. B-3). He assured the public that his side would tell the remainder of the story.

The next step in the process of qualifying the initiative for ballot was for the City Clerk to verify the signatures. A 5% random sample would be used to check the signatures. On June 24, 1985, the City Clerk announced that 58,679 valid signatures had been obtained. Provisions were available for challenging the signatures.

It did not take long for a challenge to occur. To do so, however, would represent a costly endeavor. It would cost anyone making a challenge $92,000 to verify the signatures. Nevertheless, a member of the development industry challenged the signatures on the ground that there was not enough information to determine whether the signatures were valid. More specifically, the developer disputed some signatures because the initiative petition asked for voter registration addresses, not current addresses. This could result in allowing people who did not currently live in San Diego to sign the initiative petition.

On June 28, 1985, a Superior Court judge issued a restraining order, preventing the City Council from placing the initiative

on the ballot. The judge also set a hearing date to hear the
developer's arguments for challenging the signatures; consequently, the verification process could not be commenced until
after the hearing.

The hearing was held on July 9, 1985. The Superior Court was
not persuaded by the developer's arguments. Although noting
that the initiative petitions "deviated slightly from the law,"
Judge Douglas R. Woodworth ruled that "if every 't' had to be
crossed and every 'i' had to be dotted by every petitioner in the
state, there would be simply no initiative law left" (Smolens,
1985b, p. B-1). The developer subsequently withdrew the re-
quest for an individual signature count. A second attempt by
the developer to keep the initiative off the ballot was rejected
by the 4th District Court of Appeal.

The San Diegans for Managed Growth's goal of having the
initiative placed on the ballot was finally realized on July 15,
1985. Although the City Council decided not to adopt the initiative as law, it did agree, by an 8-0 vote, to place the initiative
on the November 5, 1985 ballot.

THE PROPOSITION A CAMPAIGN

The Proposition A campaign was bitterly contested. Both
proponents and opponents of the measure continually sought
to advance their cause while attempting to discredit their opposition. To do so, each side employed a variety of tactics. Because their campaign had raised only approximately $45,000,
proponents had to rely on primarily grassroots and volunteer
support. They relied on free media coverage and volunteers
who distributed fliers and other forms of information. Mass
mailings were rare because they were so costly.

The opposition to Proposition A ran a far more sophisticated and professional campaign. In fact, they hired a political
consultant to manage their campaign. After raising more than

$700,000, they were able to utilize mass mailings, radio advertisements, telephone polls, and billboards to get their message across to the people.

The use of billboards became an issue in the campaign. Early in the campaign, proponents of Proposition A used the slogan "No L.A. ! Yes on A." That slogan would later appear in a modified version on a number of billboards paid for by the anti-Proposition A campaign. More specifically, the anti-Proposition A campaign spent substantial money to place in heavily populated areas of the city billboards containing the message "No L.A. No on A." The signs had been placed in areas where they felt the growth would occur if Proposition A passed. At one point in the campaign, an individual or individuals changed the message on some of the billboards from "No L.A. ! No on Prop. A" to "No L.A. ! Yes on Prop. A." The anti-Proposition A campaign questioned whether their opposition was employing a dirty campaign trick. The end result was that the voters were getting confused.

Debates were also used to disseminate information and to give the sides an opportunity to dispute the charges made by their opponents. In a October 9, 1985 debate sponsored by the San Diego Taxpayers Association, Republican Assemblyman Larry Stirling argued against Proposition A while City Councilman Gotch argued for it. Stirling felt that its passage would cost the city a great deal of money and that the funds could be better spent on other public activities. He also questioned whether citizens understood the complexity of land use issues and could find the time to assimilate the information needed to make an informed decision. Gotch disputed Stirling's claim that many of the issues are too complex for the citizens by suggesting the people already vote on complex issues. Moreover, Gotch felt that without Proposition A land development would occur in the outlying areas and lead to higher public service costs and other disamenities associated with population growth.

Less than a month later, Stirling debated the initiative with Mayor Hedgecock. Stirling reiterated his earlier allegations and attacked the initiative as being developed by a group of people upset with a past City Council decision. Hedgecock countered Stirling's claims by suggesting developers were, in fact, a special interest group and questioned whether, due to its past performance, the City Council even could be trusted to make the necessary land use decisions. His opinion was that the City Council could not be trusted to make the decisions.

As noted earlier, the pro-Proposition A campaign relied on, to some extent, free media coverage. A great deal of the coverage came in newspaper articles, newspaper editorials, citizen commentaries, and letters to the editor. In total, citizens witnessed a great deal of newspaper coverage on various facets of the campaign.

One of the city's newspapers, the *San Diego Union*, ran several editorials opposing the initiative. The *Union* believed the city's growth management policy was working. Passing Proposition A would limit the city's flexibility in managing growth ("Flawed remedy," 1985). In another editorial, just two days before the election, the *Union* echoed earlier statements made by the anti-Proposition A side and urged voters to vote against the initiative ("Matter of self-interest," 1985).

Readers were also able to take advantage of several commentaries about the initiative. One of them pitted a supporter of the initiative against an opponent. The supporter wondered what type of city San Diegans wanted and reemphasized the point that the City Council was not doing its job of managing the city's growth (Gotch, 1985). The opponent felt the initiative was wrong and that if the initiative passed, the future urbanizing area might be inundated with large-lot suburban development (Silverman, 1985). Ultimately, he felt the initiative was not an example of rational land use planning.

Even readers responded to the various campaigns and newspaper coverage by writing letters to the editor. A number of readers opposing the initiative complained that the initiative was developed by a group of citizens angry with the City Council. To these readers, the angry citizens were only concerned with stopping growth near them. Concomitantly, readers claimed the voters lacked the necessary expertise in land use planning to make an informed decision on the issue before them.

On the other hand, a number of readers wrote in support of the initiative. They reaffirmed the notion that the City Council had lost the people's faith. They could no longer be trusted to make the necessary land use decisions. Others commented on the opposition's "slick" campaign and said that the citizens could not be fooled by the opposition's strategy and tactics. These readers believed the voters had enough intelligence to read between the lines and make an informed decision on the initiative.

Both campaigns continued to garner support for their positions from a number of different parties. U.S. Representative Jim Bates of San Diego, an advocate of the initiative, claimed the opposition was confusing the voters and accused them of "using 'deceitful' tactics in their strategy to defeat the proposition" (Weisberg, 1985b, p. B-1). Conversely, the chairman of the San Diego County Republican Central Committee voiced that group's opposition to Proposition A by commenting that "it's such a bad proposition, I don't think it's worthy of discussion" (Weisberg, 1985a, p. B-2). Citizens for Community Planning, the major body opposing the initiative, even hired a former assistant city attorney to investigate the legality of Proposition A. Attorneys attacked the measure on the ground that it would be subject to costly legal challenges.

Support and opposition to Proposition A also came from politicians from surrounding cities. A slow-growth advocate and city councilman from the City of Escondido supported the measure because it would "help us [San Diego and Escondido] keep the borders of our respective cities from merging into 'sluberbia' as cities have in Orange and Los Angeles counties" (Okerblom, 1985, p. B-2). Opposition to the initiative came from a city councilman from the city of Del Mar who questioned the need for the initiative and wondered why another direct democracy device had not been used. More specifically, citizens should use the recall device if they were opposed to a council member's actions.

ELECTION DAY

Proposition A appeared on the November 5, 1985 ballot in the following form:

CITY OF SAN DIEGO INITIATIVE MEASURE. AMENDS THE CITY OF SAN DIEGO PROGRESS GUIDE AND GENERAL PLAN. Shall the city of San Diego Progress Guide and General Plan be amended by adding restrictions requiring that land areas which are designated as "future urbanizing" not be redesignated without voter approval?

A majority vote was required for passage.

The sample ballot that had been sent earlier to all registered voters gave them the opportunity to try deciphering arguments in favor of and against the initiative. The following were among the arguments in favor of the initiative: (a) City Council had consistently violated the adopted Growth Management Plan; (b) City Council has squandered more than half of the urban reserve; and (c) we need checks on the influence of special interests and to assure accountability of our elected officials. Arguments against the initiative included the following: (a) It will force growth into our neighborhoods; (b) we will pay higher taxes in overcrowded neighborhoods for more parks, streets, sewers, traffic lights, and police and fire protection; and

(c) it will create the "Los Angelesization" it was supposed to stop.

San Diego's voters passed Proposition A by a vote of 77,640 (56.12%) to 60,712 (43.88%). Although only 28% of the registered voters cast their votes, Proposition A became municipal law and would now be implemented by the Planning Department, Planning Commission, and City Council.

Supporters of Proposition A were elated with its passage. One of its leading supporters, Mayor Hedgecock, noted its importance by suggesting that "it is a stirring victory for the people of the city against special interests and it shows that the people are much more concerned about growth than the City Council has been" (Weisberg, 1985c, p.A-1). Other supporters echoed similar sentiments and credited the voters for seeing through the opposition's campaign of misinformation and not being misled by it.

Opponents to Proposition A claimed they knew they were fighting an uphill battle. They recognized that citizens were clearly frustrated over increased traffic congestion, smog, and other disamenities associated with population growth. Nevertheless, although out-spending their opposition by a 10-to-1 margin, they continued to feel that the citizens did not understand their campaign messages. Legal challenges to the validity and constitutionality of Proposition A were expected.

POST PROPOSITION A

The passage of Proposition A did not end the growth debate by any stretch of the imagination. In fact, the debate became even more intense. There were spirited debates over limits, in the form of the number of new homes that could be built, and other techniques to manage growth.

Proposition A would continue being a focal point in the following years. Its first ballot test came on November 4, 1986. On that date, San Diego's voters approved Proposition D—a Sorrento Valley industrial park project on urban reserve land. The project's developers swapped approximately 300 acres of land to be used as a preserve for the ability to develop the project. The La Jolla Valley project appeared again in 1987. This time the developers wanted the voters to decide whether the project's 5,100 acres should be opened for development. In June 1987 the City Council, in a 9-0 vote, agreed to send the project to the voters. On November 3, 1987, the voters rejected Proposition J—the shifting of the 5,100 acres from the Future Urbanizing to Planned Urbanizing designation.

Earlier that same year, the mayor and City Council appointed a 28-member Citizens Advisory Committee on Growth and Development, whose purposes were to update the City's Progress Guide and General Plan and to help formulate how the City should handle its anticipated growth. One product of the committee was a growth management ballot measure for the City Council. The committee met on numerous occasions over the next 2 years and even published a newsletter, called *SANDIPLAN*, to keep interested San Diegans informed of its progress.

In May 1987 a group calling itself Citizens for Limited Growth entered the growth debate. Composed of slow-growth advocates, environmentalists, academicians, and others concerned with the problems of growth, Citizens for Limited Growth emerged as a powerful interest group in the growth debates. The group was dissatisfied over the current state of affairs and the way the city was handling the growth problem. It announced its intention of developing a slow-growth initiative, called the Quality of Life Initiative, for both the City and County of San Diego. Claiming that the initiative was necessary to slow down development, Linda Martin, a leading member of the group, indicated that "we just haven't seen any proposal that attacks the problem in a way that would be effective and in a way that would stick" (Sottili, 1987, p. B-8). On

March 22, 1988, the group turned in the required petitions with more than 80,000 signatures. Later, after verification of the required number of signatures had been obtained, the City Clerk's Office, on April 1, 1988, announced that the group's initiative had qualified for the November 8, 1988 ballot. The City Council would later vote in favor of placing the initiative on the ballot. The measure would read, in part, as follows:

INITIATIVE MEASURE. AMENDS THE SAN DIEGO GENERAL PLAN.

Until standards as designated in the initiative are met, shall the city:

a. Limit residential dwelling units as follows:
   FY 1988-89: 7,000 to 9,000 dwelling units
   FY 1989-90: 6,000 to 8,000 dwelling units
   FY 1990-91: 5,000 to 7,000 dwelling units and each subsequent fiscal year through
   FY 2009-2010—4,000 to 6,000 dwelling units;

b. Develop and implement a plan for industrial and commercial development consistent with the criteria in the initiative;

c. Develop and implement an allocation system for residential development as provided in the initiative;

d. Preserve sensitive environmental lands as provided in the initiative;

e. Adopt a plan for the development of the city's sphere of influence as provided in the initiative?

The city continued its work on finding ways to handle the population growth. Recognizing that it would take some time before a new growth management strategy would be ready, the City embarked on developing a stop-gap growth measure known as the Interim Development Ordinance (IDO). The City Council, in a lengthy session, approved the IDO on July 21, 1987. The ordinance set an annual limit on residential building permits of 8,000, which would be allocated on a community-by-community basis and would be in effect from August 21, 1987, for a period of no more than 18 months—until the November 1988 election, when voters would decide the city's long-term growth strategy.

The IDO generated a great deal of discussion. Its opponents alleged that it would cause builders to go elsewhere, thereby creating dire economic repercussions for the building industry and related businesses. Citizens for Limited Growth, upset over the City Council's action, vowed to continue pursuing its proposed initiative, which would impose tougher standards on future development and growth. Its supporters countered by claiming it was an appropriate device to be employed until a permanent growth strategy could be finalized.

A major point of debate regarding the IDO was the number of exemptions it would allow. For example, among the activities exempt from the IDO, according to the 1988 San Diego Amended Ordinance 0-17015, Section 4 (A), were:

1. Low-income housing projects which meet the criteria for exemption as determined by housing policies of the San Diego Housing Commission;
2. Senior citizen housing and student dormitories as approved by a conditional use permit;
3. Construction of an individual dwelling unit conforming to existing zoning requirements on a preexisting recorded vacant lot during a separate ownership prior to the effective date of the IDO;
4. All formally adopted redevelopment plans, revitalization areas, and enterprise zones; and
5. Certain trolley and transportation corridors.

The existence of the exemptions led to countless debates. On one occasion, a property owner tearfully recalled that her husband was preparing a piece of property for sale when he passed away (O'Connell, 1987a). With financial difficulties facing her, she subsequently asked to be exempted from the IDO. The City Council granted her an exemption. On another occasion, Tim O'Connell, adviser on land use matters to the mayor, jokingly commented that "we . . . literally had a pregnant woman threatening to go into labor if we didn't approve her husband's project" (Weisberg, 1987, p. B-1). Mayor Maureen O'Connor even characterized one exemption as "making Swiss cheese out of the IDO" (Balint, 1987, p. A-1).

There was more criticism when communities were released from the IDO. The release was allowed where public facilities were adequate to accommodate the growth, and the timing and financing of constructing the required facilities were in place. Of course there were heated debates among members of the City Council on whether to release a community from the IDO. On one occasion, a member of the City Council accused the Mayor of "politicizing the issue to the point of sacrificing the best interests of the community" (O'Connell, 1987b, p. B-8).

In a related issue, the City Council had also decided to impose fees on residential development in the inner-city neighborhoods. These fees, ranging from $800 to $2,500 per residential unit, did not apply to commercial or industrial developments. They were to be used to help finance needed public facilities and services.

The debate over how to handle San Diego's growth was heating up. The Citizen's for Limited Growth's "Quality of Life Initiative"—Proposition J—had already qualified for the November 1988 ballot. After a long 16 months of work and numerous public hearings, the appointed Citizens Advisory Committee on Growth and Development finalized a growth management ballot measure.

The City Council, on August 8, 1988, in an 8-1 vote, voted to submit the measure, ultimately to be known as Proposition H, to the voters. The lone dissenting vote characterized the measure as being like "Swiss cheese, full of holes and generally unfair and uneven" (La Fee, 1988, p. B-1). The measure read, in part, as follows:

AMENDS THE CITY OF SAN DIEGO PROGRESS GUIDE AND GENERAL PLAN BY ADDING A GROWTH MANAGEMENT ELEMENT.

Shall the City adopt a Growth Management Element which:

a. Establishes a maximum limit for the next five years of 3,600 new residential units per year, and 3,990 previously approved residential units per year;

b. Protects single-family neighborhoods by restricting new development;

c. Preserves environmentally sensitive lands, including wetlands, floodplains, steep slopes, biologically sensitive lands, and significant prehistoric sites;

d. Requires that traffic generated by new development stay within road capacity;

e. Strengthens community plans by requiring periodic comprehensive updates and limiting amendments between updates;

f. Requires there be adequate public facilities and services at the time of development; and

g. Establishes regional goals for air quality, water, sewage treatment, solid waste disposal, and transportation?

Citizens were spared from a third ballot measure when a Sensitive Lands Initiative, sponsored by San Diegans for Managed Growth, failed to qualify for the ballot due to a lack of signatures. This group would eventually throw its support to Proposition J and oppose the Council-backed Proposition H. In opposing Proposition H, a member of the group commented that "the exceptions and loopholes they approved were so drastic that it came to the point where it was a slap in the face" (Weisberg, 1988a, p. B-3).

Both measures had strong supporters. Peter Navarro, one of the leaders of the Proposition J campaign, worked long hours to persuade San Diegans that Proposition J was the best and most well-thought-out initiative. He characterized Proposition J as being a "sophisticated, state-of-the-art growth management plan" that tackled a multitude of problems (Navarro, 1988, p. C-1). The opposing measure was weak and contained too many loopholes, according to many in the Proposition J camp. Council member Ron Roberts was an advocate of the Council-backed Proposition H. Noting the 2 years it took to develop, the numerous hearings that were held, and the fact that all but one member of the City Council supported it, Roberts felt Proposition H would serve the public better than the alternative ballot measure. Proposition H would help promote economic growth, help limit new residential construction, and help protect single-family neighborhoods (Roberts, 1988). Another group, the Coalition for a Balanced Environment, comprising business and community leaders, supported Proposition H and opposed Proposition J. The group would actively campaign for passage of the Council-backed measure. It would also support a County Board of Supervisors ballot measure instead of a competing measure on growth management in the unincorporated areas of San Diego County.

One recurring issue that always arises in any discussion of growth management is whether jobs will be lost as a result of managing growth. It was certainly an issue in this campaign. A 1988 study by the San Diego Economic Development Corporation (EDC) claimed that should Proposition J pass, unemployment would increase because industrial and commercial development would be limited by the initiative. Its president suggested that the reason for the study was to offer voters some information on an important, but little discussed, aspect of Proposition J (Weisberg, 1988b). The analysis was widely attacked by supporters of Proposition J. Council member Abby Wolfsheimer, a supporter of Proposition J, even asked the City Attorney to review whether the EDC's analysis was proper. She questioned whether a city-funded agency could legally take positions under municipal or state election law. The City Attorney's office eventually questioned whether EDC had overstepped the limits of using public funds for electioneering purposes when it left no question about what its position was on the ballot measure (Abrams, 1988). No sanctions were imposed on the EDC. The question of the impacts of growth controls on the economic climate of an area is still being debated.

The wording of the ballot measures' description/summary and the placement of the measures on the ballot also created some controversy. Proposition J supporters claimed that the ballot description, written by staff members of the City Attorney's office, was misleading, contained false wording, and was possibly confusing to the voters. Peter Navarro even characterized the summary as "a glaring example of favoritism" (Ristine, 1988, p. B-7). Moreover, supporters also faulted the description for not containing the title "Quality of Life Initiative." Instead, the description titled the measure "Initiative Measure. Amends the San Diego General Plan." They felt that the voters might be confused over the wording, which would hurt their chances at the ballot box.

The City Attorney's office responded to the complaints over the ballot summaries and agreed to recommend changes in the wording to the City Council. Much to the chagrin of the Proposition J supporters, the City Council, in a 4-4 tie, failed to approve the recommended wording changes.

Failing to get satisfaction from the City Council, Proposition J supporters took another course of action. They filed a petition against the City Council in Superior Court, requesting a new title and new wording. Once again, they met with no success. Superior Court Judge James R. Milliken refused to order any changes in the ballot summaries due to time constraints. As Judge Milliken ruled, "It is humanly impossible to accomplish what would be required to make a change and go forward with the election" (Weisberg, 1988c, p. B-3).

As election day got closer, supporters of Proposition H urged voters to vote for both ballot measures. This represented an interesting twist to the campaigns. They were concerned that the development-industry-backed group, San Diegans for Regional Traffic Solutions, was waging an expensive campaign to defeat both measures. Therefore, they felt passing one of the measures was better than letting the development industry pump a lot of capital into the campaign, successfully divide the voters, and defeat both measures.

In the end, voters were confronted with an extremely long and complex ballot, more than 150 pages in length and containing information on more than 35 ballot measures—15 of which were state-wide measures. The length of the ballot concerned many people. The San Diego Taxpayers Association, an interest group concerned with government spending, had earlier attributed the lengthy ballot to elected officials failing to do their jobs (Jackson, 1988). Others attributed the length to a general decline of representative government in the United States. There was also a concern that the lengthy and confusing ballot would cause many voters to stay away from the polls.

Election day saw Propositions H and J go down to defeat. Proposition H lost by a vote of 198,559 (55.5%) to 159,123 (44.5%). Proposition J lost by a larger margin—210,032 (58.7%) to 146,672 (41.3%). In addition to raising more than $1 million

Table 6.3 Sampling of Contributors Opposing Propositions H and J

Group Name	$ Amount Contributed
The Fieldstone Co.	$55,000
McMillin Development, Inc.	50,000
The William Lyon Co.	50,000
Pardee Construction	49,688
The Newland Group, Inc.	46,000
McKellar Development of La Jolla	45,000
Baldwin Builders, Inc.	40,000
California Structures	26,000
Donald L. Bren Co.	25,800
Ahmanson Development, Inc.	25,000
Daley Corporation	25,000
Stewart Title Company of San Diego	25,000
4-S Partners	25,000
Watt Political Action Committee, Inc.	21,000
Barratt American Incorporated	20,000
The Buie Corp.	20,000

SOURCE: San Diego City Clerk's Office, 1990

to defeat both measures, the development industry mounted a media blitz during the final days of the campaign that had apparently been successful.

A sampling of some of the major contributors opposing the measures can be found in Table 6.3. The pro-Proposition H and J campaign relied on much smaller contributions and more volunteer efforts. This battle on how to control San Diego's growth was over. It was now back to the drawing board.

REGIONAL CONSIDERATIONS
OF MANAGING LOCAL GROWTH

The San Diego region, of which the City of San Diego is by far the most populated city, is made up of 18 municipalities and the county-controlled unincorporated area. The entire region is projected to grow from a 1986 population of 2.1 million to 3.1 million in 2010—a 46% increase (San Diego Association of Governments, 1988). No discussion of growth management in either San Diego or any other jurisdiction in the region can be provided without mentioning the surrounding area.

It has been shown in numerous cases around the country that the land use actions of one jurisdiction can have potentially serious repercussions for the surrounding areas. For example, growth control actions in the City of San Diego could cause a premature demand for housing, schools, roads, and other public services in neighboring cities. On the other hand, neighboring cities might also benefit economically from the growth of San Diego.

With the region expected to grow 46% by the year 2010, citizens are justifiably concerned with their quality of life. Having been somewhat frustrated over the actions of local officials, citizens in a number of the region's jurisdictions have taken to the ballot box to resolve various land use matters. Table 6.4 offers a sampling of some of the ballot measures that have dealt with land use control issues in the San Diego region from 1986 to 1990. The measures dealt with such issues as requiring voter approval for any upzoning or rezoning in a city's open space and rural residential lands, placing a ceiling or cap on residential development, calling for the establishment of a citizen's committee to spell out criteria for development, and calling for a policy of allowing only such development and overall population growth as is consistent with a high quality of life for residents.

Of particular note in Table 6.4 is Proposition C, which was placed before the voters in 1988. This measure was an advisory initiative that would have given elected officials notice as to what the voters felt about the need for regional planning. Proposition C sought to demonstrate public support for regional planning and growth control measures by proposing a Regional Planning and Growth Management Review Board. This

Table 6.4 Sampling of Land Use Ballot Measures in the San Diego
Region, 1986-1990

Jurisdiction	Measure	Date	Result
Carlsbad	Proposition G	Nov. 1986	Passed
	Proposition E	Nov. 1986	Passed
Chula Vista	Proposition V	Nov. 1988	Passed
Encinitas	Proposition AA	Nov. 1988	Defeated
	Proposition BB	Nov. 1988	Defeated
Oceanside	Proposition A	Apr. 1987	Passed
	Proposition B	Apr. 1987	Defeated
Poway	Proposition FF	Nov. 1988	Passed
	Proposition GG	Nov. 1988	Defeated
San Diego County	Proposition B	Nov. 1988	Defeated
	Proposition C	Nov. 1988	Passed
	Proposition D	Nov. 1988	Defeated
	Proposition D	Nov. 1990	Defeated
Vista	Proposition A	Apr. 1987	Passed
	Proposition B	Apr. 1987	Passed

SOURCE: Caves, 1990

Board would then develop a regional growth management
plan for resolving problems associated with transportation
management, solid waste disposal, water reclamation, sewage
disposal, air quality, and growth-inducing industrial zoning.
Proposition C was approved by the voters. The growth management plan is currently being developed.

In 1990 the latest saga of ballot box planning took place in
San Diego. On November 6, 1990, voters had the opportunity
to vote on Propositions D, E, and M. Propositions D and M,
developer-supported growth initiatives, wanted to create a
Traffic Control Plan and a Comprehensive Growth Management Plan in the County of San Diego and the City of San
Diego, respectively. Recognizing that problems stemming from
rapid growth, which vary from traffic to air pollution, are inter-
related, the plans would encourage the County of San Diego
and the City of San Diego to work with neighboring jurisdic-

tions to solve regional problems. Proposition E called for a
$100-million bond sale in the City of San Diego to purchase
parkland and open space. All three measures were defeated by
the voters.

THE CONTINUING BATTLE

The growth debates of 1985, 1988, and 1990 have been decided. Citizen activism in the form of Proposition A succeeded
in the face of strong opposition from the development industry
and other parties. In 1988, with a repetition of massive development industry opposition, Propositions H and J were defeated. Did the development industry buy the election, as some
people speculate? There is no answer to this question. Did the
development industry celebrate the defeat of both ballot measures? In all likelihood, the answer is yes. They won the battle
on that occasion. However, announcing total victory would be
premature. The City is currently attempting to develop a new
growth management policy that incorporates measures all parties will support. Growth control continues to be a hot topic
debated in and out of City Council meetings. Many of the participants remain active in the debate, and some new participants have also entered the picture. With growth control being
an emotional topic, the potential for even more ballot measures
remains high. In the end, the growth wars of San Diego will
continue.

SEVEN

Seattle, Washington: Capping Downtown Growth

Seattle is consistently rated high in quality-of-life studies in the United States. It has a reputation for being one of the most livable cities in the country. Residents are proud of this distinction and strive to maintain the high quality of life they currently enjoy. However, several years ago, a number of citizens became alarmed over the amount of development occurring in the downtown area. They felt their quality of life was being jeopardized. To them, downtown growth was getting out of hand and the city's skyline, as shown in Figure 7.1, was becoming overwhelmed with skyscrapers. Citizens experienced disruptions in downtown traffic flow, witnessed a reduction in the downtown low-income housing supply, and complained about other problems associated with this growth.

Some citizens and groups called for something to be done about the downtown growth. Others called for time to let the existing planning policies do their job. Questions had to be answered: Should downtown growth be limited? Should the city impose limitations on the height and bulk of buildings in the downtown area? If the answer is yes to both questions, what

Figure 7.1. Seattle Skyline

will the impacts be on the downtown area, the city as a whole, and on the surrounding region? If the answer is no to both questions, what will the impacts of these decisions be on the aforementioned areas? A battle that would eventually polarize the community was quickly taking shape.

On May 16, 1989, the citizens of Seattle, Washington went to the ballot box to decide the fate of Initiative 31—the Citizens' Alternative Plan (CAP). This measure placed the following question before Seattle voters:

> Shall Seattle's Land Use Code be amended as it relates to downtown zoning to reduce permitted building height, re- duce bulk by reducing development bonuses for public

Table 7.1 Population

	1970	1980	1990	2000	2020
Seattle	530,831	493,846	496,254	507,068	521,720
King County	1,159,587	1,269,754	1,460,996	1,697,519	2,114,744
Seattle % of King County	46%	39%	34%	30%	25%

SOURCE: Puget Sound Council of Governments, June 1988.

and development benefits, limit the development of new office space, with exceptions for small buildings to 500,000 square feet per year through 1994 and to 1,000,000 square feet per year from 1994 through 1999, and require that a study regarding the future management of downtown growth be prepared?

BACKGROUND

As evidenced in Table 7.1, Seattle is once again experiencing population growth. From 1980 to 2020, its population is projected to increase from 493,846 to 521,720—a 5.6% increase. Note, however, that this 521,720 population figure is still below its 1970 population of 530,831. In addition, although Seattle remains the largest municipality in King County, its proportion of the total King County population is decreasing.

A number of past events contributed to the creation of the CAP Initiative. One such event occurred in 1971, when the Pike Place Market, a city landmark described by syndicated columnist Neal Peirce as "one of the great urban places" in the nation, was saved from redevelopment by an initiative (The Municipal League, 1989, p. 6).

Seven years later, in 1978, work started on replacing Seattle's Comprehensive Plan with "new land use policies which form the basis for a new zoning code and map" (City of Seattle, 1983,

p. i). Part of this process was the development and adoption of new downtown land use and transportation policies. Once adopted, these policies would serve to guide development in downtown Seattle. As part of the process, citizens were afforded the opportunity to not only help identify problems facing the downtown area but also voice their hopes for the area.

In March 1981 the City of Seattle prepared a Background Report of the Downtown Land Use and Transportation Project—a document that provided background information for both identifying and quantifying issues facing downtown Seattle and for developing alternative downtown plans. Citizens assisted in identifying the issues and developing general alternatives. In August 1981, at the end of this part of the process, the mayor and City Council adopted the Guidelines for Downtown Alternative Plan.

A task force appointed by the mayor then reviewed some 15 alternatives that had been developed by various participants in the process. Some of this information was, in turn, incorporated into The 1982 Downtown Alternative Plan, published in May 1982. This "set forth in a single document the direction and basis for development of detailed land use and transportation policies" (City of Seattle, 1983, p. ii).

In October 1983 Seattle issued a Draft Environmental Impact Statement (DEIS) for the Land Use and Transportation Plan for Downtown Seattle. This document was distributed to federal, state, local, and city agencies, civic interest groups, community councils, Seattle Public Libraries, community service centers, and the media for public comment. The DEIS examined the proposed action and four alternatives for guiding development in downtown Seattle. The proposed action would have future downtown development being guided by the policies and downtown portion of the Land Use Code resulting from the June 1983 Draft Downtown Land Use and Transportation Plan. These policies include such issues as:

Designation of land for retail, commercial/office, residential and mixed uses; an expansion area for the office core; uses permitted in the various subareas of downtown; allowable densities; off-street parking; development standards to control the impacts of development; and building heights in different parts of downtown. The policies will also establish directions for transportation, housing, human services, public open space and the street level environment; identify transportation investments within downtown and its surroundings needed to meet land use objectives; guide public capital investments; establish the City's strategy for maintaining and adding to the downtown housing supply; and define the level of services and utilities needed to support downtown development. (City of Seattle, 1984, p. i)

A Final Environmental Impact Statement (FEIS) was prepared in August 1984 that incorporated public comments on the DEIS.

On June 10, 1985, a new Land Use and Transportation Plan for Downtown Seattle was adopted. The 1985 Plan incorporated framework policies that focused on Seattle as the pre-eminent regional center as well as on downtown growth, economic development, transportation, housing, human services, urban form, culture and entertainment, and areas of varied character. According to the policy on growth:

Downtown growth shall be allowed and encouraged to the extent that water, sewer, electrical and transportation systems capacity will accommodate it at reasonable cost and provided that development furthers the environmental, social, and urban form goals herein. If it becomes apparent that the infrastructure will not accommodate development, the City shall consider limits on growth. (City of Seattle, 1985, p. 1)

Within the 1985 Plan, Seattle's downtown had been divided into 11 land use functional districts (City of Seattle, 1985, p. 65). These districts were:

1. Downtown Office Core-1 (DOC-1)
2. Downtown Office Core-2 (DOC-2)
3. Downtown Retail Core (DRC)
4. Downtown Mixed Commercial (DMC)
5. Downtown Mixed Residential (DMR)
6. Pike Market Mixed (PMM)
7. Pioneer Square Mixed (PSM)
8. International District Mixed (IDM)
9. International District Residential (IDR)
10. Downtown Harborfront-1 (DH-1)
11. Downtown Harborfront-2 (DH-2)

The DOC-1, DOC-2 and DRC district classifications are of primary importance to this research. These districts represent the following:

DOC-1: shall apply to the area of the most concentrated office activity. A large share of the downtown's future employment growth shall be accommodated within this district where the existing and planned infrastructure can accommodate growth. Although the area is intended primarily for office uses, other uses including housing, retail, hotels, and cultural and entertainment facilities shall be encouraged to add diversity and activity beyond the working day. (City of Seattle, 1985, p. 66)

DOC-2: shall apply to those areas adjacent to the office core determined appropriate for office expansion or where a transition in density to mixed other use areas is desirable. The district shall be primarily for office use with a mix of other activities encouraged to add diversity, particularly beyond the hours of the normal working day. The district shall provide scale and density transitions to adjacent areas

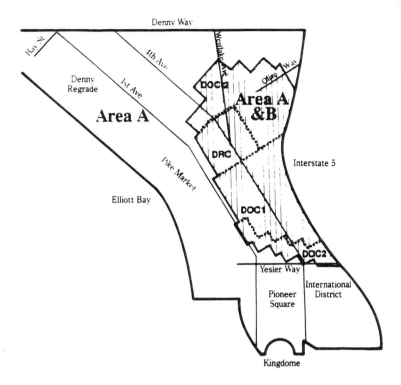

Figure 7.2. Area of Proposed Development Limitation Under CAP

and reduce pressures for development of major office uses in the retail core and adjacent residential areas. (City of Seattle, 1985, p. 69)

DRC: shall apply to the area containing the major department stores and having the greatest concentration of downtown's retail activity. The district shall be principal center of shopping for both the downtown and the region. Uses other than retail shall be allowed to the extent that they augment but do not detract from this primary function. An active and pleasant street level environment shall

be maintained through development standards specifically tailored to the unique function and character of this
area. (City of Seattle, 1985, p. 71)

Figure 7.2 indicates where the various districts can be found.

The part of the 1985 Plan garnering the most criticism was a
floor area bonus system that enabled developers to obtain additional floor area in their buildings if they provided features
determined to be of benefit to the public. For example, a bonus
from a minimum of 5,000 square feet to a maximum of 15,000
square feet was available to a developer for placing a motion
picture theater in his building—floor area increases could not
be obtained for theaters showing adult motion pictures. This
bonus was to encourage evening activity in office, retail, and
mixed-use areas. In addition, provision of space for retail
shops, restaurants, galleries, and other uses that are retail in
character would also qualify for additional floor area. Bonuses
in floor area would also be granted for small landscaped residential parcel parks used to reinforce residential areas. Additional bonuses were possible, subject to both special criteria
and review by the Director of the Seattle Department of Construction and Land Use and review by the City Council. A
listing of the general bonus features can be found in Table 7.2.
A complete listing of the bonus features of the 1985 Plan can be
found in the Appendix. The developers of the 55-story Washington Mutual Tower, as shown in Figure 7.3, took advantage
of the city's bonus system and doubled the size of the building.

The years following the adoption of the 1985 Plan have seen
some interesting debates. A number of individuals and groups
questioned the pace of downtown development, and the various externalities associated with this development, and called
for the amending of the 1985 Plan by limiting downtown development. For example, attorney Margaret Pageler, a supporter
of the CAP Initiative (31), claimed the 1985 Plan "over-rated the
amount of relief the transit tunnel will provide and under-rated

Table 7.2 General Bonus Features of the 1985 Plan

Human Services	Day Care Services
Cinema	Shopping Atrium
Shopping Corridor	Retail Shopping
Parcel Park	Residential Parcel Park
Street Park	Hillclimb Assist
Rooftop Garden—Street Accessible	Hillside Terrace
Rooftop Garden—Interior Accessible	Harborfront Open Space
Sidewalk Widening	Overhead Weather Protection
Voluntary Building Setback	Sculptured Building Tops
Short-Term Parking	Small Site Development

SOURCE: 1985 Downtown Land Use and Transportation Plan

the impact of high-rise projects already in the pipeline" (Paschall, 1989, p. C-12). In addition, she felt the 1985 Plan had been developed without neighborhood input. On the other hand, some individuals and groups felt the 1985 Plan was a good, strong plan that could be made better and opposed amending it because that would hinder Seattle's economic future and virtually stop development.

In 1986 Seattle condemned and then demolished a small commercial center in the city's retail core and hoped to see the property developed as a focal point or showpiece for downtown Seattle. The mayor and the Downtown Seattle Association (DSA)—a downtown business-oriented booster club—supported its development. However, a grassroots organization called People for an Open Westlake (POW) gathered signatures and unsuccessfully petitioned the City Council to save the site and make it a public square—a wide-open park. In 1988 Westlake Center, a 22-story office tower and retail center, opened on the site POW had wanted to use as a public square.

Downtown development continued to intensify as a public issue. As additional construction activity was taking place, citizens witnessed disruptions in traffic flow that resulted in increased levels of traffic congestion and increased citizen frustra-

Figure 7.3. Washington Mutual Tower

tions over higher parking fees, the lack of downtown parking, and the loss of affordable housing in the downtown area. However, prior to the opening of the Westlake Center, members of POW and another grassroots organization, Vision Seattle, broadened their perspectives and started focusing on the larger issue of the development of the entire downtown, not just the Westlake area. It was during this time that the CAP idea was formulated. The stage was set for an interesting public debate.

THE DEVELOPMENT OF CAP

Seattle is not the only city to either consider or employ a downtown building limit. Prior to developing CAP, proponents studied measures currently being used in Vancouver, British Columbia; Portland, Oregon; and San Francisco. In Vancouver, a city currently experiencing a building boom, the City Council limited building heights in the downtown area to 450 feet in order to protect not only views but also access to the sun. In addition, the maximum density or floor-to-area ratio (FAR) is 9:1—the building has a floor area equal to 9 times the size of the building site. The FAR is intended to "regulate bulk while allowing a developer certain freedom to decide the height of a building and its placement on the lot" (Schultz and Kasen, 1984, p. 155). Interestingly enough, while CAP's proponents pointed to Vancouver as an example of a city limiting downtown building heights, Vancouver Mayor Gordon Campbell suggested, in a speech to the Downtown Seattle Association (DSA), that broad solutions, such as CAP offered, to the problems of growth don't work. Suggesting CAP represented such a "sweeping solution," Campbell recommended that "solutions to the problems come through consistent, seemingly minor improvements to all the components that go into growing pains, such as public transportation, parking, and open space" ("CAP won't work," 1989, p. B-3).

CAP proponents also investigated the downtown building limitations found in Portland, Oregon, where buildings cannot exceed a maximum height of 460 feet and an FAR of 15:1. Although Portland's downtown problems aren't as visible as Seattle's, its City Council did, nevertheless, adopt a Downtown

Table 7.3 Summary of Downtown Office Core Density and Height
For San Francisco, Portland, and Vancouver, B.C.

	San Francisco	*Portland*	*Vancouver*
Base Floor Area Ratio	9:1	15:1	9:1
Maximum Floor Area Ratio	18:1[1]	18:1[2]	13:1[3]
Maximum Height Limit (ft.) (no exceptions)	550'	460'	450'

NOTES: 1. 18 FAR maximum with transfer of development rights from historic buildings; no maximum FAR for housing, limited only by maximum height.
2. In all zones, a 3 FAR bonus increment available; bonus features are housing, public art, day care, rooftop gardens, theaters and water features.
3. Base FAR is maximum FAR with design criteria and features negotiated; FAR may be increased for social/recreational amenities with no limit—13 FAR is maximum to date. Transfer of development rights may be negotiated with no maximum FAR set; height limit would control.
SOURCE: Office of the Mayor, City of Seattle, 1988, p. 46.

Plan in 1988 that gave bonuses to developers for providing various public amenities. These bonuses allow developers to construct bulkier buildings, not taller ones.

Finally, San Francisco's scheme, imposing a downtown office building maximum height limit of 550 feet and an FAR of 9:1, was examined. The FAR can increase to 18:1 through either the purchase or the transfer of development rights from other sites. After a series of civic battles in the 1970s and 1980s, the voters of San Francisco approved, in 1986, Proposition M, a referendum that limited or capped the amount of new office space allowed in the city to 475,000 square feet until 2000, and 950,000 square feet a year after 2000. A comparison of the limitations in these cities can be found in Table 7.3.

There has been some disagreement over the impacts of Proposition M. The Director of City Planning in San Francisco indicated that his department had not found that Proposition M had caused any adverse impacts on city development (Tang, 1989). Others suggested that rents had not changed a great deal in the downtown area. Conversely, the San Francisco Chamber

Table 7.4 Summary Comparison of Height and Density

		Existing Law	*Initiative*
DOC-1	Density	Base FAR: 10	Base FAR: 5
		Max. FAR: 20	Max. FAR: 14
DOC-1	Height (ft.)	No limit	450′
DOC-2	Density	Base FAR: 8	Base FAR: 4
		Max. FAR: 14	Max. FAR: 10
DOC-2	Height (ft.)	400′	300′
DRC	Density	Base FAR: 5	Base FAR: 2.5
		Max. FAR: 12	Max. FAR: 6
DRC	Height (ft.) (400′ with MR, PA Bonus)	240′	85′ (150′ with MR, PA Bonus)

NOTES: MR = Major Retail Store; PA = Performing Arts Center. One story equals about 12 feet. This means that a 450′ building is between 35 and 40 stories.
SOURCE: Official City Voters Pamphlet, City of Seattle, May 16, 1989

of Commerce calculated that Proposition M had cost San Francisco millions of dollars in tax revenues and fees (Liebman, 1989). There will undoubtedly continue to be strong opinions voiced regarding the impacts of Proposition M on downtown San Francisco and the surrounding area.

CAP was written after its proponents had studied alternative development regulations for the downtown office core and retail core areas in other jurisdictions. In total, CAP would amend Seattle's Land Use Zoning Code, as applied in downtown Seattle, in three ways. First, it would reduce the density and height limits, as found in the 1985 Plan, in the DOC-1, DOC-2, and DRC districts. Table 7.4 shows the differences between the 1985 Plan and CAP's limitations. Density in the downtown area is regulated by the FAR, which represents the ratio between the amount of floor area permitted in a building and the size of the lot. Second, CAP places limitations on the amount of allowable new downtown office space. The 1985 Plan does not have such limits. CAP would limit the amount of office space that could be built downtown to 500,000 square feet from 1989 through 1994, and to 1,000,000 square feet from 1995 through 1999. However, provisions exist for carrying over square footage that is not used in one year to the next year, exempting buildings of less than 50,000 square feet from the limits, and requiring that 85,000 square feet of the allowed square footage be set aside for buildings containing between 50,000 and 85,000 square feet. Finally, CAP mandates a study of its effect on the areas outside the downtown zone and the investigation of measures for the long-term management of downtown development. A copy of the complete text of the CAP can be found in the Appendix.

THE CAMPAIGN

From all available indications, the proponents of the CAP faced an uphill battle. A number of obstacles, ranging from events to individuals, confronted them. For example, they were plagued by very little interest on the part of, and lack of support from, members of the City Council to pass an interim zoning code for the downtown area. When supporters asked for Council support in January 1988, only one of nine members supported the idea of an interim zoning code. Some of this lack of support may be traced back to the fact that the 1985 Downtown Plan had been in effect for only 3 years. One additional council member would later agree to support and pass an interim zoning code.

Two months later proponents wrote a letter to the City Council, outlining their concerns about Downtown Seattle. Once again, they basically received no response to their concerns. Moreover, according to one of the proponents, the mayor appeared to be somewhat hostile to the idea of the interim zoning code.

Apparently frustrated over City Council inaction, they wrote and distributed another letter to the Council and attached a copy of the interim controls that they had drafted. A continued lack of response convinced them to redraft the controls in the form of the CAP. Proponents hit the streets during the summer of 1988 to get the number of signatures required for placing CAP on the ballot.

On June 20, 1988, Mayor Charles Royer issued his State of the City Message. In his message, Royer spoke of the uneasiness that citizens were having over growth. Acknowledging that the growth versus no-growth debate is not healthy, Royer commented:

> The loudest debate in our community is focused on our smallest neighborhood—downtown. It's ironic that so much of our attention has been focused on less than 2% of our land mass. Downtown is important to Seattle's neighborhoods and County residents alike. This thirty blocks represents more than 25 percent of the City's assessed property value and nearly 10 percent of the total assessed value Countywide. Add sales and business taxes and this little neighborhood pays about a third of the City's bills.

Although recognizing the frustrations that downtown building causes, Royer claimed proposals to limit downtown growth "are directed at the symptoms, not the problems." He continued:

> Building limits will not ease traffic congestion, reduce suburban sprawl, or preserve open space. In fact, it can be argued they will have the opposite effect. If growth of the downtown core is narrowly restricted, the pressure to build office and retail space will creep into our neighborhoods and boom into the suburbs.

Overall, Royer concluded that "rather than trying to stop development downtown, we should be attempting to harness it, better directing the value it creates toward the values we hold as a community." The pro-CAP forces now had another hurdle to surmount—Mayor Royer's opposition.

The CAP issue was already being debated in the community. On the one hand, Margaret A. Pageler—attorney, citizen activist, and CAP supporter—criticized the 1985 Downtown Plan and noted that Seattle citizens were faced with "a downtown increasingly congested, costly, and inhumane—a downtown subject to construction cycles no longer controlled by local market forces but by financial interests far removed from Seattle's residents and taxpayers" (Pageler, 1988, p. 1). Feeling there was a need for a middle ground between the political extremes of no-growth and unbridled boosterism, Pageler felt CAP represented "a reasonable proposal which provides for a decade of robust but controlled growth downtown while we take a longer look at regional capacity issues" (Pageler, 1988, p. 17).

On the other hand, some individuals opposed the idea of the CAP because Seattle's office and retail markets were healthy and didn't need government intervention. In arguing against development controls, Robert L. Aigner, who works for Coldwell Banker Commercial Real Estate Services in Seattle, suggested controlling or discouraging downtown growth would simply shift the growth to the suburbs and also slow down the search for a solution (Aigner, 1988). Others wondered if the measure was not just a little bit premature.

As the debates intensified, Mayor Royer reentered the picture by creating an Advisory Forum on Balanced Growth to examine downtown growth within a regional perspective and recommend new and "effective methods to share further the benefits of growth with all individuals and neighborhoods" (Royer, 1988, p. 2). He saw the forum as "a means of generating an informed political consensus on Seattle's role in the regional development picture" (Royer, 1988, p. 1). Not everyone applauded Mayor Royer's effort. Some felt his action was designed to not only deflect criticism of the 1985 Downtown

Plan but also take some of the momentum away from the CAP campaign. Others felt the timing was right for such a forum.

The CAP proponents continued their attempts to press the City Council for action. In an August 1988 letter to City Council member Paul Kraabel, they once again indicated the need for the CAP. And once again, their efforts were to no avail. However, with the endorsement of City Council member Virginia Galle, a summary of the CAP was presented to the City Council on September 14, 1988.

Two months later, City Council member Kraabel issued a statement regarding the CAP. He agreed that growth was an important issue facing Seattle. However, he did note that his "only philosophical disagreement with the proposal is the idea of imposing a flat limit on the amount of office space that can be built downtown in a year" (Kraabel, 1988, p. 1). The effect of doing that would cause repercussions in the surrounding urban areas. Instead, he felt "that growth is best addressed by ensuring that the undesirable aspects are mitigated through the developments themselves and anticipate that the Council will develop an alternative which embraces that approach" (Kraabel, 1988, p. 1). To him, the CAP was simply not the answer to the problem.

Recognizing citizen frustrations over the problems of growth Mayor Royer added a new twist to the debate. In a November 29, 1988 letter to Sam Smith, president of the Seattle City Council, Royer proposed an alternative to the CAP that outlined his proposed revisions to the 1985 Downtown Plan. His revision contained five major elements:

1. Reduces height and densities for new construction in the downtown office and retail cores;
2. Increases public benefits from private development—pedestrian amenities, child care space, housing, historic preservation, human services, and neighborhood open space;

3. Proposes new rules to reduce disruption caused by public and private construction activities and to control the amount of construction occurring at any one time;

4. Tightens rules for development to ensure that building is consistent with current codes and to discourage speculation; and

5. Commits the City to a longer term comprehensive planning process focused on transportation, housing affordability, and neighborhood and regional growth concerns.

He hoped this alternative would appear on the same ballot as the CAP.

The mayor's proposal met with mixed reactions. Some individuals felt it was a responsible alternative. For example, in a November 28, 1988 press statement, James Daly, Senior Principal, American Institute of Architects, claimed the proposal was "a thoughtful, studied alternative that I and many other design professionals who will use it as design guidelines can support" (Daly, 1988, p. 1). Conversely, the chairman of the DSA felt "the mayor's proposal was not that much different from the CAP proposal," and a leading supporter of the CAP proposal wondered "whether the mayor's proposal goes far enough in addressing the cumulative impact of more downtown buildings" (Ougland, 1988, p. 1). Overall, the mayor's proposal was destined to be second-guessed.

The timing of the CAP election was also subject to controversy. The mayor wanted his proposal to appear on the same spring ballot as the CAP initiative. The DSA, however, wanted the CAP initiative to appear by itself on a special May ballot. This angered some individuals. Others wondered why the City could not wait for a later election, which would have the saved the City a substantial amount of money. CAP supporters tended to feel that the DSA hoped the CAP initiative would be defeated if it were alone on a ballot. They wanted it on the September ballot, where current and prospective Council members would have to take a stand for or against the CAP.

The City Council ultimately decided in January, in a 5-4 vote
to set a May 16, 1989 election date.

Another important event occurring in January was the for
mation of a group called Citizens for a Better Downtown (CBD
by the DSA. According to its April 1989 *Downtown Update*, the
CBD was "a genuinely representative coalition of citizens ded
icated to improving downtown growth management and
deeply concerned over the possible negative impacts of [CAP
Initiative 31." It was probably the most visible and most voca
group opposing the CAP. CAP proponents felt the group wa
formed to confuse citizens about the initiative.

An unusual twist took place in January 1989. In a letter to
fellow employees, Mayor Royer urged them to "turn concern
over growth into community consensus around rationa
growth planning" and to "defeat the Citizens' Alternative Plan
initiative in May without defeating the citizens whose concern
placed CAP on the ballot." Later, complaints filed with the Of
fice of Election Administration charged Royer with using cit
facilities to produce and distribute the letter, which would be
violation of the City's Fair Campaign Practices ordinance. Roye
would later agree to pay $500 in restitution.

On March 16, 1989, the Downtown Plan Revisions Advisor
Committee, which was appointed by the mayor and the Coun
cil, presented recommendations on interim downtown control
to Paul Kraabel, chair of the Urban Redevelopment Committee
Seattle City Council. Representing a compromise between th
CAP and the 1985 Downtown Plan, these controls would tak
effect immediately if the CAP was defeated.

As the campaign came to a close, local newspapers consis
tently carried letters from citizens on how they felt about th
CAP. Supporters thought that the measure was well though
out and that failure to pass it would mean developers woul
continue to prosper at public expense. Those opposing the CA
felt that if it were passed, Seattle would be locked into some

thing that would eventually harm the city. Moreover, opponents warned of a rush on downtown development activity.

Getting out the Messages

The outcome of any election depends, in part, on how effective both sides are in relaying their messages to the public. The side opposing the CAP claimed the 1985 Downtown Plan was working and shouldn't be tossed aside. To them, approving the CAP would limit economic growth, increase traffic on existing roadways, and shift jobs to the outlying areas. On the other hand, supporters of the CAP felt something had to be done to save Seattle's neighborhoods. The impacts of rapid high-rise downtown office development hadn't been dealt with effectively. Furthermore, reasonable limits had to be set on growth. The stage was now set for the sides to get out the troops.

Both sides employed a variety of means to get their messages out to the public. For instance, debates featuring a host of individuals from both sides were popular ways of disseminating information on their positions and criticizing their opponents. Debates also afforded citizens the opportunity to obtain information that might help them clear up any misconceptions regarding the CAP initiative. Although the debates were predominantly held in various parts of the city, some were also televised so that those unable to attend in person could be informed about the issue.

Both sides of the campaign appeared to have targeted "perfect voters" to receive mailings and other inquiries—those individuals who had voted in primary and general elections in 1987 and 1988. However, a telephone poll conducted by the anti-CAP side appears to have generated the most controversy. One interviewee, previously undecided on how he was going to vote, claimed a question was so misleading that it angered him enough to decide in support of the initiative. The question would later be defended as one appropriately describing the effects of Initiative 31. The telephone poll was supposedly conducted to identify possible allies against the CAP.

Newspaper coverage of the CAP campaign was extensive. Daily newspapers, weeklies, and business journals routinely contained not only articles dealing with CAP but also pro-CAP and anti-CAP editorials. Even Seattle's two largest newspapers, *The Seattle Times* and *Seattle Post-Intelligencer,* came out in opposition to the CAP. In an April 7, 1989 editorial, the *Post-Intelligencer* called CAP a "blunt instrument" and noted that if it should pass, "the flow of low-income housing money, day-care facilities and other benefits that must be provided by developers when they build new buildings" would be halted ("Interim Controls," 1989, p. A-7). Concomitantly, placing a CAP on downtown development would lead to several undesirable but predictable consequences, such as forcing downtown office rents up and shifting growth pressures from downtown to city neighborhoods and suburbs.

The Seattle Times was just as disturbed by the CAP initiative. In a May 14, 1989 editorial, just 2 days before the election, it recommended that voters reject the CAP. Indicating that deciding such a technical land use issue by popular ballot is wrong, it claimed that "passage of CAP could plant seeds of economic mischief, provoke a costly court challenge (sections of the initiative may violate state law), and limit Seattle's capacity for participation in the regional planning loop in which all King County cities should decide growth-management issues jointly" ("Managing city growth," 1989, p. A-14).

Interestingly enough, the anti-CAP forces were disturbed with the early newspaper coverage of the campaign. One opponent felt the newspapers were failing to focus on the overall issue and instead were targeting specific events and people. For example, both newspapers ran articles profiling Walt Crowley, a spokesman for the anti-CAP campaign who was a contract employee for a public consulting firm working for the

CBD. According to one CAP opponent, Crowley became the issue, not the CAP. Ultimately, Crowley decided to continue speaking out against the CAP, but would no longer grant press interviews.

Evidently, Crowley's instincts were correct. Later, *The Seattle Times* ran a major article discussing how some people thought he had sold out his earlier beliefs (Hatch, 1989b). The article contained side-by-side photographs of him as an anti-war activist in 1971 and as an anti-CAP leader in 1989, thus giving the impression that he had sold out his earlier liberal beliefs to the Establishment. He appeared to have definitely become an issue. Nevertheless, in the end, one opponent of the CAP felt that the newspaper coverage had finally come around and dealt with the issue directly.

Direct mailings represented a popular means for anti-CAP and pro-CAP forces to get their messages across. As one might expect, the mailings were predominantly one-sided arguments that pointed out the strengths of their position while dramatizing the weaknesses of their opponents' positions.

In one of their mailings, the pro-CAP forces invoked some historical context into the campaign by noting how development interests had wanted to tear down the Pike Place Market 17 years earlier. Noting that development's "Build-Build-Build" motto would destroy the integrity and character of Seattle, the pro-CAP message attempted to show the citizens that development interests had been stopped in a previous time and could be stopped again. They wanted the citizens to answer the question: "Who *does* Seattle belong to?"

Another pro-CAP mailing urged citizens to "cut through the baloney" of the developers' arguments and consider the facts. Their goal was to counter the developers' claims by labeling them "baloney" and then counter by giving the "fact" of the matter. They also used a cartoon showing Pinocchio's nose getting larger as the developers told more lies. Pinocchio's nose grew in the shape of an increasingly larger building.

The anti-CAP campaign focused on the negatives of CAP. In one mailing, they claimed, "If Initiative 31 passes, our property taxes could rise dramatically." Mayor Royer was disturbed that the mailing showed his picture and one of his statements just below the slogan: "Keep Property Taxes Down—Vote No On Initiative 31." Royer, who had proposed an alternative to the CAP, did not endorse the mailing and noted "the whole campaign has just degenerated" (Bruscas, 1989, p. B-1). He was particularly unhappy with a statement attributed to him, saying that he would propose a multimillion-dollar bond issue to ward off the potential effects of Initiative 31. At the urging of Royer's staff, the mailing was changed to include one of his statements from an earlier (April 28, 1989) speech on downtown development. This statement read: "Since 1983, our city government has realized 32 million in real growth dollars . . . we've been able to hire 20% more police officers . . . and fund childcare in our schools." A pro-CAP spokesman claimed that this statement was just as misleading as the original statement. Nevertheless, the new statement appeared on the mailing.

Claims of a property tax increase didn't sit too well with King County Assessor, Ruthe Ridder. She was upset over a reprint of a property tax bill with "property tax increase" stamped over it. To her, the statement was misleading and was contributing "to a kind of public hysteria." (Hatch, 1989a, p. D-1). Indicating that property tax increases are limited by the State Constitution, Ridder said, "No one can say with any certainty how CAP would affect property taxes" (Hatch, 1989a, p. D-1). The field director of the anti-CAP campaign defended the mailing.

The legality of the CAP initiative was also questioned by the anti-CAP forces. In one mailing, an attorney noted the following problems:

It is one thing to send the city council a message about controlling growth—it is quite another to pass a law that won't work and will end up costing taxpayers like you and me thousands of dollars in needless court battles. Seattle needs this money to tackle real problems like drugs and crime in our neighborhoods. . . .

Initiative 31 leaves the city wide open to lawsuits challenging critical environmental review procedures that must be followed when we change land use laws. Similar zoning initiatives have been struck down by Washington courts in 1976 in Bothell and in 1980 in Bremerton, in each case after years of litigation. (Citizens for a Better Downtown, n.d.)

To further stress the point that Initiative 31 would be a bad law, the other side of the mailing indicated that if Initiative 31 passed, it will only mean "LAWSUITS"—printed some 94 times.

Another anti-CAP mailing began "Important: Economic Alert." Noting that revenues would be severely cut if CAP passed, there was a picture of downtown Seattle with a "closed" sign around it, suggesting that the city did not want any more new business.

Finally, some groups opposing the CAP sent letters to their members, urging them to vote against it. In an April 1989 letter to members of the Seattle Chapter of the American Institute of Architects, chapter President Thom Emrich, AIA, noted that although the original intent of a relatively small band of dedicated citizens was to "send a message to city government that our current plan has some flaws and needs revision," they had tended to "over-dramatize the problems and to oversimplify the solutions." Emrich continued by commenting that "CBD zoning is far too complex an issue to be decided in such a manner by even the best-informed citizenry."

Cartoons and posters were also used to dramatize the positions of the various campaigns. As previously mentioned, pro-CAP forces used a drawing of Pinocchio that showed his nose growing in the shape of an increasingly larger skyscraper as developers lied about the CAP. *The Seattle Times,* on April 26, 1989, depicted a Godzilla-like monster, wearing a CAP button, who was tearing off the tops of buildings while a "voice" suggested that CAP would be around for only a couple of years. The CBD even offered a picture of an outdoorsman carrying a chain saw, with CAP written on the chain, sawing the tops off buildings. "NO" appeared in bold type beside the outdoorsman.

The Seattle Chapter of the AIA also produced a poster to dramatize its opposition to the CAP. Their poster showed a skyscraper acting as a missile going down into a field, with a caption: "Don't turn growth into an unguided missile." At the bottom of the poster, the AIA listed some of the negative things associated with the CAP: severely limiting growth in the Downtown Core, making efficient light rail transit unworkable, increasing traffic volumes on existing roadways, and sending jobs and tax revenues out of the city. These were the general negative messages the anti-CAP forces were trying to relay to the public.

Getting out the Troops

The "Battle for Seattle," as it was termed on at least one occasion, attracted the attention of a multitude of groups. Many saw the election as one pitting David against Goliath, with David being the citizen and Goliath being the downtown development interests. Others saw it as community groups versus the well-financed, economic-based growth machine. Regardless of how the two sides were labeled, a variety of groups participated to varying degrees in the election. Table 7.5 provides a sampling of the many groups that participated in the election.

Difficulty in generating campaign contributions jeopardizes the ability of a group to advance its causes. While a number of

Table 7.5 Participating Groups in the CAP Campaign

Groups Supporting the CAP

Vision Seattle
Allied Arts
League of Women Voters of Seattle
Seattle Citizens' Summit
Seattle Community Council Federation
Seattle Neighborhood Coalition
Sensible Growth Alliance
Downtown Human Services Council
District Democratic Committees
Church Council of Greater Seattle
Sierra Club

Groups Opposing the CAP

Citizens for a Better Downtown (CBD)
Downtown Seattle Association (DSA)
Greater Seattle Chamber of Commerce
King County Labor Council
Seattle Chapter—American Institute of Architects (AIA)
Washington State Labor Council

SOURCE: Compiled by author

individuals and groups donated their time, expertise, and labor, funds were needed for printing and circulating campaign fliers, leaflets, and other materials. According to the office of the City Elections Administrator, both sides were required by law to disclose where they received their campaign funds and how much they received. Overall, as of July 10, 1989, the pro-CAP campaign had raised approximately $30,000, while the anti-CAP campaign had raised close to $200,000.

The pro-CAP campaign was essentially a grassroots effort. Contributions of $5, $10, and $20 were not uncommon. According to one source, its biggest contribution was $1,705, which included a $605 loan, and came from a community activist (Hatch, 1989, p. B-10).

Table 7.6 Main Contributors to the Anti-CAP Campaign

Group	Dollars Donated
Developers	$26,200
Banks	22,530
Contractors	19,460
Manufacturers	15,500
Real Estate	14,784
Utilities	12,000
Architects and Engineers	10,850
Hotels	10,300
Business Associations	8,937
Lawyers	6,150
Accountants	5,325
Retailers	4,900
Unions	4,290

SOURCE: *The Seattle Times*, May 7, 1989, B-10.

While the pro-CAP campaign received the vast majority of its funds from individuals, the anti-CAP campaign did not appear to have received a great deal of campaign cash support from individual contributors. Instead, it relied on contributions from groups operating in the downtown area. For example, according to one report, the DSA spent more than $30,000 to oppose the CAP prior to its being certified for the ballot. Table 7.6 shows the groups that donated the most money to defeat the CAP.

THE ELECTION AND ITS AFTERMATH

On May 16, 1989, the voters of Seattle passed the CAP by a vote of 44,826 (62%) to 27,971 (38%). This was a turnout of only 25% of the 291,903 registered voters eligible for the election. The result was that the city would limit the height, density, and number of skyscrapers in downtown Seattle. The measure could not be amended until 2 years after its passage.

Pro-CAP forces claim that the people's voting verified their frustrations with what was happening in the downtown area. The disamenities associated with downtown development were getting out of hand. Pro-CAP support came primarily from Seattle's white middle-class communities, while opposition centered around various wealthy white neighborhoods and minority neighborhoods. The latter neighborhoods, in all likelihood, voted against the CAP for fear of losing employment opportunities.

The anti-CAP forces blamed their defeat on a number of factors. First, they appeared to question whether the citizens understood the messages they were trying to get across to them. Second, they felt their campaign started late and then had difficulty raising funds. This was because some developers remained neutral in the campaign. Moreover, people may have become upset over some of their campaign tactics and materials.

Since CAP's passage, Mayor Royer has attempted to mediate the differences between the two sides. The anti-CAP forces wanted to challenge the measure in court. The pro-CAP forces wanted to incorporate CAP into municipal law. In the end, a competitive review process has been implemented that allocates the downtown building permits under the CAP. The review process incorporates context, siting, design, environmental, and transportation impacts as criteria.

Legal issues and concerns still surround the CAP. Acknowledging some of the concerns, attorney G. Richard Hill, vice-chair of the American Bar Association's land use planning and zoning committee, suggested the following:

> Whatever the results of a legal challenge, fueled by frustration over traffic congestion and rapid development, [it] has resulted in the destruction of a carefully crafted and innovative downtown plan. The development (and political)

landscape will never be quite the same as it was before the
CAP initiative voters took matters directly into their hands
(Hill, 1989, p. 33).

Only time will tell whether Hill's statements will come true.

On May 28, 1991, some two years after Seattle's voters approved the CAP, the Seattle City Council revised CAP to
allow buildings to exceed the downtown height limit. Debate
continues on whether the CAP should have been amended or
left alone.

EIGHT

Conclusions

The use of direct democracy has enjoyed a long tradition in the United States. Its use is supported by some individuals and opposed by others. Proponents argue that the voters are informed enough on the issues to cast an informed, intelligent vote. Opponents claim that the voters lack the information needed to make informed decisions and should let the elected officials do their jobs. Debates on whether direct democracy should be used to decide state and local issues are certain to continue.

Land use remains an important issue in many areas across the United States. In fact, land use concerns are either near or at the top of many public policy agendas. And citizens will continue monitoring the land use decisions of their elected officials. If citizens perceive that the officials are deciding issues contrary to already adopted plans and policies, or if they simply do not like the direction the city is taking, they may turn to direct democracy to decide various public issues. Depending on the area and whether they possess the power, citizens may be able to remove an elected official by recall; propose a legislative policy and place it before the voters via the initiative process; or reject various legislative actions taken by the legislative body (i.e., city council, board of supervisors) via the referendum process.

The case studies examined in this book demonstrate why citizens in Barnstable County, Massachusetts; Portland, Maine; San Diego, California; and Seattle, Washington; turned to the ballot box to decide important land use policy issues. The campaigns in each of the areas pitted grassroots organizations against a well-financed opposition. The grassroots organizations focused on the negative externalities associated with growth, while the opposition countered with warnings that jobs would be lost and the economic development of the areas would be severely jeopardized if the ballot measures were passed. This well-financed opposition could be easily characterized as the "growth machine" (Molotch, 1976; Logan and Molotch, 1987).

CASE STUDIES

Growth pressures and concerns over the area's water supply and the problems associated with growth led to the development of two nonbinding public policy questions in Barnstable County, Massachusetts. One question dealt with a moratorium on development; the other covered the creation of the Cape Cod Commission—a regional land use planning and regulatory agency for Barnstable County. Both measures were passed by the voters. Unlike the other ballot measures examined in this book, voter approval of the latter measure did not actually create the agency. Voter approval was only the first step. The next step was for the Cape Cod Commission Act to be approved by the State House, the State Senate, and the governor. After a somewhat lengthy period of time, the measure was approved by the aforementioned parties and eventually ratified by the voters. The Cape Cod Commission is currently functioning as the regional land use planning and regulatory body for

Barnstable County. It has been heralded as a bold regional planning measure in Massachusetts and its activities are being closely watched and examined by numerous bodies.

In Portland, Maine, citizens became alarmed over an attempt to change the city's working waterfront into a mixed-use area. Citizens and groups banded together and developed the Working Waterfront Initiative—a ballot measure to protect the working waterfront by prohibiting non-marine uses on it. The proponents of the measure felt allowing mixed uses would ultimately destroy an essential part of Portland's history—the working waterfront. Development interests argued that failing to allow mixed uses on the waterfront would hurt the city economically. Proponents believed the waterfront could be a more valuable economic asset to the city with proper marketing and development. The measure was passed by the voters, and the marketing and development of the working waterfront is currently underway.

San Diego continues to experience growing pains. Growth control is constantly being debated. Like the citizens in other parts of California, San Diegans are not shy about turning to the ballot box if they feel officials are unresponsive to their desires or if they do not like the direction in which the city is headed. San Diego's growth wars have pitted the usual development interests against a variety of interest groups. While the former argue that jobs will be a casualty under a growth control scenario, the latter have argued that the costs of not controlling population growth (i.e., increased traffic congestion, environmental degradation, loss of open space, and so on) outweigh its benefits.

Proposition A was passed by the voters in 1985. However, in recent years, except for a regional advisory initiative on planning for growth at the regional level, development interests have emerged victorious in the growth wars. This has certainly not discouraged some groups. They continually monitor the city's actions and will not hesitate to start the initiative process again. The growth wars are far from over in San Diego—self-proclaimed as "America's Finest City."

Concerns over the continued development of downtown Seattle prompted various individuals and groups there to develop an initiative to reduce density and height limits, reduce the amount of new office space that may be built downtown, and require the city to study the effects of the measure on the surrounding area. These parties were concerned with increasing levels of traffic congestions, the disappearance of small businesses, the loss of low-income housing in the downtown area, and a general lessening of the downtown quality of life. They were concerned with the "Manhattanization" of Seattle's skyline and wanted to prevent the further destruction of the downtown environment. As was the case in the other areas examined in this book, the same types of participants took part in the debate—development and associated business interests and a variety of grassroots organizations. In a hotly contested debate, residents of Seattle saw charges and counter-charges thrown by all parties. The campaign drew extensive media coverage, as did the measures in other states. The measure was passed by the electorate; nevertheless, both sides are continuing to monitor downtown development.

CONCLUDING COMMENTS

The increasing use of the initiative and referendum to decide land use issues suggests that additional research is needed. Among the research questions that need to be addressed in the future are:

1. Why are citizens turning to the initiative or referendum?
2. Who participates in the land use debates?
3. What do citizens think of the use of the initiative and referendum to decide a land use issue?

4. What effects have the measures had on the community once they were passed by the electorate?
5. What are the effects of passing a ballot measure on the surrounding region?

Reasonable individuals and groups will continue to debate the virtues and vices of the initiative and referendum. While many citizens and groups feel that using such measures allows them to bypass an unresponsive legislative body, others are leery of continued use. In a recent issue of the *Journal of the American Planning Association,* Callies and Curtin (1990, p. 222) argued that "whatever the cause, planning and zoning by popular vote is fraught with peril for the wise use of land and for sound planning." To them and others, resorting to the initiative ignores the planning process and could result in people making uninformed decisions on complex issues. Conversely, McClendon (1990, p. 223) feels the initiative and referendum represent "valuable procedures for encouraging more direct democratic participation in local planning and zoning issues," and supports their use when citizens are confronted with unresponsive public officials. Nonetheless, the California Supreme Court stated, in *Amador Valley Joint Union High School District v. State Board of Equalization,* 22 Cal. 3d 208, 228 (1978):

> The initiative is in essence a legislative battering ram which may be used to tear through the exasperating tangle of the traditional legislative procedure and strike directly toward the desired end. Virtually every type of interest group has on occasion used this instrument. It is inefficient as means of legislation in that it permits very little balancing of interests or compromise, but it is designed primarily for use in situations where the ordinary machinery of legislation has utterly failed in this respect.

Moore (1987, p. 301) has even commented on how earlier political theorists would view the way people are currently using the initiative and referendum:

> If Rousseau and Madison were alive today it is likely they would be satisfied with the use of the initiative by the people. We still have the representative government that Madison advocated, yet we also preserve the democratic voice that Rousseau praised. Although the use of the initiative has increased dramatically in recent years, it is still only used as an adjunct to the legislative process. This is how initiative should be employed. It is not a panacea; it is merely the populace's insurance policy against unresponsive government. Both models can coexist because neither usurps the other's power but only checks it. The courts have taken the appropriate judicial course in upholding the use of the initiative in zoning.

The stakes involved in land use decisions are high. The planning process should be allowed to function. Citizen participation must be an integral part of the process. If the process is flawed, and citizen input is either lacking or ignored by the appropriate officials, citizens may have to turn to another course of action.

Appendix

City of Portland
May 5, 1987

SHALL THE FOLLOWING ORDINANCE ENTITLED: "LAND USE CODE AMENDMENT TO BE ENACTED BY INITIATIVE" BE ADOPTED?

Purpose: To secure the Portland waterfront for marine uses.

In order to secure the Portland waterfront for marine uses, no uses shall be permitted within the area bounded by the Tukeys Bridge and the Veteran's Memorial Bridge lying between and including the waters of the Fore River, Portland Harbor and Casco Bay, excluding the Casco Bay Islands, and the water side of a line running down the middle of Commercial Street, India Street, Fore Street and the Eastern Promenade other than those accessory to fishing activities, maritime activities, functionally water-dependent activities or authorized public uses as these terms are defined below.

Without limitation and not withstanding the provisions of the Portland Land Use Code, particularly Division 4, R-3 Residential Zone; Division 8.5, R-OS Recreational and Open Space Zone; Division 14, I-2 and I-2b Industrial Zones; Division 15, I-3 and I-3b Industrial Zone; Division 18, W-1 Waterfront Zone; Division 18.5, W-2 Waterfront Zone; and any other Division, Zone, or Section of the Code purporting to authorize pier and/or land uses of any kind, there shall not be permitted in the area described in the first paragraph:

(1) Hotels, motels, boatels and residential uses.

(2) Office, industrial, commercial, research and institutional uses and facilities which not accessory to the activities defined below.

Definitions.

(1) FISHING ACTIVITIES means activities required for, supportive of or commonly associated with fishing, such as fin fish and shell fish processing, storage, marketing and handling, the manufacturing and sale of bait, nets and other fishing supplies, and the manufacture, sale, installation and repair of fishing boats, engines and equipment, and ground level parking incidental to any such uses.

(2) MARITIME ACTIVITIES means activities required for, supportive of or commonly associated with the construction, repair, operation, storage, loading and unloading of boats, waterfront dock and port facilities, marinas, navigation aids, boat fuel and equipment supply, ground level parking incidental to such uses and other activities the primary purpose of which is to facilitate maritime trade.

(3) FUNCTIONALLY WATER DEPENDENT ACTIVITIES means activities that require, for their primary purpose, a location on the waterfront or that require direct access to the water and which cannot relocate away from the water.

(4) AUTHORIZED PUBLIC USES means uses of facilities which are publicly owned and designed for a public purpose, together with public utility facilities, and equipment storage and other facilities necessary for public safety.

Because of the significance of this amendment to development activities within the defined waterfront area and the potential for long-run harm which development inconsistent with this amendment will have for all of the citizens of the City of Portland, the provisions hereof, if subsequently accepted by the voters of the City of Portland, shall be applicable to all pending proceedings, applications and petitions commenced after December 22, 1986, which is the date of the filing of this initiative in the City Clerk's office of the City of Portland.

Each and every provision of this amendment is severable. If any provision is determined to be invalid by a court of competent jurisdiction, or the application of any provision to any person or circumstance is determined to be invalid by such a court, such invalidity shall not affect any other provisions or the applications to any person or circumstance.

City of San Diego Proposition A

A. CITY OF SAN DIEGO INITIATIVE MEASURE. AMENDS THE CITY OF SAN DIEGO PROGRESS GUIDE AND GENERAL PLAN. Shall the City of San Diego Progress Guide and General Plan be amended by adding restrictions requiring that land areas which are designated as 'future urbanizing' not be redesignated without voter approval?

This proposition requires a majority vote.

Add to the Progress Guide and General Plan for the City of San Diego, Document Number 76485, at page 35 immediately following the caption "Future Urbanizing Areas" the language of the proposed initiative measure which is underlined.

Future Urbanizing Areas

Land within the future urbanizing designation which is zoned agricultural or low density residential-recreational use for extended periods of time should be given tax relief through preferential tax assessments. This can be accomplished through the use of the Williamson Act which requires the designation of land as an "agricultural preserve" or as open space pursuant to the General Plan or specific plans based on the overall program to guide growth. The designation of land in this category is not permanent, it is an interim or urban reserve designation. Its purpose is to preclude premature development and to guide urbanization.

Section 1. "No property shall be changed from the 'future urbanizing' land use designation in the Progress Guide and General Plan to any other land use designation and the provisions restricting development in the future urbanizing area shall not be amended except by majority vote of the people voting on the change or amendment at a City wide election thereon."

Section 2. Definitions. "For purposes of this initiative measure, the following words and phrases shall have the following meanings:

(a) "Progress Guide and General Plan shall mean the Progress Guide and General Plan of the City of San Diego, including text and maps, as the same existed on August 1, 1984."

(b) " 'Change of Designation' or 'changed from Future Urbanizing' shall mean the removal of any area of land from the future urbanizing designation."

(c) " 'Amendment' or 'amended' as used in Section 1 shall mean any proposal to amend the text or maps of the Progress Guide and General Plan affecting the future urbanizing designation as the same existed in the Progress Guide and General Plan on August 1, 1984 or the land subject to said designation on August 1, 1984, except amendments which are neutral or make the designation more restrictive in terms of permitting development."

Section 3. Implementation. "The City Council, City Planning Commission, and City staff are hereby directed to take any and all actions necessary under this initiative measure, including but not limited to adoption and implementation on any amendments to the General Plan and zoning ordinance or City Code, reasonable necessary to carry out the intent and purpose of this Initiative measure. Said actions shall be carried forthwith."

Section 4. Guidelines. "The City Council may adopt reasonable guidelines to implement this initiative measure following notice and public hearing, providing that any such guidelines shall be consistent with the intent and purpose of this measure."

<u>Section 5. Exemptions for Certain Projects.</u> "This measure shall not prevent completion of any project as to which a building permit has been issued pursuant to Section 92.02.03(a) of the San Diego Municipal Code prior to the effective date of this measure; provided, however, that the project shall cease to be exempt from the provisions of Section 91.02.0303(d) of the San Diego Municipal Code or if the said permit is suspended or revoked pursuant to Section 91.02.0303(e) of the San Diego Municipal Code."

<u>Section 6. Amendment or Repeal.</u> This measure may be amended or repealed only by a majority of the voters voting at an election thereon.

<u>Section 7. Severability.</u> "If any section, subsection, sentence, phrase, clause, or portion of this initiative is for any reason held to be invalid or unconstitutional by any Court of competent jurisdiction, such decision shall not affect the validity of the remaining portions of this Initiative and each section, subsection, sentence, clause, phrase, part of portion thereof would have been adopted or passed irrespective of the fact that any one or more sections, subsections, sentences, clauses, phrases, parts or portions be declared invalid or unconstitutional."

City of Seattle
Initiative Measure No. 31

AN INITIATIVE pertaining to land use; amending chapter 23.49; establishing and amending heights for buildings in certain downtown zones; changing the bonus system in certain downtown zones; modifying the floor area ratios in certain downtown zones and requiring that studies be performed.

WHEREAS, overdevelopment of downtown office space create substantial economic costs because of the transportation, utility and service improvements which make it necessary; and

WHEREAS, the expenditure of disproportionately large amounts of public funds on improvements made necessary by downtown overdevelopment occurs at the expense of Seattle's residential neighborhoods; and

WHEREAS, thousands of units of downtown low-income housing have been lost in recent years to office development, with thousands of additional units in danger of demolition; and

WHEREAS, the city-subsidized replacement of downtown low-income lost solely because of office overdevelopment will cost taxpayers millions of dollars, which could better be spent for other purposes if such housing were preserved; and

WHEREAS, overdevelopment of downtown office space will adversely affect the city's residential neighborhoods, driving up the price of homes, depriving middle income families of the option of living in Seattle, and increasing the likelihood of residential up-zones in single family areas; and

WHEREAS, the rapid proliferation of large downtown office towers is creating a windy, dark, crowded and unpleasant environment in which to work and shop; and

WHEREAS, overdevelopment of downtown office space threatens the economic viability of older, architecturally-significant structures and historic districts downtown; and

WHEREAS, speculative office development has displaced many of the small retail businesses which are important to the continued economic vitality of our city center, and to its continued usefulness to Seattle residents; and

WHEREAS, orderly, predictable and aesthetically pleasing growth in downtown Seattle is in the best long-term economic interest of the city's residents, while concurrent construction of a number of downtown skyscrapers disrupts business, restricts the use of the streets, and makes downtown an unpleasant place in which to live, work or shop; and

WHEREAS, the present Downtown Plan allows for greater and more rapid growth of office space than is good for the ultimate economic well-being and livability of the city; and

WHEREAS, certain features of the present Downtown Plan fail to address the undesirable economic, social and environmental impacts brought about by overdevelopment of downtown office space.

BE IT ENACTED BY THE CITY OF SEATTLE:

<u>Section 1.</u> SMC Section 23.49.008A is amended to read as follows:

A. Maximum structure height shall be designated on the Official Land Use Map, Chapter 23.32, except that:

1. The Council shall determine the maximum permitted height when a major retail store or performing arts theater bonus is approved in Downtown Retail Core zones pursuant to Section 23.49.096; provided, that such height shall not exceed ~~four hundred (400')~~ <u>one hundred and fifty feet (150').</u>

2. Any property in the Pike Market Mixed zone that is subject to an urban renewal covenant may be built no higher than the height permitted by the covenant for the life of the covenant.

3. <u>Structures in the Downtown Office Core 1 zone shall not exceed a height of 450 feet.</u>

4. <u>Notwithstanding any contrary designation on the Official Land Use Map, the maximum height of structures in the Downtown Retail Core zones shall be 85 feet, except as otherwise specified in subparagraph A.1 of this section.</u>

5. <u>Notwithstanding any contrary designation on the Official Land Use Map, structures in the Downtown Office Core 2 zones that are designated for a permitted height of 400 feet may not exceed a maximum height of 300 feet.</u>

<u>Section 2.</u> SMC Chapter 23.49 is amended by adding a new Section 23.49.011 to read as follows:

<u>23.49.011 Maximum Annual Development of Office Space</u>
<u>The following provisions establish the maximum number of square feet of usable new office space for which the City may issue building permits on an annual basis, as well as exceptions to these limitations.</u>

A.1. <u>If this ordinance takes effect before July 1, 1989, the City may not, during the summer of 1989, issue building permits for more than 500,000 square feet of usable new office space in downtown, including all downtown zones. If this ordinance takes effect on or after July 1, 1989, the City may not, during the</u>

remainder of 1989, issue building permits for more than 250,000 square feet of usable new office space in downtown, including all downtown zones.

A.2. Except as otherwise provided in Sub-Section A.3 below, the City may not, in any calendar year from 1990 through 1994 issue building permits for the construction of more than 500,000 square feet of usable new office space in downtown, including all downtown zones.

A.3. If, in any calendar year from 1990 through 1994, the City does not issue building permits for the construction of 500,000 square feet of usable new office space, then the difference between the square footage for which building permits have been issued and 500,000 square feet shall be available in the next calendar and subsequent years. In no event, however, may the City issue building permits for more than 1,000,000 square feet of usable new office space in any calendar year through 1994.

B.1. Except as otherwise provided in Sub-Section B.2 below, the City may not, in any calendar year from 1995 through 1999, issue building permits for the construction of more than 1,000,000 square feet of usable new office space in downtown, including all downtown zones.

B.2. If, in any calendar year, from 1995 through 1999, the City does not issue building permits for 1,000,000 square feet of usable new office space, then the difference between the square footage for which building permits have been issued and 1,000,000 square feet shall be available in the next and subsequent calendar years. In no event, however, may the City issue building permits in any calendar year from 1995 through 1999 for more than 2,000,000 square feet of usable new office space.

C.   Any building which contains less than 50,000 square feet of usable new office space is exempt from the provisions of this Section 23.49.011.

D.   Except as provided in Sub-Section E below, building permits will be issued on a first-come, first-served basis annually under rules adopted by the Department of Construction and Land Use, or pursuant to such other reasonable mechanism established by DCLU after public comment and hearing.

E.   Of the maximum allowable square footage for usable new office space allowed under Sub-Section A or B above, building permits for 85,00 square feet per year shall be reserved for buildings containing between 50,000 and 85,000 square feet of usable new office space. Permits for these buildings will be issued on a first-come-first-served basis annually under rules adopted by the DCLU, or pursuant to such other reasonable mechanism established by DCLU after public comment and hearing. Any square footage of usable new office space reserved under this subsection E which is not used in any calendar year shall be carried over to the next calendar year and subsequent years to be available for buildings containing between 50,000 and 85,000 square feet of usable new office space.

Section 3. SMC Section 23.49.048B is amended to read as follows:

B.   Permitted FAR
     Permitted FAR shall be as follows:

FLOOR AREA RATIO

Base	Maximum with Bonus for Public Benefit Features Other Than Housing or TDR Other Than from Low Income Housing	Maximum with Housing Bonus or Transfer of Development Rights from Low Income Housing or Landmark Structure	Maximum with Transfer of Development Rights from Low Income Housing
~~10~~	~~15~~	~~20~~	
5	7	10	14

Section 4. SMC Section 23.49.068B is amended to read as follows:

B. Permitted FAR
    Permitted FAR shall be as follows:

FLOOR AREA RATIO

Base	Maximum with Bonus for Public Benefit Features Other Than Housing or TDR Other Than from Low Income Housing	Maximum with Housing Bonus or Transfer of Development Rights from Low Income Housing or Landmark Structures	Maximum with Transfer of Development Rights from Low Income Housing
~~8~~	~~11~~	~~14~~	
4	6	8	10

Section 5. Section 23.49.096B 4 a. is amended to read as follows:

An increase in the height up to ~~400~~ 150 feet may be permitted when the primary objective described above will be furthered and:

Section 6. SMC Section 23.49.098B is amended to read as follows:

FLOOR AREA RATIO

Base	Maximum with Bonus for Public Benefit Features Other Than Housing or Transfer of Development Rights[1]	Maximum with Bonus for Public Benefit Features. Including Housing Where Permitted as Shown on Map IVA	Maximum With Major Retail Store or Preforming Arts Theater Bonus	~~Maximum with Preforming Arts Theater Bonus~~
~~5~~	~~7~~	~~9~~	~~11~~	~~12~~
2.5	3.5	4	6	

Section 7. SMC Section 23.84.040 is amended by adding the following definition:
Usable New Office Space

The floor area of a structure, which floor area is available for lease, sale or occupancy as office use, whether such floor area is created by new construction or by conversion from other use.

Section 8. The Office of Long Range Planning or other appropriate City agency is directed to monitor and study what effect, if any, this ordinance will have on areas outside the Downtown Zone. Specifically, the agency shall evaluate whether changes are needed to the neighborhood commercial, commercial and other zones within the city to maintain downtown as the center for dense commercial use, and to prevent adverse development in the city's neighborhoods. The agency shall report to the City Council on a regular basis regarding the progress of its study. The final report on this study, and recommendations regarding any necessary zoning changes, shall be presented to the City Council within six months of the effective date of this ordinance.

Section 9. The Office of Long Range Planning or other appropriate City agency is directed to study measures for the long-term management of downtown development, including a permanent annual limitation on the issuance of building permits. Specifically, the study shall evaluate what measures are appropriate to control the pace, scale and impacts of downtown development, and to prevent construction cycles harmful to downtown and to the city's neighborhoods. The report to the City Council on this study shall be presented no later than January, 1998. This study shall address the following factors, among others, in determining long-term growth management measures:

a. Progress toward implementation of a regional light-rail or other transportation system capable of adequately serving downtown and regional needs;
b. Compliance with downtown housing and low-income housing goals, including those set by the 1985 Downtown Plan;
c. Development pressures in the city's neighborhoods which may result from downtown office development;

   d.   The effect which downtown office development may have on the affordability of housing in the city's neighborhoods;

   e.   The cost of infrastructure and utility improvements required to serve new downtown office development, and the manner in which such improvements are to be financed;

   f.   Levels of service at downtown intersections, and other measures of traffic and parking capacity; and

   g.   Attainment of clean air standards as prescribed by the Puget Sound Air Pollution Control Authority.

Section 10. This ordinance shall take effect on the earliest date authorized under Article IV, Section 1 of the City Charter.

Section 11. If any provision of this ordinance or its application to any person or circumstance is declared illegal, the remainder of the ordinance or its application to other persons or circumstances shall not be affected thereby. The City Attorney is directed to fully defend against any challenge to this ordinance and/or its application to any person or circumstance.

---

1. As permitted by Section 23.49.102A

Incentive System

Policy 23 Floor Area Bonus System

Incentives for the inclusion of features determined to be of benefit to the public shall be provided by granting additional floor area in conformance with the downtown policies and the density regulations of the appropriate land use district classification. The value of the bonus shall reflect both public priority for the feature and the cost of providing it. The total of all additional development rights granted for public benefit features shall be limited by a maximum floor area ratio.

Guideline 1: <u>General Bonus Features</u>. Additional development rights shall be granted for the following features in conformance with the regulations of the appropriate land use district classification:

a. <u>Human Services.</u> Up to 10,000 square feet of space provided at reduced rents for eligible public or private health or human service organizations shall be granted a floor area increase. Alternatively, a bonus shall be granted for a voluntary agreement to contribute funds to the Downtown Health and Human Services Fund in accordance with Policy 13: Health and Human Services. To allow facilities to locate near target populations, this incentive bonus shall apply in all downtown areas where floor increases are permitted.

b. <u>Day Care Services.</u> Up to 3,000 square feet of space provided at reduced rents to eligible nonprofit or for-profit day care centers shall be granted a floor area increase. To qualify, day care facilities must provide services at rates affordable to the range of income levels representative of the downtown work force. Day care space in excess of 3,000 square feet shall be granted a floor area increase as a human service facility.

c. <u>Cinema</u>. To encourage evening activity in office, retail and mixed use areas additional floor area shall be granted for motion picture theaters, ranging in size from a minimum of 5,000 square feet to a maximum of 15,000 square feet. Floor area increases shall not be granted for cinemas used for exhibiting adult motion pictures.

d. <u>Shopping Atrium.</u> To encourage intensification of retail shopping activity in the retail core and adjacent areas, floor area increases shall be granted for public spaces ranging in size from 4,000 square feet to 15,000 square feet which provide a combination of retail shopping and passive recreational spaces directly accessible from the street. These will be interior spaces with high ceilings, seating and landscaping surrounded by shops and services which may be on several levels.

e. <u>Shopping Corridor.</u> To enhance pedestrian circulation as well as provide for additional retail frontage, floor area increases shall be granted for through-block passages lined with shops connecting parallel avenues in the retail core and adjacent areas. The minimum width of the corridor shall be 20 feet and maximum width subject to the bonus shall be 30 feet.

f. Retail Shopping. Provision of space for retail shops, restaurants, personal services, amusement establishments, galleries and other uses that are retail in character shall be granted additional floor area. Banks, airline ticket agencies, travel agencies and similar uses shall not qualify for this incentive. Qualifying uses shall be granted a floor area increase in all areas, except the retail core, when fronting on any Class I Pedestrian Street and along street parks in commercial areas. Up to .5 FAR not to exceed 15,000 square feet may be bonused.

g. Parcel Park. Small landscaped open spaces which include retail activity and are suited to a variety of activities shall be granted additional floor area. Parcel parks shall be at least 3,000 square feet in size; the maximum area eligible for a bonus shall be 7,000 square feet. The park shall be within 3 feet of the sidewalk level along the primary street frontage. To avoid disruption of the street wall, the street opening shall be limited, and only one parcel park shall be permitted per street front. Additional floor area shall be granted for parcel parks in all downtown office and mixed commercial areas.

h. Residential Parcel Park. Additional floor area shall be granted for small landscaped residential parcel parks to reinforce residential areas, and provide neighborhood public space for passive and active recreational activities. The minimum size of a residential parcel park shall be 2,000 square feet and the maximum area eligible for this incentive shall be 12,000 square feet. Street frontage requirements shall be similar to parcel parks. Floor area increases for this incentive shall be limited to mixed use residential areas where floor area increases are permitted.

i. Street Park. Additional floor area shall be granted for participation in the development of street parks abutting new projects in accordance with an adopted street park development procedure. This incentive shall be granted only for specified improvements along designated street parks, in accordance with Guideline 3 of Policy 22: Open Space.

j. Rooftop Garden—Street Accessible. Additional floor area shall be granted for the inclusion of open space on roof tops near street level which improve the appearance of the cityscape from street level and the upper floors of surrounding buildings. Street accessible rooftop gardens shall be landscaped open space directly accessible and visible from the street or other public space.

The elevation of the minimum area required shall not exceed 4 feet above the point where public access is provided from a street or public open space. Within the garden terracing shall be allowed to increase the elevation and permit uses at street level beneath the garden. The minimum areas shall be 1,500 square feet and the maximum area eligible for a floor area increase shall be 20 percent of the site area. Additional floor area for this feature shall be granted in all office and mixed commercial areas.

k. Rooftop Garden—Interior Accessible. Additional floor area shall be granted for landscaped public open spaces located on the rooftops to a maximum of 240 feet above grade. Rooftop gardens shall be directly accessible from the elevator lobby of the floor on which they are located. Identification of the location of the rooftop garden shall be posted at the main entrance of the building and in each elevator. The minimum area shall be 2,000 square feet and the maximum area eligible shall be a 30 percent of the area of the site. Floor area increases for rooftop gardens shall be granted in all office and mixed commercial areas.

l. Hillclimb Assist. Additional floor area shall be granted for pedestrian corridors that incorporate mechanical features such as elevators or escalators, across sites with slopes of 10 percent or more to aid pedestrian movement up and down steep slopes connecting two parallel avenues. The minimum clear width of the corridor shall at no point be less than 10 feet, with an average width of 15 feet. Hillclimb assists shall be limited to one per block and floor area may be granted in all office and mixed commercial areas where grades exceed 10 percent.

m. Hillside Terrace. Additional floor area shall be granted for public open space extensions of the sidewalk on steeply sloping streets which promote a better relationship between the building and sidewalk and make travel on foot more pleasant. The terrace shall extend along the majority of the street frontage of the site and include shopping uses. The minimum width shall be 10 feet and the maximum area eligible for this incentive shall be 6,000 square feet. This incentive shall be allowed on sites with at least a 10 percent slope in office and mixed commercial areas.

n. Harborfront Open Space. Additional floor area shall be granted for open space which improves public circulation between the waterfront and upland areas and conforms with guidelines developed for the Alaskan Way Harborfront Public Improvement

Plan. The open space shall have frontage on Alaskan Way or have direct access to it through a public space. The bonused space shall have seating and be landscaped; have a minimum dimension of 40 feet and a minimum area of 4,000 square feet; and be within three feet of the elevation of Alaskan Way. The maximum area eligible for this incentive shall be equivalent to 30 percent of the area of the site.

o. Sidewalk Widening. Additional floor area shall be granted for sidewalk widening when buildings are set back from the street property line to meet the minimum sidewalk width requirement in accordance with the Pedestrian Street Classification schedule of Guideline 4, Policy 8: Street Classification System.

p. Overhead Weather Protection. Additional floor area shall be granted for overhead weather protection which covers portions of the sidewalk. Included shall be nonstructural features like canopies, awnings, and marquees and structural features like building overhangs and arcades. This incentive shall apply along all streets designated Class I Pedestrian Streets in accordance with Policy 8: Street Classification System. The maximum extent of covered street frontage for which additional floor area is granted shall be 100 percent of the total street frontage of the site, the minimum width shall be 6 feet.

q. Voluntary Building Setback. Additional floor area shall be granted for voluntary building setbacks which increase the landscaped area along street parks in mixed use residential areas where floor area increases are permitted. To be eligible for this incentive, the setback must reinforce the character of the street park and provide a unifying element within the residential area. To be eligible for added floor area the setback shall be a minimum of five feet from the street property line, a maximum of ten feet and extend along the entire street frontage of the site.

r. Sculptured Building Tops. Additional floor area shall be granted for reductions in bulk within the upper floors of structures in office areas to improve the appearance of the downtown skyline and provide light and air to the street. Additional floor area shall be granted for the total amount of area by which each floor is reduced. The total area eligible for a bonus shall be 30,000 square feet.

s. Short Term Parking. Additional floor area shall be granted for provision of short-term parking to meet shopper and visitor parking needs in retail areas. Short term parking shall be marketed, priced or operated in such a manner as to discourage its use for parking durations longer than six hours. At least 25 spaces in excess of the minimum required accessory to other uses on the site must be provided; a maximum of 200 spaces shall be eligible for bonus. The parking may be constructed above or below grade.

t. <u>Small Site Development.</u> Additional floor area shall be granted for development of sites less than 15,000 square feet in area in office and retail areas and for existing structures on sites of less than 7,200 square feet in mixed residential areas to encourage smaller structures that will add diversity to downtown, reduce development pressures on older structures and preserve a more human scale in the streetscape. Additional floor area shall be granted for development on sites less than 15,000 square feet in area in mixed commercial zones: (1) for sites located on the same block as Office Core-1 districts; and (2) for sites subject to the view corridor setback requirements of Policy 17: Street Level Views. The bonus shall be an increased FAR on sites located in the office, retail, mixed commercial and mixed residential areas where a floor area increase is allowed.

Guideline 2: Special Criteria. Certain bonuses shall be subject to special criteria and review by the Director of DCLU and will not be automatically granted.

a. <u>Performing Arts Theater.</u> To promote downtown as a center for cultural and entertainment activities, to foster the arts in the City, and attract people to office areas during evening hours, bonuses shall be granted for facilities expressly designed for the production and presentation of legitimate live performances. Theaters ranging in size from 200 to 3,000 seats plus support areas such as the lobby, stage, and production storage space shall be eligible to receive a bonus. Bonuses shall be subject to special evaluation criteria to ensure that there is a long term demand for a theater of the proposed design and size, and that there is a sound financial plan for long term operation and management of the theater.

b. <u>Public Display Space.</u> Bonuses shall be granted for interior public space used to preserve and exhibit natural, scientific, historical, cultural or literary objects of interest or works of art by public or private nonprofit organizations. A minimum of 2,500 square feet of exhibit space shall be provided at street level and the maximum bonusable size shall be 10,000 square feet. Bonuses shall not be granted for commercial gallery or display space or for building lobby space. This bonus shall be subject to special evaluation criteria to ensure that there is public demand for the proposed exhibit facility and a sound financial plan for long term operation and management. A bonus for up to 30,000 square feet of display space for the major facility of an existing established museum may be granted through administrative criteria and review procedure.

c. <u>Urban Plaza.</u> Bonuses shall be granted for the provision of major public open spaces integrated with the downtown transit system and open space network in areas of concentrated office development. Urban plazas shall be major public open spaces at least 6,000 square feet in size, bonusable up to 15,000 square feet. Plazas shall be strategically located to denote important places within downtown, create a focus for surrounding development, and increase light and air within the public street environment. This bonus shall be subject to special evaluation criteria to ensure locations where large open spaces would complement the proposed transit system, open space network and an active street level environment.

d. <u>Transit Station Access.</u> To integrate the pedestrian network with the proposed transit system and to minimize sidewalk conflicts, bonuses shall be granted for provision of transit station access associated with private development. Bonuses shall be available for three kinds of access: 1) mechanical access where the transit station is generally below the access point necessitating elevators and escalators for convenient travel; 2) grade level access where topographic conditions allow access approximately level with the station mezzanines and opportunities for daylight into stations and 3) provision of an easement on the private development site for public construction of the transit station access.

The bonus shall be granted in office and retail areas on sites proximate to the transit stations up to a maximum of 30,000 square feet of additional floor area. Approval shall be subject to special evaluation criteria to ensure that the location and design of the transit station access is well integrated with the transit system and street level pedestrian network.

e. <u>Public Atrium.</u> To provide weather protected space within office areas for passive recreational activities, temporary arts events and other public gatherings, bonuses shall be granted for the provision of skylighted public atriums. This bonus shall be subject to special evaluation criteria to ensure that the space is a functionally independent part of the building, separated from building lobbies and internal circulation paths, and has direct access to a street or public open space. The minimum areas shall be 2,000 square feet; up to 5,000 square feet shall be eligible for a bonus.

f. <u>Housing.</u> Residential units affordable to households with incomes not exceeding 150 percent of the median income for the Seattle area shall be eligible for floor area increases in accordance with Policy 11: Housing Preservation and Policy 12: Housing Development.

Guideline 3: <u>Council Conditional Use</u>. Certain bonuses shall be subject to review and approval by City Council. Since these bonuses allow exceptions to density, height and development standards in highly sensitive areas of downtown, they may be granted outright, granted with conditions or denied.

a. <u>Major Retail Store.</u> Bonuses may be granted for development which includes space for major new retail firms with established reputations that will attract customers from a regional area. Bonuses shall be granted only in the retail core for major retail stores which must be at least 80,000 square feet in size; the maximum floor area eligible for a bonus shall be 200,000 square feet. Since this bonus allows exceptions to density, height and setback regulations for the retail core, City Council review and approval shall be required, in conformance with Policy 30: Downtown Retail Core.

b. <u>Performing Arts Theaters in the Retail Core.</u> To promote downtown as a center for cultural and entertainment activities, to foster the arts in the City, and attract people to the retail core during afternoon and evening hours, bonuses shall be granted for facilities expressly designed for the production and presentation of legitimate live performances. The same size, design and evaluation criteria shall be used as for the performing arts theater bonus in Guideline 2; however, since in the retail core this bonus will allow exceptions to height, density and development standards, City Council review and approval shall be required in conformance with Policy 30: Downtown Retail Core.

c. <u>Water Dependent Incentive.</u> To encourage retention and development of new water dependent uses, height and lot coverage exceptions may be developments which include a significant water dependent use on waterfront lots in the downtown harborfront. This bonus shall be subject to development standards and performance criteria of Policy 36: Downtown Harborfront-1 and Shoreline Environment, and shall require City Council review and approval.

Guideline 4: Value of Floor Area Increases. Floor area bonuses shall reflect the value of the increased development rights in each area where bonuses are allowed and the cost to provide the desired feature. In establishing bonus ratios the value of the increased development rights shall be discounted to provide an economic incentive.

Guideline 5: Art in Public Spaces. To add interest and enrich the quality of public spaces each interior and exterior public benefit feature which includes a commonly accessible open space and may be incorporated through a variety of means. The art may be part of wall or paving surfaces, elements of landscaping, fountains, or free standing sculpture.

Art work shall be included in the following public benefit features:
Shopping Atrium
Shopping Corridor
Parcel Park
Residential Parcel Park
Street Park
Rooftop Garden, Street Accessible
Rooftop Garden, Interior Accessible
Hillside Terrace
Harborfront Open Space

Urban Plaza
Public Atrium
Performing Arts Theater

Guideline 6: Floor Area Exemptions. All features meeting the standards of the public benefit features rule, whether granted a floor area bonus or not shall be exempt from the calculation of permitted FAR regardless of the maximum bonusable area limitations. The floor area exemption for street level retail shall be governed by the density and use schedule of the land use district where the bonus is allowed.

Guideline 7: Street Wall Exemptions. All street frontage along public open spaces meeting the criteria of the public benefit features rule whether granted a floor area bonus or not shall be exempt from the requirements of Policy 18: Street Level Development Standards.

Guideline 8: Performance Evaluation. After 1 million square feet of office space has been bonused in DOC 1 through the incentive bonus system, if less than 40 percent of the square footage is achieved through the combination of housing bonus or TDR, then the bonus tiering system will be adjusted so that it would have resulted in 40 percent of bonused square footage being housing or TDR. If less than the equivalent of 70,000 square feet is achieved through the human services and day care bonuses, a specific human services and day care set-aside will be established in the amenities portion of the bonus system.

SOURCE: Land Use & Transportation Plan for Downtown Seattle
Adopted June 10, 1985, by Resolution 27281

References

Abourezk, J. 1977. Statement. Pp. 6-8 in *Hearings Before the Subcommittee on the Constitution of the Committee on the Judiciary. United States Senate. Ninety-Fifth Congress, 1st Sess. on S.J. Res. 67*. Joint resolution proposing an amendment to the Constitution of the United States with respect to the proposal and the enactment of laws by popular vote of the people of the United States, December 13, 14, 1977.

Abrams, M. 1988. "EDC may be linked with Prop. J." *San Diego Union* (October 27): p. 3.

Adrian, C. R. and C. Press. 1968. *Governing Urban America*. 3rd. ed. New York: McGraw-Hill.

Aigner, R. L. 1988. "City's office market is healthy and does not require intervention." *Puget Sound Business Journal* (May 30): pp. 1, 10.

American City Corporation, The. 1982. *Development Program for Portland, Maine, Waterfront*. Columbia, MD: The American City Corporation.

Andrews, T. H. 1990, April 2. Letter to the Portland City Council.

Arnstein, S. R. 1969. "A Ladder of Participation." *Journal of the American Institute of Planners* 35 (July): 216-224.

Association for the Preservation of Cape Cod, Inc. 1988, June 8. Press Release. Orleans, MA: Association for the Preservation of Cape Cod, Inc.

Austin, D. M. 1972. "Resident Participation: Political Mobilization or Organizational Co-optation." *Public Administration Review* 32 (September): 409-421.

Babcock, R. F. 1966. *The Zoning Game: Municipal Practices and Policies*. Madison: University of Wisconsin Press.

Babcock, R. F. 1976. "Eastlake v. Forest City Enterprise: A Comment by Richard F. Babcock." *Land Use Law and Zoning Digest* 28 (8): 3-4.

Bair, F. H., Jr. 1976. "Eastlake v. Forest City Enterprises: A Comment by Fred H. Bair, Jr." *Land Use Law and Zoning Digest* 28 (8): 5-6.

Baker, G. E. 1977. "The Impulse for Direct Democracy." *National Civic Review* 66 (January): 19-23, 35.

Baldassare, M. 1981. *The Growth Dilemma*. Berkeley: University of California Press.

Balint, K. 1987. "5,000 new homes permitted by growth-limit exemption." *San Diego Tribune* (December 2): pp. A-1, A-12.

"Ballot: Words and propositions." 1987. *Portland Evening Express* (April 29): p. 6.

Beatley, T. 1989. "The Role of Expectations and Promises in Land Use Decisionmaking." *Policy Sciences* 22 (March): 27-50.

Berman, D. R. 1975. *State and Local Politics*. Boston: Holbrook Press.

Bosselman, F. and D. Callies. 1971. *The Quiet Revolution in Land Use Controls*. Washington: Council on Environmental Quality.

Bowman, A. O'M. and R. C. Kearney. 1986. *The Resurgence of the States*. Englewood Cliffs, NJ: Prentice-Hall.

Bradbury, D. 1987. "Realtor: Don't limit waterfront." *Portland Evening Express* (March 11): p. 34.

Bradley, J. 1985. "Why community planners oppose Proposition A." *San Diego Union* (November 2): p. B-11.

Bradley, T. 1987. "Vote lightens planners' agenda." *Portland Press Herald* (May 7): p. 13.

Branch, M. C. 1985. *Comprehensive City Planning: Introduction & Explanation*. Chicago: APA Planners Press.

Brower, D. 1980. "Courts Move Toward Redefinition of General Welfare." Pp. 144-150 in F.C. Schnidman and J. Silverman (eds.) *Management and Control of Growth: Updating the Law*. Vol. 5. Washington: Urban Land Institute.

____ et al. 1976. *Urban Growth Management Through Development Timing*. New York: Praeger.

Bruscas, A. 1989. "Final CAP attack draws fire from Royer." *Seattle Post-Intelligencer* (May 13): pp. B-1, B-2.

Burke, E. M. 1968. "Citizen Participation Strategies." *Journal of the American Institute of Planners* 34 (September): 287-294.

Burrows, L. B. 1978. *Growth Management: Issues, Techniques and Policy Implications*. New Brunswick, NJ: Center for Urban Policy Research.

Calavita, N. and R. Caves. n.d. "The Attitudes of Planners and the Public Towards Growth." Unpublished paper, San Diego State University.

California Association of Realtors. 1989. *Matrix of Land Use Planning Measures, 1971-1989*. Los Angeles: California Association of Realtors.

California Office of Planning and Research. 1980. *The Growth Revolt: Aftershock of Proposition 13?* Sacramento: California Office of Planning and Research.

Callies, D. L. 1976. "The Supreme Court is Wrong About Zoning by Popular Vote." *Planning* (August). Reprinted in F. C. Schnidman and J. Silverman (eds.) 1980. *Management and Control of Growth: Updating the Law*. Vol. 5. Washington: Urban Land Institute.

Callies, D. and D. J. Curtin. 1990. "On the Making of Land Use Decisions through Citizen Initiative and Referendum." *Journal of the American Planning Association* 56 (Spring): 222-223.

Callies, D. L., N. C. Neuffer, and C. P. Caliboso. 1989. *Ballot Box Zoning in Hawaii: Initiative, Referendum and the Law.* Honolulu: The Land Use Research Foundation of Hawaii.

"CAP won't work, warns mayor of Vancouver, B.C." 1989. *Seattle Post-Intelligencer* (May 13): p. B-3.

Cape Cod Planning and Economic Development Commission. 1988. *Cape Cod's Future.* Barnstable, MA: Cape Cod Planning and Economic Development Commission.

Cape Cod Planning and Economic Development Commission. 1989. *Annual Report for the Fiscal Year 1989.* Barnstable, MA: Cape Cod Planning and Economic Development Commission.

Carr, J. H. and E. E. Duensing, eds. 1983. *Land Use Issues of the 1980s.* New Brunswick, NJ: Center for Urban Policy Research.

Carter, S., K. Bert, and P. Nobert. 1974. "Controlling Growth: A Challenge for Local Government." Pp. 265-277 in *The Municipal Year Book 1974.* Washington: International City Management Association.

Castrodale, B. 1988. "Local builders 'mad' as hell." *Cape Cod Times* (June 9): pp. 1, 11.

Caves, R. W. 1980. "Downzoning in a Changing Urban Environment." *Real Estate Issues* 5 (Fall/Winter): 12-15.

_____. 1990. "Determining Land Use Policy Via the Ballot Box: The Growth Initiative Blitz in California." *Land Use Policy* 7 (January): 70-79.

Chesley, R. A. 1984. "The Current Use of the Initiative and Referendum in Ohio and Other States." *University of Cincinnati Law Review* 53 (Spring): 541-560.

Citizens for a Better Downtown. n.d. "Initiative 31 is a bad law!" Seattle: Citizens for a Better Downtown.

City of Portland, Maine. 1982. *Strategies for the Development and Revitalization of the Portland Waterfront.* Report prepared for the Portland City Council.

City of Portland, Maine, City Clerk's Office. 1989. *Voting Figures for the May 5, 1987, election.* Portland, ME: City Clerk's Office.

City of San Diego, California. 1967. *Progress Guide and General Plan* (Approved July 20). San Diego: City of San Diego.

_____. 1979. *Progress Guide and General Plan* (Approved February 26). San Diego: City of San Diego.

City of San Diego, California, Growth Management Review Task Force. 1984. *Task Force Report to the City Council.* San Diego: City of San Diego.

City of San Diego, California, Planning Department. 1986. *Background Summary: City of San Diego Growth Management Program.* San Diego: City of San Diego Planning Department.

City of Seattle, Washington. 1983. *Draft Environmental Impact Statement for the Land Use and Transportation Plan for Downtown Seattle, Vol.1.*

_____. 1984. *Final Environmental Impact Statement for the Land Use and Transportation Plan for Downtown Seattle, Vol. 1.*

_____. 1985. *Land Use & Transportation Plan for Downtown Seattle.* Adopted June 10, 1985, by Resolution 27281.

Clawson, M. 1972. *Suburban Land Conversion.* Baltimore: Johns Hopkins University Press.

_____., ed. 1973. *Modernizing Urban Land Policy*. Baltimore: Johns Hopkins University Press.

Cobb, R. W. and C. D. Elder. (1983). *Participation in American Politics: The Dynamics of Agenda-Building*. 2nd ed. Baltimore: Johns Hopkins University Press.

Cole, R. L. 1974. *Citizen Participation and the Urban Policy Process*. Lexington, MA: Lexington Books.

Concerned Citizens for Portland's Waterfront. n.d. *The Waterfront Referendum*. Portland, ME: Concerned Citizens for Portland's Waterfront.

Cooper, S. 1986. "Growth Control Evolves in Boulder." Pp. 35-44 in D. R. Porter (ed.) *Growth Management: Keeping on Target?* Washington: Urban Land Institute.

Council of State Governments. 1976. *State Growth Management*. Lexington, KY: Council of State Governments.

Council on Environmental Quality. 1976. *The Growth Shapers*. Washington: Government Printing Office.

Cronin, T. E. 1989. *Direct Democracy: The Politics of the Initiative, Referendum, and Recall*. Cambridge, MA: Harvard University Press.

Cunningham, J. V. 1972. "Citizen Participation in Public Affairs." *Public Administration Review* 32 (October): 589-602.

Curtin, D. J., Jr., and M. T. Jacobson. 1989. "Growth Management by the Initiative in California: Legal and Practical Issues." *The Urban Lawyer* 21 (Summer): 491-510.

Dahl, R. A. 1961. *Who Governs? Democracy and Power in an American City*. New Haven: Yale University Press.

_____. 1982. *Dilemma of Pluralist Democracy*. New Haven, CT: Yale University Press.

Daly, J. 1988, November 28. Press Statement: Response to Mayor Royer's Proposed Alternative to CAP.

DeGrove, J. 1984. *Land, Growth & Politics*. Chicago: APA Planners Press.

DeGrove, J. M. 1987. "Balanced Growth in Florida: A Challenge for Local, Regional and State Governments." *New Jersey Bell Journal* 10 (3): 38-50.

_____ and W. J. deHaven-Smith. 1988. "Resource Planning and Management Committees: Implementing Florida's Critical Area Program." Pp. 157-175 in W. J. deHaven-Smith (ed.) *Growth Management Innovations in Florida*. Monograph #88-1. Fort Lauderdale: Florida Atlantic University and Florida International University Joint Center for Environmental and Urban Problems.

Delafons, J. 1969. *Land-Use Controls in the United States*. Cambridge: The MIT Press.

DeLeon, R. E. and S. S. Powell. 1989. "Growth Control and Electoral Politics: The Triumph of Urban Populism in San Francisco." *Western Political Quarterly* 42 (June): 307-331.

Domhoff, G. W. 1967. *Who Rules America?* Englewood Cliffs, NJ: Prentice-Hall.

_____. 1986. "The Growth Machine and the Power Elite: A Challenge to Pluralists and Marxists Alike." Pp. 53-73 in R. J. Waste (ed.) *Community Power: Directions for Future Research*. Newbury Park, CA: Sage.

"Dorler: Closed door policy." [Opinion] 1986. *Portland Evening Express* (November 13): p. 10.

Durkee, M. P., M. T. Jacobson, T. C. Wood, and M. H. Zischke. 1990. *Land-Use Initiatives and Referenda in California*. Point Arena, CA: Solano Press.

Dye, T. R. 1985. *Politics in States and Communities*. Englewood Cliffs, NJ: Prentice-Hall.

_____. 1987. *Understanding Public Policy*. 6th ed. Englewood Cliffs, NJ: Prentice-Hall.

Eastman, H. 1985. "Squelching Vox Populi: Judicial Review of the Initiative in California." *Santa Clara Law Review* 25 (Autumn): 529-554.

Eddins, T. W. and J. S. Ono Hall. 1990. Note. "Zoning by Initiative in Hawaii." *The University of Hawaii Law Review* 12 (Summer): 181-214.

Eu, M. F. 1988a. *A History of the California Initiative Process*. Sacramento: California Secretary of State.

_____. 1988b. *California's Ballot Initiative*. Sacramento: California Secretary of State.

Feagin, J. 1988. "Tallying the Social Costs of Urban Growth Under Capitalism: The Case of Houston." In S. Cummings (ed.) *Business Elites and Urban Development*. Albany: State University of New York Press.

Ferland, J. 1982a. "Tide swelling to keep city waterfront as it is." *Portland Evening Express* (March 9): pp. 1, 12.

_____. 1982b. "Mayor defends development of waterfront." *Portland Evening Express* (March 10): pp. 1, 8.

_____. 1982c. "Round one: Waterfront wins allies." *Portland Evening Express* (March 12): pp. 1, 12.

_____. 1982d. "American City's Connolly returns fire." *Portland Evening Express* (March 19): pp. 1, 13.

_____. 1982e. "$64 million plan strongly opposed." *Portland Evening Express* (March 19): pp. 1, 14.

Fleischmann, A. and J. R. Feagin. 1987. "The Politics of Growth-Oriented Urban Alliances: Comparing Old Industrial and New Sunbelt Cities." *Urban Affairs Quarterly* 23 (December): 207-232.

Ford, H. J. 1924. *Representative Government*. New York: Henry Holt.

Fountaine, C. L. 1988. "Lousy Lawmaking: Questioning the Desirability of Legislating by Initiative." *Southern California Law Review* 61 (March): 733-776.

Fralin, R. 1978. *Rousseau and Representation: A Study of the Development of His Concept of Political Institutions*. New York: Columbia University Press.

Freilich, R. H. and D. B. Guemmer. 1989. "Removing Artifical Barriers to Public Participation in Land-Use Policy: Effective Zoning and Planning by Initiative and Referendum." *The Urban Lawyer* 21 (Summer): 511-556.

Gardner, C. M. 1987. "Munjoy Hill group elects candidates backing controls." *Maine Sunday Telegram* (April 26): p. 26.

Giftis, S. H. 1984. *Law Dictionary*. New York: Barron's.

Gleeson, M. E. et al. 1975. *Urban Growth Management Systems: An Evolution of Policy Related Research*. Planning Advisory Service Report, Nos. 309-310. Chicago: American Society of Planning Officials.

Glenn, P. G. 1978. "State Law Limitations on the Use of Initiatives and Referenda in Connection with Zoning Amendments." *Southern California Law Review* 51: 265-306.

Glickfeld, M., L. Graymer, and K. Morrison. 1987. "Trends in Local Growth Control Ballot Measures in California." *UCLA Journal of Environmental Law and Policy* 6: 111-159.

Goetz, J. E. 1987. "Direct Democracy in Land Use Planning: The State Response to Eastlake." *Pacific Law Journal* 19 (April): 793-844.

Gotch, M. 1985. "Proposition A, Pro: Initiative will let citizens regain control of city's future." *San Diego Union* (October 24): Commentary, p. B-7.

Governor's Task Force on Urban Growth Patterns. 1989. *Final Report.* Tallahassee, FL: Governor's Task Force on Urban Growth Patterns.

Grossman, B. F. 1981. "The Initiative and Referendum Process: The Michigan Experience." *Wayne Law Review* 28 (Fall): 77-136.

Gunn, P. F. 1981. "Initiatives and Referendums: Direct Democracy and Minority Interests." *Urban Law Annual* 22: 135-159.

Hamilton, D. 1989. "Dome duo grabs Act." *The Register* (August 10): pp. 1-3.

"Harbor: Keep mixed use." [Editorial] 1987a. *Portland Evening Express* (March 6): p. 16.

"Harbor: The intent is clear." [Editorial] 1987b. *Portland Evening Express* (April 8): p. 6.

Hartzer, T. J. 1976. "Eastlake v. Forest City Enterprises: A Comment by Timothy J. Hartzer." *Land Use Law and Zoning Digest* 28 (8): 6-8.

Hatch, W. 1989a. "Walt Crowley: Liberal entrepreneur dogged by accusations that he's sold out." *The Seattle Times* (April 12): pp. 3-A, 22-A.

_____. 1989b. "Anti-CAP group attracts $180,000 in donations: Supporters of initiative raise much less—$14,000." *Seattle Times/Seattle Post-Intelligencer* (May 7): p. B-10.

_____. 1989c. "Anti-CAP flier misleads, says official: Assessor takes issue with claim proposal would increase tax rates." *The Seattle Times* (May 10): pp. D-1, D-2.

Hawley, W. D. and F. M. Wirt, eds. 1974. *The Search for Community Power.* 2nd ed. Englewood Cliffs, NJ: Prentice-Hall.

Healy, R. and J. Rosenberg. 1979. *Land Use and the States.* 2nd ed. Baltimore: Johns Hopkins University Press.

Hedgecock, R. 1985. "In Support of Proposition A: Statement of Mayor Roger Hedgecock." *APA San Diego Section Local Planning Journal* (October): 2, 5.

Hill, G. R. 1989. "Seattle's Voters Cap Downtown Development." *Urban Land* 48 (August): 32-33.

Holmes, R. 1986. "Visionary movement under way on Cape." *Cape Cod Times* (October 1): pp. 1-2.

_____. 1988a. "Tsongas 'astonished' by support for moratorium." *Cape Cod Times* (June 5): pp. 1, 14.

_____. 1988b. "Builders mounting opposition to moratorium." *Cape Cod Times* (June 9): p. 1.

_____. 1988c. "EPA official supports Cape Cod building ban." *Cape Cod Times* (August 26): pp. 1, 14.

Home Builders Association of Cape Cod. 1988, September 22. *Position Paper on the "M" Word*. Sandwich, MA: Home Builders Association of Cape Cod.

Home Builders Association of Massachusetts. 1988, June 24. *Moratorium Update*. Boston: Home Builders Association of Massachusetts.

Hunter, F. 1953. *Community Power Structure*. Chapel Hill: University of North Carolina Press.

Hyink, B. L., S. Brown, and E. W. Thacker. 1973. *Politics and Government in California*. 8th ed. New York: Thomas Y. Crowell.

"Interim controls best for Seattle." 1989. *Seattle Post-Intelligencer* (April 7): p. A-10.

Jackson, K. 1988. "S.D. watchdog group takes stance on ballot measures." *San Diego Union* (September 22): p. B-4.

Jacobs, C. E. and A. D. Sokolow. 1970. *California Government: One Among Fifty*. London: Collier-Macmillan.

Johnston, R. A. 1980. "The Politics of Local Growth Controls." *Policy Studies Journal* 9 (Winter): 427-439.

Kelso, W. A. 1978. *American Democratic Theory: Pluralism and Its Critics*. Westport, CT: Greenwood.

Kemper, J. R. 1976. "Annotation: Adoption of Zoning Ordinance or Amendment Thereto as Subject of Referendum." Pp. 1030-1060 in *72 American Law Reports, 3d*. Rochester, NY and San Francisco: Lawyers Cooperative Publishing and Bancroft-Whitney.

Kraabel, P. 1988, November 9. Statement on CAP Initiative.

Kreitzer, D. 1985, January 28. Statement of David Kreitzer, Chairman, San Diegans for Managed Growth.

La Fee, S. 1988. "Council's growth limits headed for ballot." *San Diego Tribune* (August 9): pp. B-1, B-4.

Langton, S. 1979. "American Citizen Participation: A Deep-Rooted Tradition." *National Civic Review* 68 (September): 403-410, 422.

Lassar, T. J. 1987. "Ballot-Box Growth Control." *Planning* 46 (March): 26-27.

Leonard, D. 1985. "In Opposition to Proposition A: Citizens for Community Planning." *APA San Diego Section Local Planning Journal* (October): 2, 5.

Levy, J. R. 1988. *Contemporary Urban Planning*. Englewood Cliffs, NJ: Prentice-Hall.

Lewis, S. 1975. "The Jury's Out on Growth Control." *Planning* 41 (January): 8.

Liebman, L. 1989. "How San Francisco fares under CAP called Proposition M." *Puget Sound Business Journal* (April 24): pp. 3A, 22A.

Logan, J. R. and H. L. Molotch. 1987. *Urban Fortunes: The Political Economy of Place*. Berkeley: University of California Press.

Lourie, D. A. 1990, March 8. City of Portland, Maine, Memorandum to R. B. Ganley, City Manager, on Initiative and Referendum Ordinance.

Lovell, J. 1987. "Waterfront vote divides Portlanders." *Maine Sunday Telegram* (May 3): pp. 1, 20.

Lucas, J. R. 1976. *Democracy and Participation*. Middlesex, UK: Penguin.

Madigan, M. 1985. "The Unmanageable Initiative." *BIA Builder* (October): 20-21.

Magleby, D. 1984. *Direct Legislation: Voting on Ballot Propositions in the United States*. Baltimore: Johns Hopkins University Press.

____. 1986. "The Politics of Direct Democracy." *State Government* 59 (Spring):
31-39.

____. 1988. "Taking the Initiative: Direct Legislation and Direct Democracy in
the 1980s." *PS 21* (Summer): 600-611.

"Managing city growth with CAP initiative." 1989. *The Seattle Times* (May 14)
p. A-14.

Mandelker, D. R. 1988. *Land Use Law.* 2nd ed. Charlottesville, VA: Michie.

Maraziti, J. J., Jr. 1987. "Morris 2000: A Citizens' Forum for Regional Problem
Solving." *New Jersey Bell Journal* 10 (3): 28-37.

"Matter of self-interest." [Editorial] 1985. *San Diego Union* (November 3): p. C-2.

McClendon, B. W. 1990. "An Alternative Proposal." *Journal of the American Plan
ning Association* 56 (Spring): 223-225.

McNulty, B. 1986. "Other uses of waterfront favored." *Portland Press Herald* (Jan
uary 15): p. 23.

McNulty, B. 1987a. "Waterfront inventory readied." *Portland Evening Express*
(March 4): pp. 1, 16.

____. 1987b. "Decision on marinas delayed: Council listens to arguments." *Port
land Evening Express* (March 5): p. 3.

____. 1987c. "Waterfront group hits wording of ballot issue." *Portland Evening
Express* (April 7): pp. 1, 14.

Meck, S. 1976. "Eastlake v. Forest City Enterprises: A Comment by Stuart
Meck." *Land Use Law and Zoning Digest* 28 (8): 8-10.

Melious, J. O. 1988. "Growth Management by Local Initiatives: 'Grass Roots'
Planning in California." *Land Use Law and Zoning Digest.* 40 (May): 3-8.

Mill, J. S. 1873. *Considerations on Representative Government.* New York: Henry
Holt.

Mills, C. W. 1956. *The Power Elite.* New York: Oxford University Press.

Milton, S. 1989a. "Land-use authority worries bankers." *Cape Cod Times* (April
5): pp. 1, 10.

____. 1989b. "Land-use bill wins key vote." *Cape Cod Times* (October 4): pp. 1, 7.

Mitau, G. T. 1966. *State and Local Government Politics and Processes.* New York:
Scribner.

Molotch, H. 1976. "The City as a Growth Machine." *American Journal of Sociology*
82 (2): 309-330.

Moore, D. 1987. Comment. "The Use of Initiatives in Municipal Zoning." *Uni
versity of Missouri-Kansas City Law Review* 55 (2): 284-301.

Morone, J. 1990. *The Democratic Wish: Popular Participation and the Limits of Amer
ican Government.* New York: Basic Books.

Municipal League, The. 1989. "CAP: Challenging a Planning Orthodoxy." *Issue
Brief* 5 (May): 5-8.

Murphy, E. D. 1987a. "Waterfront users face moratorium dilemma." *Portland
Evening Express* (March 17): pp. 1, 14.

____. 1987b. "Waterfront coalition cites condo fears." *Portland Evening Express*
(March 26): pp. 1, 12.

____. 1987c. "City faces waterfront crossroads." *Portland Evening Express* (April
27): pp. 1, 14.

____. 1988. "Head of waterfront panel questions Dorler appointees." *Portland Evening Express* (May 17): pp. 1, 12.

National Academy of Sciences. 1972. *Urban Growth and Land Development: The Land Conversion Process.* Washington: National Academy of Sciences.

Navarro, P. 1988. "Proposition J: Citizen initiative offers tighter rein on growth of San Diego." *San Diego Union* (August 28): pp. C-1, C-7.

New Jersey State Planning Commission. 1988. *Communities of Place: A Legacy For the Next Generation.* Vol. 1. The Preliminary State Development and Redevelopment Plan for the State of New Jersey. Trenton: New Jersey State Planning Commission.

Nickerson, S. n.d. *What is the moratorium?* Unpublished paper.

" 'No' to No Growth." 1988. *Zoning News* (December): 3.

Oberholtzer, E. P. 1971. *The Referendum in America.* New York: Da Capo Press.

O'Connell, J. 1987a. "City grants 30 building permits for hardship." *San Diego Union* (November 18): p. B-3.

____. 1987b. "Release from IDO snagged." *San Diego Union* (November 25): pp. B-1, B-8.

Okerblom, J. 1985. "30,000-plus acres at stake." *San Diego Union* (October 27): pp. B-1, B-2.

Orman, L. 1984. *Ballot-Box Planning: The Boom in Electoral Land-Use Control.* Public Affairs Report 25. (December). Berkeley: Bulletin of the Institute of Governmental Studies, University of California.

Ougland, M. 1988. "CAP alternative under fire." *Seattle Daily Journal of Commerce* (December 1): p. 1.

Pageler, M. A. 1988. "Basic assumptions of the downtown plan are no longer valid." *Puget Sound Business Journal* (May 30): pp. 1, 11, 17.

Paris, J. S. 1977. Note. "Use of Referendum in Zoning." *Stanford University Law Review* 29 (April): 819-851.

Pascall, G. 1989. "Would CAP plan on growth be best for region in the long run?" *Seattle Times/Seattle Post-Intelligencer* (January 1): p. C-12.

Pateman, C. 1970. *Participation and Democratic Theory.* Cambridge: Cambridge University Press.

Patterson, T. W. 1988. *Land Use Planning: Techniques of Implementation.* Rev. ed. Malabar, FL: Robert F. Krieger.

Pennock, J. R. 1979. *Democratic Political Theory.* Princeton: Princeton University Press.

Perry, N. 1987. "Legislative delegation majority backs ban." *Portland Evening Express* (April 30): pp. 1, 10.

Platt, R. H. 1976. *Land Use Control: Interface of Law and Geography.* Resource Paper No. 75-1. Washington: Association of American Geographers.

Polsby, N. W. 1980. *Community Power and Political Theory.* 2nd. ed. New Haven: Yale University Press.

Popper, F. J. 1981. *The Politics of Land Use Reform.* Madison: University of Wisconsin Press.

Porter, D. R., ed. 1986. *Growth Management: Keeping on Target?* Washington: Urban Land Institute.

232   LAND USE PLANNING

Portland Chamber of Commerce. 1987, March 16. Statement. Portland, ME: Portland Chamber of Commerce.

Prokop, D. 1988. "Developers Fight Back." *California Journal* 19 (October): 444-448.

Radar, S. G. 1983. "Rezoning by Referendum and the Right of Due Process Under the Florida Constitution." *Florida Bar Journal* 57 (Ocotber): 556-560.

Ranney, A., ed. 1981. *The Referendum Device.* Washington: American Enterprise Institute for Public Policy Research.

Rawson, D. S. 1987. "Water's boiling in Portland." *Portland Press Herald* (May 1): p. 6.

"Readers Write." 1987a. *Portland Evening Express* (April 24): p. 16.

_____. 1987b. *Portland Evening Express* (May 2): p. 10.

Reilly. W., ed. 1973. *The Use of Land: A Citizens' Policy Guide to Urban Growth.* New York: Crowell.

Ricci, D. M. 1971. *Community Power and Democratic Theory.* New York: Random House.

Riker, W. 1986. *The Art of Political Manipulation.* New Haven: Yale University Press.

Ristine, J. 1988. "Group balks at wording on growth." *San Diego Tribune* (August 26): pp. B-1, B-7.

Roberts, R. 1988. "Proposition H: City Council's plan drawn to serve the entire community." *San Diego Union* (August 28): pp. C-1, C-7.

Rosenberg, R. H. 1984. "Referendum Zoning: Legal Doctrine and Practice." *University of Cincinnati Law Review* 53 (Spring): 381-433.

Rousseau, J. J. 1953. "The Social Contract." In *Political Writings.* Translated by F. Watkins. Edinburgh: Thomas Nelson.

Royer, C. 1988, June 2. Press Release.

Salvato, G. M. 1986. "New Limits on the California Initiative: An Analysis and Critique." *Loyola of Los Angeles Law Review* 19 (May): 1045-1096.

San Diego Association of Governments. 1987. "Series 7 Regionwide Forecast, 1985-2010." *SANDAG INFO* 1 (January-February). San Diego: San Diego Association of Governments.

_____. 1988. "Series 7 Growth Forecast." San Diego: San Diego Association of Governments.

Sanford, K. 1988, June 17. Press Release.

Schmidt, D. D. 1989. *Citizen Lawmakers: The Ballot Initiative Revolution.* Philadelphia: Temple University Press.

Schultz, M. S. and V. L. Kasen. 1984. *Encyclopedia of Community Planning and Environmental Management.* New York: Facts on File.

"S.D. slow-growth petitions filed." 1988. *San Diego Union* (March 23): p. B-3.

Siemon, C. L., W. U. Larsen, and A. Fleming. 1988. "Downtown/Areawide DRIs: The Benefits to Growing Communities." Pp. 133-155 in W. J. deHaven Smith (ed.) *Growth Management Innovations in Florida.* Monograph #88-1 Fort Lauderdale: Florida Atlantic University and Florida International University Joint Center for Environmental and Urban Problems.

Sierra Club, San Diego Chapter. 1985. "Initiative Contest Announced." *Hi Sierran* (May): 1.

Silverman, S. 1985. "Proposition A, Con: Measure would prohibit planning, permit rural sprawl." *San Diego Union* (October 24): Commentary, p. B-7.

Sleeper, F. 1987. "Waterfront issue debated." *Portland Press Herald* (April 22): p. 17.

Smolens, M. 1983. "Hedgecock will unveil city growth reform plan." *San Diego Union* (October 14): pp. A-1, A-4.

____. 1985a. "Managed growth supporters file 75,000 signatures." *San Diego Union* (June 13): p. B-3.

____. 1985b. "Bid to block growth plan is rejected." *San Diego Union* (July 10): pp. B-1, B-8.

Sottili, C. 1987. "Initiative drafted to slow growth." *San Diego Union* (May 28): pp. B-1, B-8.

Stone, C. R. 1989. *Urban Regimes: Governing Atlanta, 1946-1988.* Lawrence: University of Kansas Press.

Tallian, L. 1977. *Direct Democracy: An Historical Analysis of the Initiative, Referendum, and Recall Process.* Los Angeles: People's Lobby.

Tang, T. 1989. "Learning to live with trimmed towers: The cappings of San Francisco's skyline suggests that Seattle's CAP will not produce dire results." *Seattle Weekly* (April 5): pp. 23-24.

Thompson, D. F. 1976. *John Stuart Mill and Representative Government.* Princeton: Princeton University Press.

Turner, R. S. 1990. "Intergovernmental Growth Management: A Partnership Framework for State-Local Relations." *Publius: The Journal of Federalism* 20 (Summer): 79-97.

Vogel, R. K. and B. E. Swanson. 1989. "The Growth Machine Versus the Antigrowth Coalition: The Battle for Our Communities." *Urban Affairs Quarterly* 25 (September): 63-85.

Walker, J. L. 1966. "A Critique of the Elitist Theory of Democracy." *American Political Science Review* 60 (June): 285-295.

Waste, R. J., ed. 1986. *Community Power: Directions for Future Research.* Newbury Park, CA: Sage.

____. 1987. *Power and Pluralism in American Cities: Researching the Urban Laboratory.* New York: Greenwood.

"Waterfront proposals." 1982. *Portland Evening Express* (April 27): p. 8.

Waterfront Task Force. 1990, April. *Waterfront Task Force Recommendations.* Portland, ME: Waterfront Task Force.

Webster, D. H. 1958. *Urban Planning and Municipal Public Policy.* New York: Harper & Brothers.

Weintraub, D. M. 1983. "La Jolla Valley: Urban Panacea or Intrusion on Grand Design." *Los Angeles Times* [San Diego County Edition] (October 9): pp. II-1, 8.

Weir, G. 1987. "Waterfront businesses' fate debated." *Portland Evening Express* (May 2): p. 12.

Weisberg, L. 1985a. "Opposition to Prop. A voiced by GOP's central committee." *San Diego Union* (October 15): p. B-2.

____. 1985b. "Bates attacks strategy of foes of Proposition A." *San Diego Union* (October 18): pp. B-1, B-7.

234 LAND USE PLANNING

_____. 1985c. "Voters pass control on city growth." *San Diego Union* (November 6): pp. A-1, A-8.

_____. 1987. "City slow-growth policy sometimes causes tears." *San Diego Union* (December 13): pp. B-1, B-6.

_____. 1988a. "Group hits city plan for growth." *San Diego Union* (August 19): p. 3.

_____. 1988b. "Job loss seen in growth initiative." *San Diego Union* (August 26): pp. B-1, B-7.

_____. 1988c. "Rewording of ballot summaries denied by judge." *San Diego Union* (September 27): p. B-3.

Whitehill, L. 1985. "Direct Legislation: A Survey of Recent Literature." *Legal Reference Services Quarterly* 5 (Spring): 3-45.

Wilcox, D. F. 1912. *Government by All the People.* New York: MacMillan.

Working Waterfront Coalition. n.d. Campaign Material. Portland, ME: Working Waterfront Coalition.

_____. n.d. Statement. Portland, ME: Working Waterfront Coalition.

_____. 1987a, February. *Developing the Working Waterfront in Portland, Maine.* Position Paper. Portland, ME: Working Waterfront Coalition.

_____. 1987b, April 25. Campaign Letter. Portland, ME: Working Waterfront Coalition.

_____. 1987c, April 30. Press Release. Portland, ME: Working Waterfront Coalition.

Zimmerman, J. F. 1986. "Populism Revisited." *Statement Government* 58: 172-178.

Bibliography

BOOKS

Altshuler, A. 1970. *Community Control.* New York: Pegasus.

Bachrach, P. 1967. *The Theory of Democratic Elitism.* Boston: Little, Brown.

Brugmann, B. and G. Sletteland, eds. 1971. *The Ultimate Highrise: San Francisco's Mad Rush Toward the Sky.* San Francisco: San Francisco Bay Guardian Books.

Carr, R. H., M. H. Berstein, and W. F. Murphy. 1965. *American Democracy in Theory and Practice: Essentials of National, State, and Local Government.* 3rd ed. New York: Holt, Rinehart & Winston.

Crouch, W. W., J. C. Bollens, and S. Scott. 1977. *California Government and Politics.* 6th ed. Englewood Cliffs, NJ: Prentice-Hall.

Cummings, S., ed. 1988. *Business Elites and Urban Development.* Albany: State University of New York.

Curtin, D. J., Jr. 1988. *California Land-Use and Planning Law.* Berkeley: Solano.

deHaven-Smith, W. J., ed. 1988. *Growth Management Innovations in Florida.* Monograph #88-1. Fort Lauderdale: Florida Atlantic University and Florida International University Joint Center for Environmental and Urban Problems.

Dvorin, E. P. and A. J. Misner. 1967. *Introduction to California Government.* Reading, MA: Addison-Wesley.

Dye, T. R. 1986. "Community Power and Public Policy." Pp. 29-51 in R.J. Waste (ed.) *Community Power: Directions for Future Research.* Newbury Park, CA: Sage.

Fainstein, S. S., N. I. Fainstein, and P. I. Armstrong. 1986. *Restructuring the City.* Rev. ed. White Plains, NY: Longman.

Fainstein, S. S. et al. 1986. "San Francisco: Urban Transformation and the Local State." Pp. 202-244 in S. S. Fainstein et al. *Restructuring the City*. White Plains, NY: Longman.

Feagin, J. 1983. *The Urban Real Estate Game*. Englewood Cliffs, NJ: Prentice-Hall.

Fesler, J. W., ed. 1967. *The 50 States and their Local Governments*. New York: Knopf.

Gottdiener, M. 1987. *The Decline of Urban Politics: Political Theory and the Crisis of the Local State*. Newbury Park, CA: Sage.

Harrington, M. 1970. *Toward a Democrat Left*. New York: Harper & Row.

Harvey, R. B. 1970. *The Dynamics of California Government and Politics*. Belmont, CA: Wadsworth.

Henig, J. R. 1985. *Public Policy and Federalism: Issues in State and Local Politics*. New York: St. Martins Press.

Jefferson, T. 1939. *Democracy*. Selected and Arranged With An Introduction by S.K. Padover. New York: Greenwood.

Kingdon, J. W. 1984. *Agenda, Alternatives, and Public Policies*. Boston: Little, Brown.

Kotler, M. 1967. *Neighborhood Government*. Indianapolis: Bobbs-Merrill.

Lee, E. C. 1981. "The American Experience, 1778-1978." Pp. 46-74 in A. Ranney (ed.) *The Referendum Device*. Washington: American Enterprise Institute for Public Policy Research.

____ and Hawley, W. D. 1970. *The Challenge of California with a concise introduction to California Government*. Boston: Little, Brown.

Lowi, T. J. 1969. *The End of Liberalism*. New York: Norton.

Mandelker, D. R. 1971. *The Zoning Dilemma*. Indianapolis: Bobbs-Merrill.

McKelvey, B. 1963. *The Urbanization of America, 1860-1915*. New Brunswick, NJ: Rutgers University.

Molotch, H. L. 1988. "Strategies and Constraints of Urban Elites." Pp. 25-47 in S. Cummings (ed.) *Business Elites and Urban Development*. Albany: State University of New York Press.

Nelson, R. H. 1980. *Zoning and Property Rights: An Analysis of the American System of Land-Use Regulation*. Cambridge: The MIT Press.

Peterson, P. E. 1973. *City Limits*. Chicago: University of Chicago Press.

Price, C. M. 1987. "Direct Democracy at the Local Level." Pp. 97-109 in R. S. Ross (ed.) *Perspectives on Local Government in California*. Belmont, CA: Star.

Rohan, P. J. 1989. *Zoning and Land Use Controls*. Vol. 7. New York: Matthew Bender.

Ross, M. J. 1987. *California: Its Government and Politics*. 3rd ed. Belmont, CA: Brooks/Cole.

Schnidman, F. and J. Silverman, eds. 1980. *Management and Control of Growth: Updating the Law*. Vol. 5. Washington: The Urban Land Institute.

Schumpeter, J. A. 1950. *Capitalism, Socialism and Democracy*. New York: Harper & Brothers.

Scott, R. W., ed. 1975. *Management and Control of Growth: Issues, Techniques, Problems, Trends*. Vol. 1. Washington: Urban Land Institute.

Stone, C. N. 1986. "Power and Social Complexity." Pp. 77-113 in R.J. Waste (ed.) *Community Power: Directions for Future Research*. Newbury Park, CA: Sage.

Swanstrom, T. 1988. "Urban Populism, Uneven Development, and the Space for Reform." Pp. 121-152 in S. Cummings (ed.) *Business Elites and Urban Development.* Albany: State University of New York Press.

Whitt, J. A. 1982. *Urban Elites and Mass Transportation.* Princeton: Princeton University Press.

Wirt, F. M. 1974. *Power in the City: Decisionmaking in San Francisco.* Berkeley: University of California Press.

Wolff, R. B. 1968. *The Poverty of Liberalism.* Boston: Beacon.

ARTICLES, REPORTS, PAPERS

Albrecht, D. E., G. Bultena, and E. Hoiberg. 1986. "Constituency of the Anti-growth Movement: A Comparison of the Growth Orientations of Urban Status Groups." *Urban Affairs Quarterly* 21 (June): 607-616.

American Planning Association. 1985. "Ballots Cast on Growth and Environmental Controls." *Zoning News* (December): 1-2.

____. 1986a. "Is Growth Management Really Alphabet Soup?" *Zoning News* (December): 2.

____. 1986b. "L. A. to Vote on Growth Controls." *Zoning News* (September): 3.

Barnett, M. 1979. "The growing pains of the Central Coast region." *California Journal* 10 (February): 70-72.

____. 1980. "How California cities are curbing residential growth." *California Journal* 11 (December): 475-477.

Bell, C. and C. Price. 1988. "Lawmakers and Initiatives: Are ballot measures the magic ride to success." *California Journal* 19 (September): 380-384.

Berg, L. L. and C. B. Holman. 1989. "The Initiative Process and Its Declining Agenda-Setting Value." *Law and Policy* 11 (October): 451-469.

Berwanger, C. 1987. "Land Use Planning by Initiative." *Los Angeles Lawyer* 9 (January): 43-49.

Bone, H. A. and R. C. Benedict. 1975. "Perspectives on Direct Legislation: Washington State's Experience 1914-1973." *Western Political Quarterly* 28 (June): 330-351.

Borchers, P. J. 1989. "California Local Initiatives and Referenda: An Argument for Keeping the Progressive Flame Burning." *Pacific Law Journal* 21 (October): 119-145.

Bryan, F. M. 1978. "Does the Town Meeting Offer an Option for Urban America." *National Civic Review* 67 (December): 523-527.

Buck, C. 1987. "Reforming the Initiative: Is the process bankrupt?" *California Journal* 18 (August): 395-397.

Bundy, R. 1988. "Ballot Box Planning is Clear Evidence of a Planning Failure." *San Diego Planning Journal* (December): 6.

Callies, D. 1980. "The Quiet Revolution Revisited." *Journal of the American Planning Association* 46 (April): 135-144.

Caves, R. W. 1987. "Defining Urban Regions: Land Use and Legal Considerations." *Urban Resources* 5 (Winter): 23-26, 60-61.

Chinitz, B. 1990. "Growth Management: Good or Bad?" *Journal of the American Planning Association* 56 (Winter): 3-8.

Colburn, G. A. 1985. "San Diego: Beyond Spit and Polish." *Planning* 51 (November): 4-10.

Colinvaux, C. M. and S. D. Galowitz. 1989. "A Modest Proposal: The Cape Cod Referendum for a Moratorium on New Development." *Harvard Environmental Law Review* 13 (Summer): 559-584.

Dalton, L. C. 1989. "The Limits of Regulation: Evidence from Local Plan Implementation in California." *Journal of the American Planning Association* 55 (Spring): 151-168.

DeGrove, J. M. and N. E. Stroud. 1987. "State Land Planning and Regulation: Innovative Roles in the 1980s and Beyond." *Land Use Law and Zoning Digest* 39 (March): 3-8.

Drager, K. 1982. "Local ballot issues: 'No' to taxes, strikes and shocks." *California Journal* 13 (December): 443.

Fitzgerald, M. 1979. "Initiative fever: Many try, but few reach the ballot." *California Journal* 10 (December): 433-434.

Hahn, G., III, and S. C. Morton. 1977. Note. "Initiative and Referendum—Do They Encourage or Impair Better State Government?" *Florida State University Law Review* 5: 925-950.

Hallman, W. W. 1972. "Federally Financed Citizen Participation." *Public Administration Review* 32 (September): 421-427.

Hart, D. K. 1972. "Theories of Government Related to Decentralization and Citizen Participation." *Public Administration Review* 32 (October): 603-621.

Hubbard, C. F. 1988. "Questioning the Florida Rule on Rezoning Single Parcels of Land by Referendum." *Florida State University Law Review* 4 (Summer): 121-141.

Jordan, D. J. 1979. Note. "Constitutional Constraints on Initiative and Referendum." *Vanderbilt Law Review* 32 (5): 1143-1166.

Kahn, V. 1985. "California's 80-year Romance." *Planning* 51 (May): 13-15.

Kemper, J. R. 1976. "Annotation: Adoption of Zoning Ordinance or Amendment Thereto Through Initiative." *72 American Law Reports, 3d.*: 991-1015. Rochester, NY and San Francisco: Lawyers Cooperative Publishing and Bancroft-Whitney.

Leary, P. 1987. "Power to the People? A Critique of the Florida Supreme Court's Interpretation of the Referendum Power in Florida Land Company v. City of Winter Springs, 427 So.2d 170 (Fla. 1983)." *Florida State University Law Review* 15 (Winter): 673-686.

Lee, E. C. 1979. "The Initiative and Referendum: How California Has Fared." *National Civic Review* 68 (February): 69-76, 84.

Longhini, G. 1985. "Ballot Box Zoning." *Planning* 51 (May): 11-13.

Lowe, C. J. 1982. "Restrictions on Initiative and Referendum Powers in South Dakota." *South Dakota Law Review* 28 (Winter): 53-87.

Lowenstein, D. H. 1983. "California Initiatives and the Single-Subject Rule." *UCLA Law Review* 30 (June): 936-975.

McFarland, J. 1984. "Progressives and the Initiative: Protestant reformers who thought politics was sin." *California Journal* 15 (October): 388-389.

Misczynski, D. J. 1986. "The Growth of Growth Control." *San Diego Planning Journal* (July): 2.

Neiman, M. and R. O. Loveridge. 1981. "Environmentalism and Local Growth Control: A Probe into the Class Bias Thesis." *Environmental Behavior* 13 (6): 759-772.

Oren, C. N. 1976. Comment. "The Initiative and Referendum's Use in Zoning." *California Law Review* 64 (January): 74-107.

Orman, L. 1986. "Ballot Box Planning: A Growing Trend?" *Western City* 62 (November): 3-4.

Popper, F. J. 1988. "Understanding American Land Use Regulation Since 1970." *Journal of the American Planning Association* 54 (Summer): 291-301.

Porter, D. R. 1989. "San Diego's Brand of Growth Management: A for Effort, C for Accomplishment." *Urban Land* 48 (May): 21-27.

Price, C. M. 1975. "The Initiative: A Comparative State Analysis and Reassessment of a Western Phenomenon." *Western Political Quarterly* 28 (June): 243-262.

____. 1981. "The mercenaries who gather signatures for ballot measures." *California Journal* 12 (October): 357-358.

____. 1988. "Initiative Campaigns: Afloat on a sea of cash." *California Journal* 19 (November): 481-486.

Schmidt, D. D. 1982. "Initiative Pendulum Begins Leftward Swing." *Public Administration Times* 5 (September 15): 1, 10.

Shipley, M. S. 1986. "The Initiative Process in Missouri: A Call for Statutory Change." *Missouri Law Review* 51 (Winter): 215-238.

Sirico, L. J., Jr. 1980. "The Constitutionality of the Initiative and Referendum." *Iowa Law Review* 65 (March): 637-677.

State of California, Office of Planning and Research. 1980. "The Growth Revolt: Aftershock of Proposition 13?" Sacramento: Office of Planning and Research.

Strange, J. H. 1972. "The Impact of Citizen Participation on Public Administration." *Public Administration Review* 32 (September): 457-470.

Toussaint, C. T. 1978. "Citizen Access and Participation are Keys to Effective Government." *National Civic Review* 67 (December): 508-511.

Tymkovich, T. M. 1982. Note. "Referendum and Rezoning." *University of Colorado Law Review* 53 (Summer): 745-764.

Witt, J. and J. Sammartino-Gardner. 1988. "Growth Management v. Vested Rights: One City's Experience." *The Urban Lawyer* 20 (Summer): 647-675.

Wood, T. C. 1989. "Must Cities Defend the Indefensible?" *Western City* 65 (December): 22-24, 44.

Working Waterfront Coalition. 1988. Press Release. (March 28). Portland, ME: Working Waterfront Coalition.

Zeiger, E. H., Jr. 1990. "Limitations on the Use of Initiative and Referendum in Controlling Land Use Disputes." *Zoning and Planning Law Report* 13 (March): 17-22.

Zell, E. S. 1989. "Contra Costa County Links Transportation Tax to Growth Management." *Urban Land* 48 (June): 6-10.

Zimmerman, J. F. 1987a. "Initiative, Referendum and Recall: Government by Plebiscite?" *Intergovernmental Perspective* 13 (Winter): 32-35.
____. 1987b. "The Initiative and the Referendum: A Threat to Representative Government." *Urban Law and Policy* 8 (June): 219-253.

NEWSPAPERS

Bruscas, A. 1989. "City questions expenditures in opposition to initiative." *Seattle Post-Intelligencer* (March 25): pp. A-1, A-4.
"Cape delegation 'united' behind amended Cape Commission Act bill." 1989. *The Register* (June 22): p. 7.
Cohen, T. 1986. "Group uses poster in waterfront plea." *Portland Press Herald* (February 5): p. 9.
Corr, O.C. 1989. "Controversy put CAP on a spokesman's replies." *Seattle Post Intelligencer* (April 3): p. A-4.
Ferland, J. 1982a. "Project opposition makes for some surprising allies." *Portland Evening Express* (March 9): pp. 1, 12.
____. 1982b. "Waterfront accord reached." *Portland Evening Express* (April 22): pp. 1, 14.
"Flawed remedy" [Editorial]. 1985. *San Diego Union* (October 24): p. B-6.
Fox, L. 1988. "Cape Builders Tackle Tsongas on Building Ban." *Cape Cod Business Journal* (July): pp. 3-4.
Frammolino, R. 1984. "La Jolla Valley loses planning panel vote." *Los Angeles Times* [San Diego County Edition] (February 13): p. II-4.
"Harbor: A 'working' waterfront." [Editorial] 1987. *Portland Evening Express* (March 12): p. 8.
Hatch, W. 1989. "Anti-CAP campaign poll stirs controversy." *The Seattle Times* (April 21): pp. C-1, C-2.
McNulty, B. 1987a. "Councilors cool to referendum." *Portland Evening Express* (March 19): pp. 1, 8.
____. 1987b. "Court orders change on ballot." *Portland Press Herald* (April 24): p. 9.
Milton, S. 1989a. "Coalition to lobby for land-use panel." *Cape Cod Times* (April 3): p. 3.
____. 1989b. "Doane lobbying violates law, legislator says." *Cape Cod Times* (May 11): pp. 1, 7.
____. 1989c. "Assembly endorses commission." *Cape Cod Times* (June 8): p. 3.
____. 1989d. "Hundreds back land-use agency." *Cape Cod Times* (September 26): pp. 1, 12.
____. 1989e. "Attempts to weaken Cape bill repelled." *Cape Cod Times* (September 28): pp. 1, 8.
Moseley, D. 1988. "Construction Limits Premature: Interview with Larry Liebman." *Puget Sound Business Journal* (May 30): pp. 4, 14-15.
Murphy, E. D. 1986. " 'Slow down': Waterfront growth fought." *Portland Evening Express* (October 20): pp. 1, 16.

_____. 1987a. "Coalition asks ballot change." *Portland Evening Express* (April 22): pp. 1, 8.

_____. 1987b. "Groups mushroom during debate." *Portland Evening Express* (April 28): pp. 1, 6.

_____. 1987c. "Zoning battle lines drawn." *Portland Evening Express* (April 29): pp. 1, 36.

Nelson, R. T. and D. Norton. 1989. "Royer letter referring to CAP draws fire." *The Seattle Times* (February 7): pp. B-1, B-2.

Peratta, E. 1988. "Council exercises caution on zoning." *Portland Evening Express* (March 29): pp. 1, 8.

Ristine, J. 1988. "City puts slow-growth measure on ballot." *San Diego Tribune* (May 3): p. B-3.

"Skeptics wary of county 'power grab.' " 1987. *Cape Cod Times* (November 10): pp. 1, 11.

Smolens, M. 1983. "Panel backs mayor on growth: But full council may not block outlying developing." *San Diego Union* (December 8): pp. A-1, A-6.

Walford, J. 1989. "The Political Scene: The Larger Issue for Paul Doane." *The Cape Codder* (February 26): pp. 14-15.

Weir, G. 1987. "New group opposes waterfront vote." *Portland Evening Express* (April 2): p. 12.

Weisberg, L. 1985a. "Both sides fight fiercely." *San Diego Union* (October 27): pp. B-1, B-2.

_____. 1985b. "Stirling, Hedgecock debate Proposition A." *San Diego Union* (November 2): p. B-3.

_____. 1988. "City slow-growth measure to make November ballot. " *San Diego Union* (April 2): pp. B-1, B-4.

Index

About the Author

Roger W. Caves is a Professor of City Planning and the Coordinator of the interdisciplinary Urban Studies Program with the School of Public Administration and Urban Studies at San Diego State University. His principal interests are land use control policy, growth politics, housing policy, and land use and environmental law issues. He has published in such journals as *Urban Studies, Cities, Land Use Policy, Journal of Urban Planning and Development,* and *Real Estate Issues.* He has presented the findings of his research to groups in the United States, Mexico, Scotland, Great Britain, Yugoslavia, Canada, and the Netherlands.